Authentic New Orleans

Authentic New Orleans

Tourism, Culture, and Race in the Big Easy

Kevin Fox Gotham

NEW YORK UNIVERSITY PRESS
New York and London

NEW YORK UNIVERSITY PRESS
New York and London
www.nyupress.org

Library of Congress Cataloging-in-Publication Data
Gotham, Kevin Fox.
Authentic New Orleans : tourism, culture, and race in the Big Easy /
Kevin Fox Gotham.
p. cm.
Includes bibliographical references and index.
ISBN-13: 978-0-8147-3185-7 (cloth : alk. paper)
ISBN-10: 0-8147-3185-6 (cloth : alk. paper)
ISBN-13: 978-0-8147-3186-4 (pbk. : alk. paper)
ISBN-10: 0-8147-3186-4 (pbk. : alk. paper)
  1. City promotion—Louisiana—New Orleans—History. 2. Tourism
—Louisiana—New Orleans—History. 3. Culture and tourism—
Louisiana—New Orleans—History. 4. Carnival—Louisiana—New
Orleans—History. 5. Exhibitions—Louisiana—New Orleans—
History. 6. New Orleans (La.)—History. 7. New Orleans (La.)—
Social life and customs. I. Title.
HT325.G68 2007
306.09763—dc22   2007023495

New York University Press books are printed on acid-free paper,
and their binding materials are chosen for strength and durability.

Manufactured in the United States of America
c 10 9 8 7 6 5 4 3 2 1
p 10 9 8 7 6 5 4 3 2 1

Contents

Preface

Research for this book began during my first few years as an assistant professor in the sociology department at Tulane University. Within months of moving to New Orleans in 1997, I became fascinated by the strong sense of place identity that seemed to radiate through the city's neighborhoods and institutions, despite the trenchant inequalities and antagonisms that marked everyday life. I quickly learned that one of the most recognized terms residents use to describe New Orleans is "authentic," an undefined and elusive referent that nevertheless makes up the city's everyday vocabulary. New Orleans is a place of distinctive authenticity, people would tell me, because of the unique "culture" that has developed over the centuries. The central components of this unique culture include jazz music and jazz funerals, creole cuisine, French and Spanish architecture, streetcars, historic neighborhoods, multiplicity of festivals and Mardi Gras, and famous cemeteries—the "cities of the dead," where bodies are buried above the ground. Interwoven with these signifiers of local culture is a tapestry of diverse ethnic histories and identities built up over three centuries of shifting group migrations into the bustling and footloose city.

As time went by, I gradually came to appreciate the subtle cues of place character that define New Orleans: the diverse musical genres broadcast on WWOZ, the community radio station; the climax of festivity that occurs on Fat Tuesday; the charm of the French Quarter and the Garden District; and the revelry of Jazz Fest, among many other symbolic indicators of authenticity. I became interested in how tourism practices, modes of staging, and visualization seemed to interpenetrate with meanings of local culture. I began to explore tourism as a set of social practices and collective representations—vocabularies, symbols, or codes—that structure people's definitions of culture and frame their assertions of authenticity. By 2001, I was deeply involved in participant observation and ethnographic work in the city. I attended dozens of meetings of homeowner associations, neighborhood coalitions, historic preservation societies, tourism organizations, and other groups to talk with them about the relationship of tourism, local culture, and racial and class inequalities. I was intrigued by the strong positions that some locals took in defense of tourism as an agent of cultural authentication versus others who condemned tourism as a pathological force of cultural degradation. This book is my journey to understand historically how local debates and conflicts about tourism and authenticity have played out in New Orleans.

The phrase " 'authentic' New Orleans" does not mean an immutable or objective reality but refers to a plurality of idealized representations of the city that residents, organizations, and tourism boosters have constructed over the decades. Like all constructions of reality, the term "authentic" New Orleans is a malleable, fabricated, and heterogeneous category that different groups use to define urban culture, create and express identities, and reinterpret the past. Like the terms "place" and "culture," authenticity is deceptively slippery and often taken as a historic given in New Orleans. As my book documents, symbols and framings of authentic New Orleans have always been in flux and transformation. On the one hand, I analyze the social construction of authentic New Orleans as a conflictual and contested process by which different groups and interests struggle to legitimate their own collective beliefs and values as authoritative representations of local culture. On the other hand, I analyze authentic New Orleans as a manufactured image, whereby powerful tourism interests project onto local culture what they believe are tourists' expectations and preferences—stereotyped images of the city. Overall, the purpose of my book is to understand and explain the ways in which local people have defined authenticity over time, the role of power and conflict in the construction of the authentic, and various historically changing ways in which tourism practices have shaped and (re)defined what is authentic.

During the course of researching and writing this book, I received a great deal of support from a wide variety of people and organizations. First and foremost, a tremendous thanks to all of those individuals who offered firsthand knowledge and shared experiences about New Orleans: Drew Bevolo, Jean Boebel, Bill Borah, Jimmy Cahn, Nathan Chapman, Lucy Chun, Jay Cicero, Geoff Coates, Sandra Dartus, Betty Decell, Patricia Gay, Beverly Gianna, John Hankins, Arthur Hardy, Dorian Hastings, Scott Hutcheson, Pres Kabacoff, Blaine Kern, Errol

Laborde, Tony Marino, Ed Melendez, Milton Melton, Kim Priez, Lyn Reed, Toni Rice, Arthur Roger, Louis Fergusson Saenz, Steve Scalia, Henri Schindler, George Schmidt, Henry Schmidt, Sandy Shilstone, Liz Tahir, and Judy Weitz. I also thank representatives of the many local groups and organizations who volunteered to meet with me and share information: New Orleans Metropolitan Convention and Visitors Bureau, New Orleans Tourism Marketing Corporation, New Orleans Multicultural Tourism Network, Mardi Gras World, Arts Council of New Orleans, Preservation Resource Center, Ethnic Heritage Preservation Council, African American Preservation Council, French Quarter Business Association, Asian Pacific Society of New Orleans, New Orleans Sports Foundation, Urban Conservancy, French Quarter Citizens, Experience New Orleans, New Orleans Museum of Art, Historic Restoration Incorporated, Association of Communities for Reform Now, Save Our Cemeteries, and the Vieux Carre Property Owners, Residents, and Associates. I thank the City Planning Commission, the Mayor's Office, the New Orleans Metropolitan Convention and Visitors Bureau, and the New Orleans Tourism Marketing Corporation for working with me in organizing service learning projects for my undergraduate students to learn about tourism and place promotion.

Like all researchers, I owe a special debt to the archivists and librarians who organize and manage historical collections, manuscripts, and ephemera. Especially helpful to me was Art Carpenter of Loyola University who guided me toward the Lafcadio Hearn Collection, Mayor Moon Landrieu's papers, and other manuscripts pertaining to the postwar era. Irene Wainwright and Wayne Everard of the City Archives at the New Orleans Public Library helped me find old newspaper articles and information on 1984 Louisiana World Exposition collection. Irene was especially helpful in locating photographs and old prints. I also thank the staff of the Williams Research Center for directing me to manuscripts on the 1884 World's Industrial and Cotton Centennial Exposition, the Federal Writers Project of the Works Progress Administration (WPA), and the William Russell Jazz Collection, among other materials. Tremendous thanks go to Wilbur Meneray, Leon Miller, Ken Owen, Robert Sherer, and Anne E. Smith at the Tulane University Special Collections. These individuals introduced me to vertical file material, and a variety of manuscripts and collections on New Orleans history, culture, and tourism. Ken Owen and Wilbur Meneray were especially patient and understanding as I examined hundreds of photographs and prints trying to decide which to include in the book. In addition, I thank the staff of the Howard-Tilton Library at Tulane University for directing me to the index of the *Times-Picayune* newspaper. This source allowed me to locate and cross-reference newspaper articles about the French Quarter, Carnival and Mardi Gras, the 1984 Louisiana World Exposition, and other important topics from the early 1970s forward.

I express my appreciation to the staff of the Louisiana and Special Collections at the University of New Orleans for introducing me to the New Orleans Chamber of Commerce collection. In addition to examining published material and reports of the many committees, bureaus, and departments of the Chamber, I accessed minutes of every meeting of the Convention and Visitors Bureau and the Publicity Bureau from the 1910s through 1979 (the last year on record). The records of the Association of Commerce (renamed the Chamber of Commerce of the New Orleans Area in 1950) offer an inside perspective into the workings of a powerful group of economic elites. Members viewed themselves as the civic guardians of New Orleans culture, and the minutes of meetings are infused with a political messianism. As the twentieth century unfolded, businessmen worked tirelessly to construct and disseminate images of local culture to the world through the institutional channels of the emerging tourism and convention industry. In analyzing the Chamber of Commerce collection and other archival materials, I was interested in detecting patterns in how New Orleans political and economic elites, cultural authorities, and grassroots organizations planned and acted to create tourism institutions and policies. I was also interested in uncovering the bases of social conflicts and struggles over the development of tourism and promotional strategies. My book does not focus on the psychological aspects of tourism or on issues of tourist consent, reception, or motivation in searching for the so-called authentic. Why people travel to New Orleans or other cities is not the key subject of the book, though I do talk a great deal about the motivations of elites in working to transform New Orleans to attract visitors.

I also thank the forty-six people who volunteered their time to be interviewed for this research project. In-depth, semistructured interviews were conducted from 2003 to 2006 and were gathered through a snowball sample that included fifteen white males, sixteen white females, nine black males, five black females, and one Asian female. These interviewees were long-term residents and included current or former tourism professionals, leaders of historic preservation societies, civil rights activists, neighborhood coalition leaders, and city planners. Interviews generally lasted between one and three hours, and all interviews were transcribed. To protect the confidentiality of my interviewees, I have changed their names and do not reveal the organizations they are affiliated with.

I used interviews to compare and contrast experiences, understandings, and framing strategies that people developed to construct New Orleans as an authentic place. Interviews complemented my newspaper and archival data and helped me identify the key actors, organized interests, and structures and networks responsible for building new global-local connections that linked New Orleans with an expanding international tourism industry in the decades after World War II. In my interviews, I asked questions about the history and organization of the tourism industry, the role of local culture and historic preservation in the development of tourism venues, conflicts over tourism in New Orleans, and the effect of tourism on local culture. I also asked interviewees to tell me their views of how other aspects of New Orleans life and culture had changed over the decades: residential life, city neighborhoods, jobs and the economy, schools and the education system, race and ethnic relations, Carnival, festivals, and so on. Thus, I used a loosely structured interview protocol that contained a set of general and specific questions. Intensive, semistructured interviews gave participants room to articulate their experiences, to speak about past events and happenings, and to elaborate at length on different points. This interviewing format also allowed me to probe for clarification when needed and helped create an opportunity to uncover rich data. Broadly, the interview data provided an added resource for triangulating data sources —archival data, government documents, oral histories and other qualitative data, and secondary sources—to enhance validity and reliability and to contribute to scholarship in tourism, urban culture, and urban sociology.

I also give heartfelt thanks to the scholars who read and commented on early drafts of this book and related papers and manuscripts. I benefited enormously from the comments of Richard Lloyd, who read the revised manuscript and offered poignant criticism and suggestions for revision. Joel Devine also took the time to provide very thoughtful and engaging feedback. I also thank the colleagues in my department who were kind enough to share their opinions of this research at several symposia: Michele Adams, Carl Bankston, April Brayfield, Tim Brezina, Xiaojin Chen, Jim Elliott, Scott Frickel, Beth Fussell, Martha Huggins, Mimi Schippers, and Jocelyn Viterna. Thanks to Elyshia Aseltine for helping to transcribe interviews and to collect and analyze the data.

I had opportunities to present my research at a number of professional conferences, including annual meetings of the American Sociological Association, the Midwest Sociological Society, the Southern Sociological Society, the Immigrant Tourist Industry workshop at the University of Amsterdam in 2003, and the Just City Conference held at the Center on Metropolitan Studies in Berlin during May 2006. Thanks to the organizers, commentators, and audience members, especially Hugh Bartling, Bob Beauregard, James Dowd, Susan Fainstein, Miriam Greenberg, Marilyn Halter, Ray Hutchison, Marina Karides, John Logan, Setha Low, Harvey Molotch, Berndt Ostendorf, Jan Rath, David Redmon, Oliver Schmidt, and Florian Urban.

Thanks also to friends, colleagues, and others who shared their keen insights, criticisms, and wisdom: Vern Baxter, Regina Bures, Ben Campkin, Stephen Fowlkes, Tim Gibson, Mark Gottdiener, Arnold Hirsch, Peter Kivisto, Dan Krier, Lauren Langman, Mick Lauria, Patrick Le Gales, Mark Lowes, David McBride, Milagros Pena, Bill Swart, and Michael Timberlake. I thank the anonymous reviewers of the work I submitted to scholarly journals, including the *International Journal of Urban and Regional Research, Urban Studies, Urban Affairs Review,* and *City: Analysis of Urban Trends, Culture, Theory, Policy, Action*. Thanks to graduate students for suggestions and stimulating interaction: Jay Arena, Krista Brumley, Jennifer Day, Farrah Gafford, Jeannie Haubert, and Andrea Wilbon. I thank Marc Pagani for permission to include his photographs in chapter eight. I also thank Tulane University Special Collections and the City Archives and Louisiana Division of the New Orleans Public Library for permission to use scanned prints in the book.

Ilene Kalish is a fabulous editor, and her efforts on behalf of this book have been extensive and much appreciated. Ilene worked with me in the months after Hurricane Katrina in sending the early manuscript out for review and encouraging me in the revision process. In terms of the production of this book, Salwa Jababo must be singled out for the extent of her influence, especially her cordial replies to my incessant emails during 2006 and 2007. I am especially grateful to both Ilene and Salwa for helping me develop and clarify points and enliven the style of the book.

I thank all the friends and neighbors who my wife and I were able to reconnect with after being displaced by Hurricane Katrina in September 2005. These people are in the urban trenches, fighting every day to rebuild their homes and lives in the constrained context of post-Katrina New Orleans. I owe all these people a special debt of appreciation for their leadership and inspiration. It is my fervent hope that the embers that glow brightly in their struggles and actions will be used by others to light a fire of urban activism that will help inspire the creation of a just and equitable New Orleans.

Finally, I send all my love to my wife, Adele, and my daughter, Audrey, who was born while I was writing this book. Adele has been rock solid in supporting me during his seemingly endless project. Audrey forced me to become a master of time management and, more important, provided welcome distraction with diaper changes and occasional strolls through the National Zoo. I am delighted to share this accomplishment with both of them.

1

Introduction
Authentic New Orleans

In the days following the devastation unleashed by Hurricane Katrina, media outlets from around the world broadcasted riveting images of stranded residents, widespread physical damage, and flooded neighborhoods. News coverage of the aftermath revealed that the vast majority of people left behind in New Orleans were poor, African American, and elderly. Subsequent analysis confirmed the unequal effect of the hurricane's damage, showing that almost one-half of the people living in damaged areas were African American and over 45 percent of homes were occupied by renters.[1] Since the hurricane, residents have been returning to the city, even though physical destruction is widespread. The process of rebuilding the economic base, public school systems, legal and government infrastructures, and transportation systems is likely to take years.

The demographic and population consequences of the evacuation of tens of thousands of people remain unclear. The physical damage was extensive and uneven. Some of New Orleans's famous tourist attractions like the French Quarter and the Audubon Zoo suffered little negative impact from the hurricane, whereas others such as City Park and the city's famous cemeteries experienced major damage. Moreover, while the Uptown area and Garden District neighborhood escaped severe flooding, other neighborhoods such as the Ninth Ward, Treme, Marigny, and Broadmoor remained largely unoccupied months after the storm. Katrina's forced displacement of residents and destruction has not only exposed the fault lines of race and class but also inspired debate over whether New Orleans's rich culture and distinctive authenticity have been lost forever. No one knows what will come of the dispersal of New Orleans's music and artistic life, or whether the thousands of artists and musical transients will become transplants.

Since the havoc, journalists, scholars, and others have presented the world with at least three contrasting scenarios for New Orleans's future, scenarios that reflect different interpretations of the city's past development as a tourist destination. One interpretation views the city as a twenty-first-century Pompeii, where the ravages of Katrina have wiped clean the enriching and vibrant culture that used to undergird and support a flourishing tourism sector. According to popular writer Anne Rice, Hurricane Katrina "has done what racism couldn't do, and what segregation couldn't do either. Nature has laid the city waste—with a scope that brings to mind the end of Pompeii."[2] Displaced musicians, preservationists, and others assert that what made New Orleans unique was the unbroken traditions of jazz music, creole architecture, and delicious cuisine. "The flavor and physical setting of the city's culture is locked up in the vernacular wooden houses of the nineteenth century," according to historian S. Frederick Starr, "and I fear from them now. [Are city officials] going to seize on this as an opportunity for mass demolition, in order to build something akin to Houston?"[3] "It's Armageddon for the culture," according to one New Orleans pianist; "it's the ephemeral folk expression in New Orleans that is gone," echoes one archeologist.[4] In an op-ed piece titled "Requiem for the Crescent City," *Washington Post* journalist Eugene Robinson eulogized that the "old New Orleans is dead" because "the people who made it special are gone and so is the path for them to come back."[5] "In 2025, I can practically write the tourist-guide spiel," according to local architect Allen Eskew; "the dark history will be buried, along with the black bodies. And that means a lot of black culture will be buried along with it."[6] These views suggest that the scattering of residents throughout the nation has eroded the tight-knit communities that used to be the seedbeds of cultural invention in the city. In this scenario, the rebuilding of New Orleans will be akin to the banalization of the city and its transformation into a culturally empty place divested of authenticity and communal value.

A second interpretation is that a reconstructed New Orleans will emerge, one displaying the features of a Disney theme park or Las Vegas–style entertainment destination. In this vision of the future, the resurrected city will be sanitized of its past charm and turned into a culturally and ethnically homogenous city that is an artificial and contrived version of its old urban self. "Will this quirky and endlessly fascinating place become an X-rated theme park, a Disneyland for adults?" Tulane

University history professor Larry Powell asked in a speech. "Is it fated to be the place where Orlando embraces Las Vegas? That's the American Pompeii I apprehend rising from the toxic sludge deposited by Lake Ponchartrain: an ersatz city, veritable site of schlock and awe."[7] According to filmmaker Ken Burns, the "spectacular vernacular architecture is all but destroyed. . . . I'm worried the money will come pouring in and what we'll wind up with is a bigger, gaudier New Orleans, like Las Vegas."[8]

In this interpretation, people worry about the taming of New Orleans's improvisational impulse and the loss of creative culture embodied in the characters and eccentrics that once populated the city's neighborhoods. "New Orleans is the most African of American cities, and those who have been displaced and potentially have the fewer resources to return are a core of this culture," according to Danille Taylor, dean of humanities at Dillard University. "It'll be a Disneyland if those people aren't there."[9] This sense of unease is fueled by the slow progress of rebuilding and eerie rumors that city leaders are courting global entertainment chains and casinos to locate to New Orleans to supply the capital to rebuild the city. Mayor C. Ray Nagin's initial proposal to create a casino district to stimulate rebuilding was quickly retracted in the face of intense opposition by local groups and the state governor's office. "They're trying to mold this city into a pseudo-Disneyland, gambling center, party center, a facade," remarked one local artist. "I . . . fear the Disneyfication of the French Quarter with all this money: people coming and buying up bars, music clubs, old restaurants—and naming drinks 'Katrina,' " complained another resident.[10] These lamentations reflect a feeling that the 20 percent of the city that did not flood, including the Uptown area and French Quarter, will retain their tourist appeal and anchor the broader transformation of the city into a Disney-like theme park to entertain visitors. In this scenario, the cultural richness of pre-Katrina New Orleans will become a fossilized relic to amuse visitors.

A third interpretation views post-Katrina rebuilding as helping to foster a new appreciation and rebirth of local culture that will enliven and mobilize people to create new bases of urban authenticity. While some residents are deeply cynical and pessimistic about the future, others are hopeful that the distinctive way of life that residents nurtured for generations will act to stimulate and support a phoenix-like recovery that will animate and reinvent local heritage. "The New Orleans Area is steeped in tradition, but it is also a place that re-invents itself when need be," according to the *New Orleans Times-Picayune* newspaper.[11] Long-term residents and people who love the city have long championed New Orleans as one of the last authentic places in the nation. These people maintain that New Orleans's unique sense of culture and place has been the bulwark against the homogenizing tendencies that have overtaken metropolitan America. While the spread of suburban-style strip malls, theme parks, chain stores, and other standardized and generic experiences have come to define many places, New Orleans has been a cultural "other" that has managed to retain an individuality and authenticity of its own. New Orleans is "a citadel against the McNuggeting of America. It seemed to resist the homogenization seen in many cities," according to *Denver Post* journalist William Porter. "For me, New Orleans is one of the few authentic places left in our landscape, and that compounds the tragedy," remarks filmmaker Ken Burns. "No other city is so equipped to deal with [Hurricane Katrina]," according to Louis Edwards, novelist and associate producer of the Jazz and Heritage Festival. "Think of the jazz funeral. . . . In New Orleans we respond to the concept of following tragedy with joy. That's a powerful philosophy to have as the underpinning of your culture."[12]

In the months since Katrina roared ashore, a plethora of books and articles have appeared proclaiming New Orleans to be one of America's most beloved cities. Titles such as *My New Orleans: Ballads to the Big Easy by Her Sons, Daughters, and Lovers*; *Why New Orleans Matters*; and *Very New Orleans: A Celebration of History, Culture, and Cajun Country Charm* serve as timely and timeless tributes to the powerful spirit that defines the city. On the local level, a quiet but urgent conversation about New Orleans's cultural survival and its sense of authenticity radiates through city streets and major institutions. Prognostications about loss and decline juxtapose with tales of resilience and strength in the face of adversity. While to some the future looks bleak and the city will never be the same, others look to the Katrina tragedy as an opportunity to face the quintessential challenge of rebuilding and reinventing the cultural heart of America.

Questions about New Orleans's future are intertwined with symbols of solidarity and division that seek to make explicit, and more comprehensible, a city's conflicting conceptions of itself and its past. In writing this book, I try to illuminate the interlocking nature of conflicts over race, culture, and authenticity in New Orleans and trace historically how tourism practices have displayed and articulated these conflicts. For more than a century, New Orleans has been a complex and constantly mutating city in which meanings of place and community have been inexorably intertwined with tourism practices. This book examines the historical growth and expansion of the tourism industry in New Orleans, the role of tourism in transmitting symbols of local culture and authenticity, and the influence of race and racial inequalities on tourism practices. For decades, scholars have derided tourism as a global process of standardization and cultural homogenization that annihilates the unique features and genuineness of places and creates what sociologist Dean MacCannell calls "staged" authenticity.[13] Others have viewed tourism as a set of discrete economic activities, a mode of consumption, or a spatially bounded locality or "destination" that is subject to external forces producing impacts. In contrast, I view tourism as a highly complex set of institutions and social relations that involve capitalist markets; state policy; and flows of commodities, cultural forms, and people. In this conception, tourism is not exogenous to localities but is embedded within broader patterns of metropolitan development and sociospatial inequality. My goal is to investigate the processes of authentication through which different groups and interests make claims for local authenticity and attempt to legitimate their constructions of race and culture. I examine the historical development of racial meanings of local authenticity, analyze how conflicts over tourism have changed over time, and address wider issues concerning the relationship between tourism and the construction of place identity.

The connections between race, culture, and tourism are important for understanding the historical development of New Orleans and its future in the aftermath of Katrina. Terms such as "whiteness," "blackness," "creole," "diversity," and "multiculturalism" have long been major signifers of local identity, as a well as sources of division and conflict. Today, these categories are fueling local and national debates over who owns New Orleans, which groups should be allowed to return, and how the city should be rebuilt. Likewise, discussions about the role of tourism in the rebuilding process are sparking conflict over which cultural symbols and images reflect the "authentic" New Orleans and who should define what is local authenticity. Popular discussions frequently employ reified and stereotyped designations that obscure the historically changing nature of race, culture, and place. Scholars have pointed out that race and culture are socially constructed categories that have an emergent and variable quality rather than being fixed or immutable group characteristics.[14] In New Orleans, racial and ethnic group distinctions, as well as cultural designations, have always been politically contested and subject to intense debate and protest. Moreover, the constructed and contingent nature of race and culture have been reinforced by the inherently fluid, situational, and fabricated nature of authenticity.[15] Authenticity is a notoriously labyrinthine concept that can refer to a variety of idealized representations of culture, identity, place. While authenticity may be a socially constructed representation of reality, it has always been real in its consequences as different groups and organized interests have struggled to create and legitimate meanings of an authentic New Orleans. Broadly, in this book I seek to provide deep understanding into the changing role of tourism discourses and practices in the creation and transformation of New Orleans's urban iconography.[16]

Historians such as Catherine Cocks, Jane C. Desmond, Harvey Newman, Hal Rothman, John F. Sears, and Marguerite S. Shaffer, among others, have unearthed a wealth of data that describe the role tourism has played in the development of national and local identities and in places of cultural significance.[17] Yet many of these historical accounts lack empirical specificity and have made little progress in theorizing the development of tourism and its attendant spatial manifestations. Moreover, many accounts of tourism present it as either primarily negative (a destroyer of cultures and local traditions) or primarily positive (bringing a wealth of new products, ideas, and economic opportunities to people). Thus, the historical trajectories and path dependencies of tourism development remain underresearched, both empirically and theoretically. Another problem is the lack of serious examination of the connections between race and tourism. Many studies merely assert the importance of race and racial discrimination without an appreciation of their socially constructed and changing meanings. In this book, I analyze the changing linkages between tourism and race to show how specific racial meanings and manifestations of discrimination were institutionalized within the tourism industry during the twentieth century. At the same time, I examine the role of social movements and protest groups in using tourism discourses and practices to challenge social inequalities and contest marginalization.

Tourism from Above and Below

A major goal in this book is to develop a theoretically driven explanation of the historical development of tourism and its articulation with local actions and broader socioeconomic processes. For years, scholars have assailed tourism as a force of globalization that hollows out the rich texture and distinctiveness of local relations and their creations, and thereby corrupts authentic cultural spaces.[18] According to critics, tourism transforms local culture into abstract, manufactured, and simulated social forms that are estranged from communal life and devoid of authenticity. Other more celebratory accounts have viewed tourism as a force of diversification that promotes cultural invention and innovation.[19] Rather than embracing either/or explanations of tourism, I develop a both/and conceptualization that views tourism as an amalgam of both homogenizing forces of sameness and uniformity, and diversifying forces of difference and hybridity. I advance this conceptualization by distinguishing between *tourism from above* and *tourism from below*, a distinction that can help us get a better sense of how tourism can promote as well as destabilize and undermine local traditions and cultures.

Tables 1.1 and 1.2 present a schematic overview of the major processes, structures and networks, and key actors and organizations in New Orleans associated with tourism above and below. Broadly, tourism from above and tourism from below are not independently given sets of phenomena (a dualism) but a duality; they are an interplay that presupposes each other. Thus, tourism from above processes do not exist "apart" from localities but are embedded in networks and organizations that facilitate some forms of action and decision making in particular locales while discouraging others. To be specific, tourism from above and below and their related processes exist in a reciprocal and reflexive relationship. Grasping that tourism embodies contrasting tendencies at once—that it can be a force of homogenization and heterogeneity, globalization and localization—is crucial to articulating the multiple dimensions of tourism and avoiding one-sided and reductive conceptions.

Tourism from above draws our attention to the role of capital flows, communication and transportation technologies, and legal modes of governance and regulation that have evolved over time to encourage travel and coordinate different forms of tourism and entertainment. The concept also refers to a mix of the extralocal processes of globalization,

TABLE 1.1
Topology of Tourism from Above

Processes	Structures and Networks	Key Actors and Organizations in New Orleans
Globalization Commodification Rationalization Disneyization Branding	International Tourism Networks and Associations: • World Tourism Organization (WTO) • International Association of Convention and Visitors Bureaus (IACVB) • Hospitality Sales and Marketing Association International (HSMAI) • International Hotel and Restaurant Association (IH&RA) • Hospitality Financial Technology Professionals (HFTP) • International Council on Hotel, Restaurant, and Institutional Education (ICHRIE) • Travel and Tourism Research Association (TTRA) • Destination Marketing International (DMI) • World Travel and Tourism Council (WTTC) • International Ecotourism Society (TIES) • World Tourism Foundation (WTF) U.S. Tourism Networks and Associations: • American Resort Development Association (ARDA) • American Hotel & Lodging Association (AH&LA) • Travel Industry Association of America (TIA) Public-Private Networks (government, corporations, and private nonprofit organizations): • U.S. Government Office of Travel and Tourism Industries (OTTI) • State government offices of tourism and cultural development • City government tourism agencies and regulatory bodies • Convention and Visitors Bureaus (CVBs) • Tourism marketing corporations • Chain hotel & entertainment firms • Schools of hospitality and tourism business	New Orleans Metropolitan Convention and Visitors Bureau (NOMCVB) New Orleans Tourism Marketing Corporation (NOTMC) New Orleans Multicultural Tourism Network (NOMTN) New Orleans Sports Foundation New Orleans Hotel-Motel Association Audubon Institute Harrah's Casino and other gambling establishments New Orleans City Council; departments and offices of economic development: tourism, film, art, music; historic and cultural district regulatory commissions, etc.

TABLE 1.2
Topology of Tourism from Below

Processes	Structures and Networks	Key Actors and Organizations in New Orleans
Localization Hybridization Creolization Distinctiveness Heterogeneity	Aesthetic networks • Arts councils, galleries, and museums • Grassroots cultural organizations (art, music, cuisine) • Schools of art, music, cuisine Residential networks • Neighborhood coalitions • Resident associations Heritage networks • Local historical societies • Music heritage foundations • Local historic preservation organizations • Festival volunteer organizations Media networks • Community radio stations • Local newspapers • Public television stations	Arts Council of New Orleans Community Arts Center (CAC) Preservation Resource Center (PRC) Save Our Cemeteries Carnival Krewes French Quarter Festivals, Inc. Jazz and Heritage Foundation New Orleans Music Colloquium New Orleans Jazz Orchestra Urban Conservancy

commodification, rationalization, Disneyization, and branding that are historically changing and uneven. *Globalization* implies the intensification of social and geographical interconnectedness and an accelerated circulation of people, capital, information, and cultural symbols on a worldwide scale. *Commodification* is the conversion of local products, cultures, and social relations and identities into saleable products that are sold on markets for profitable exchange. *Rationalization* refers to a process in which social actions and interactions are based on considerations of efficiency and calculation rather than on motivations derived from custom, tradition, or emotion. Specifically, rationalization is a long yet uneven historical process of applying formal planning, systematic organization, and sophisticated technology to enhance the tourist appeal of local cultures, traditions, and products. *Disneyization* refers to the spread of theme-park characteristics to cities and the increased use of theming techniques, the promotion of corporate brands, and the dominance of security and surveillance in the production of entertainment spaces.[20] Urban *branding* is the most recent extension of the commodification and rationalization process associated with tourism from above and implies the marketing of a corporate-oriented version of urban culture as an object of consumption. The significance of branding, as opposed to advertising and conventional place promotion, is that the distinction between the real city and imagined city implodes and advertised representations become the indicators and definers of urban reality. The branded city establishes and reproduces an infinite set of referentials between entertaining products, spectacular images, and pleasurable experiences in which one referent connects with all the other through highly charged associations across time and space.[21]

Tourism from below refers to the range of framing strategies, symbols, aesthetic codes, and other expressive resources that local people and groups create and use in everyday life to stimulate cultural invention, construct local authenticity, and promote tourism at a grassroots level. Several scholars have used the term "glocalization" to emphasize the integration of the global-local and of homogeneity-heterogeneity in the development of transnational processes.[22] Glocalization is akin to "hybridization" and refers to the intersection of global processes with local actions that result in novel and unique cultural creations in different geographic areas. A similar term, "localization," can be defined as a process by which local actors and organizations appropriate "global" imagery and symbols to reinforce "local" sentiments and inscribe "local" meanings into products and cultural creations. The term "creolization" appears in writings on globalization and postmodernity to explain the mixing of different cultures and identities in an age of migration and enhanced mobility. Scholars have also used creolization to refer to both cultural mixing and cultural adaptation, as different groups assimilate themselves to living in a new environment.[23] What has not been the subject of much research is how grassroots organizations and other local groups have used tourism institutions and practices to construct "glocal" cultures and place identities. While researchers argue that local authenticities are always hybrid and can result from creolization, it is not clear how extralocal processes interconnect with local actions to produce heterogeneity and diversity. In short, tourism from below draws our attention to how seemingly remote and distant processes are mediated at various spatial and institutional levels, from the macrolevel of globalized institutions to the microlevel of people's day-to-day lives. Such a perspective adjudicates between a top-down approach that stresses the role of global factors in driving tourism, and a bottom-up approach that focuses on the role of local influences and particularizing forces.

As a sensitizing device, the tourism from above and below heuristic suggests a set of relationships, including structures, networks, and organizations for illuminating the diverse connections between tourism and metropolitan development, urban culture, and constructions of authenticity.[24] The categories listed in tables 1.1 and 1.2 do not exhaust the historical possibilities, nor do they constitute a comprehensive framework to explain the development of tourism everywhere and at all times. The structures, networks, and organizations associated with tourism from above in table 1.1 have evolved since the nineteenth century to produce and coordinate travel flows and create different varieties of tourism. We could include railroads, airlines, travel firms, and many government agencies and regulatory bodies as major actors affiliated with tourism from above. For tourism from below, the key actors and organizations that I identify in table 1.2 are not the only actors that could be listed in the figure, but they are major forces in the promotion of local culture and have played strategic and important roles in defining the metropolitan area as a unique and distinctive place over the past half century. We could add a variety of historic landmarks commissions, historic preservationist societies, music commissions, and nonprofit organizations under the rubric of tourism from below. My goal is not to identify every single actor and tourism organization but to analyze and explain the changing connections between the actors, structures and networks, and major processes.[25]

A major goal of this book is to apply and develop the tourism from above and below heuristic to illustrate the interactive relationships between the global and the local in the development of urban tourism. My investigation eschews a notion of the global and the local as abstract levels of analysis and concentrates on the linkages that constitute the global-local or micro-macro duality. On the one hand, I wish to understand the conditions under which tourism practices can reinforce trends toward the standardization and homogenization of culture and space. To do so, I examine the historical development of tourism organizations and marketing strategies and the role they have played in fabricating a touristic notion of authenticity to attract visitors to New Orleans. On the other hand, I wish to know whether tourism practices can generate and support cultural diversification and promote the growth of new identities and authenticities. To do so, I investigate the actions of local groups in harnessing and incorporating tourism discourses and practices into their tactics of cultural invention to help preserve longstanding traditions (localization) or help generate new traditions (hybridization or creolization).[26]

As sociologists of culture have noted, "tradition" is not just inherited from the past but is socially "constructed" through everyday social activities and practices, taking place amid material needs and social circumstances. Harvey Molotch, William Freudenberg, and Krista E. Paulsen's work on the etiology of place character; Wendy Griswold and Nathan Wright's work on the endurance of regional cultures; and Thomas Hylland Eriksen's and Ulf Hannerz's works on "creolization" suggest that the creation of traditions and other forms of cultural innovation are the result of recontextualization, mixing of different identities, and mergers of symbols.[27] This processual and hybrid view of culture draws attention to how the production and maintenance of cultures and traditions take places as people interact, create meaning, and produce and reproduce shared understandings of their behavior. This action-based approach views culture as fluid, situational, changeable, and emergent. What is important is not whether cultures or traditions are "real" or "authentic" but, rather, the ways that arguments about authenticity have been framed to influence public debate, contest policies, neutralize counterarguments and opposition, and mobilize constituents. I am interested in how claims about culture, tradition, identity, and authenticity have often been interpreted and reshaped to fit the exigencies of the present, including local debates over tourism and its consequences. In short, the distinction of tourism from above and below eschews a notion of an "authentic place" corrupted by tourism and examines how tourism can be a mechanism for creating and maintaining place character, including articulating local identities and generating place-specific forms of collective action.

New Orleans Tourism before Hurricane Katrina

New Orleans confronts us as a city of paradox, irony, and contradiction. Long known as the Crescent City, the metropolis has been condemned as a city of vice and decadence and celebrated as a place of joyous culture and unforgettable charm.[28] The New Orleans metropolitan statistical area has traditionally included Orleans Parish, Jefferson Parish, St. Bernard Parish, St. Charles Parish, and St. Tammany Parish (fig. 1.1). A county in the state of Louisiana is called a "parish." Before the Hurricane Katrina disaster, the metropolitan area contained approximately 1.1 million residents. Tourism in the New Orleans metropolitan area has grown tremendously over the past century. In the early 1900s, river-based commerce, cotton trade, and a growing market for leisure and amusement dominated the New Orleans economy. During this time, sections of New Orleans became oriented toward leisure and entertainment: public parks, sports grounds, theaters, art galleries, shopping and so on. The city's "red light" district and jazz culture left an indelible image in the minds of travelers and served for decades as a magnet to draw people to experience the "sin" industry. The discovery of oil in the early decades of the twentieth century spearheaded a tremendous growth of the chemical and petroleum industry, and by World War II, the city had established itself as a hub for military shipbuilding and manufacturing. Throughout the decades, political and economic elites promoted images of New Orleans as a charming city with beautiful and historic architecture, outstanding cuisine, excellent music, and Mardi Gras. By the middle of the century, the economy had a tripartite base made up of the oil industry, the port industry, and the tourism industry.[29] During the 1950s, New Orleans city officials and elites began devising strategies to increase tourist travel to enhance the economic pros-

Fig. 1.1. Greater New Orleans. (Reproduced by permission of Tulane University, Howard-Tilton Memorial Library, Special Collections)

perity and fiscal status of the central city. Dwindling urban population, the eroding manufacturing base, and burgeoning suburban development during the 1960s raised the specter of economic stagnation and created the context for city leaders to accelerate the development of tourism in the city.[30]

Over the decades, political and economic elites have forged close institutional links and developed several public-private partnerships in pursuit of tourism as a strategy to encourage inward investment and urban revitalization. This tourism strategy has included the building of a domed stadium, a festival mall, a massive convention center, new office towers in the Central Business District, a major theme park, and a World War II museum. The city has also staged many mega-events, including the 1984 World's Fair, periodic Super Bowls and (Nokia) Sugar Bowls, the NCAA (National Collegiate Athletic Association) basketball tournaments, the Jazz and Heritage Festival, the Essence Festival, and so on. The hotel industry has grown considerably over the past few decades, as indicated by the skyrocketing number of hotel rooms in the metropolitan area. The number of hotel rooms increased from 4,750 in 1960, to 10,686 in 1975 and 19,500 in 1985. In 1990, the metropolitan area had approximately 25,500 hotel/motel rooms. This figure increased to 28,000 in 1999 and to more than 33,000 by 2004. The convention market has also grown immensely since the 1960s. The city hosted 172 conventions in 1960; 1,000 conventions in 1975; 1,453 conventions in 1990; 2,485 conventions in 1995; and 3,556 conventions in 2000.[31] Overall convention attendance increased more than twenty times from 1960 to 2001, a development that reflects the growth of a tourism infrastructure of hotel and motel accommodations, restaurants, festival promotions, university programs in tourism management and service, professional sports, and so on. Other tourism developments that have occurred in the 1990s and later include the legalization of gaming in Louisiana, the creation of the New Orleans Tourism Marketing Corporation (NOTMC), the establishment of the New Orleans Multicultural Tourism Network (NOMTN), the creation of the Mayor's Office of Tourism and Arts, and the expansion of Convention and Visitors Bureau efforts to market the region to international tourists.

New Orleans has long been known as a city with dramatic and troubling disparities. In 1960, the urban population peaked at 640,000 residents and declined in every decade thereafter. Between 1960 and 2000, the city lost a total of 156,000 people. Over the decades, weak job growth and the loss of jobs in the chemical and petroleum industries have depressed the metropolitan economic base and contributed to an 18 percent poverty rate in 2000, making New Orleans the sixth poorest of the 100 largest metropolitan areas in the nation. The region's class inequalities interlock with racial inequalities. In 1960, whites made up 62.6 percent of the city's population and blacks were 37.2 percent. As of the 2000 census, blacks made up 66.7 percent of the Central City's population, and whites were 26.6 percent (table 1.3). In 2005, blacks made up 84 percent of the city's poor population, with a high percentage living in segregated neighborhoods. According to the Brookings Institution, before Katrina, 43 percent of poor blacks in New Orleans lived in extreme poverty (census tracts with at least 40 percent of the population living below the federal poverty levels). In 2000, black median household income in the city was almost half the amount of white median income ($21,461 as contrasted to $40,390); the black poverty rate was more than three times higher than the white poverty rate (35

TABLE I.3
Total and Racial Population in the New Orleans Metropolitan Statistical Area (MSA), Central City, and Suburban Areas (1980, 1990, and 2000)

	Year	Total Population	White Population	Black Population	Hispanic Population	Other Races (non-Hispanic)
MSA	1980	1,303,800	814,193	419,630	50,961	19,016
			62.4%	32.2%	3.9%	1.5%
	1990	1,285,270	762,697	443,97	152,53	26,039
			59.3%	34.5%	4.1%	2.0%
	2000	1,337,270	731,514	498,569	58,454	49,098
			54.7%	37.3%	4.4%	3.9%
Central City	1980	557,515	224,694	304,673	19,226	8922
			40.3%	54.6%	3.4%	1.6%
	1990	496,938	164,457	306,129	15,900	10,452
			33.1%	61.6%	3.2%	2.1%
	2000	484,674	128,871	323,392	14,826	7,585
			26.6%	66.7%	3.1%	3.0%
Suburbs	1980	719,567	565,925	112,643	31,149	9850
			78.6%	15.7%	4.3%	1.4%
	1990	764,208	577,583	135,309	36,034	15,282
			75.6%	17.7%	4.7%	2.0%
	2000	827,357	581,772	171,711	43,032	30,842
			70.3%	20.8%	5.2%	3.7%

SOURCE: U.S. Census Bureau, Census of Population and Housing, 1980, 1990, and 2000. Data supplied by the State of the Cities Data System (SOCDS), http://socds.huduser.org/. Central City includes New Orleans, LA. Suburbs include all areas of the MSA outside of New Orleans, LA, and Slidell, LA.

percent compared with 11 percent); and poor blacks were almost four times as likely to live in areas with extreme poverty (43 percent of poor blacks lived in concentrated poverty while only 11 percent of poor whites did).[32] As result, by the time Katrina came ashore, New Orleans had become a place of glaring racial and class inequalities, a place where poor African Americans were segregated and spatially isolated from the rest of the population.

In short, over the past several decades New Orleans has experienced dramatic losses in urban population, stagnant incomes, and persistent poverty and racial inequality. These conditions reflect the multidecade erosion of the chemical and petroleum industry and port industry and the rise of a service sector tourism economy dominated by low-wage, nonunion jobs. In 1999, according to Bureau of Labor Statistics, New Orleans had 16,000 hospitality and hotel workers, with 90 percent of the workforce in the city being African American.[33] Over the past decade, trade unions have campaigned fiercely to organize New Orleans hospitality workers, with the aim of increasing benefits and wages. Labor struggles in the hotel sector reached a crescendo in 2002 when voters overwhelmingly approved a city minimum wage hike to achieve a "living wage" for working people. This vote was dealt a major blow later in September 2002, when the Louisiana Supreme Court declared the living wage victory unconstitutional.[34] These battles are the most recent manifestations of the long history of class strife and racial struggle in New Orleans. Broadly, class and racial conflict in tourism illustrate the social relations of exploitation behind the production of tourist images and hospitality services. My historical examination highlights the changing nature of race and class in struggles over meanings of authenticity and explains how tourism practices are intimately linked with social inequalities.

Authentic New Orleans

This book addresses the links between the past and present in New Orleans to explore the historical development of tourism with an eye to making discoveries that might be helpful in understanding the links between race, culture, and authenticity. While classic works such as John Urry's *The Tourist Gaze* and Dean MacCannell's *The Tourist: A New Theory of the Leisure Class* and *Empty Meeting Grounds: The Tourist Papers* are extremely important, because of the broad and generalized perspective they bring to the study of tourism, the kind of rich detail and investigative specificity of a historical case study can offer a researcher empirical and theoretical gains in understanding larger social complexes of actors, actions, and motives.[35]

Case studies have a rich tradition in sociology and are becoming increasingly popular within urban scholarship on tourism, metropolitan development, and urban culture and politics, as illustrated by Mark Gottdiener, Claudia Collins, and David Dickens's *Las Vegas: The Social Production of an All-American City*; Richard Lloyd's *Neo-Bohemia: Art and Commerce in the Postindustrial City*; Christopher Mele's *Selling the Lower East Side: Culture, Real Estate, and Resistance in New York City*; and David Grazian's *Blue Chicago: The Search for Authenticity in Urban Blues Clubs*.[36] This renewed interest in case study research comes from the increasing recognition that contextual factors specific to the city under study complicate cross-city generalizations about tourism.

Susan Fainstein and Dennis Judd suggest that local contextualities render the tourism process to have a relevant degree of place specificity: "Variation in the impacts of tourism and its multiple meanings . . . call for an examination of individual cases."[37] As far as tourism is an expression of larger social, economic, and political relations, the development of tourism in any particular city will express the particularities of the place in the making of its urban space. In short, place matters in the study of tourism because an analysis of *why* and *how* tourism develops will need to take into account *where* and *when* it develops.

To begin, I investigate the rise of early tourism practices and the development of a nascent tourism industry during the late nineteenth century and early twentieth century. In chapter 2, I explore the demise of the antebellum Carnival and the origin of the modern Mardi Gras celebration during the middle of the nineteenth century. Any discussion of tourism and culture in New Orleans must deal with the city's signature celebration and the part it has historically played in both reflecting and reproducing class and racial conflicts in the city. The early development of tourism in New Orleans is associated with elite efforts to transform Mardi Gras from an indigenous festival into rationalized spectacle. In chapter 3, I examine the mobilization of business elites in the planning and staging of the World's Industrial and Cotton Centennial Exposition in New Orleans in 1884 and 1885. This exposition was the largest world's fair of its time and helped nurture the growth of new business networks and cultural organizations to promote the city on global scale.

As I point out in later chapters, New Orleans has long had a penchant for international expositions and the efforts to attract world's fairs in 1884, 1915, and 1984 reflect the mobilization of local elites to harness tourism flows and build attractions as expedients to economic revitalization and urban place building. International expositions exemplify the articulation of tourism from above and below. On the one hand, expositions represent local efforts to create an ephemeral and large-scale display of local artifacts, foods, and customs to a worldwide audience. On the other hand, expositions comprise a series of extralocal networks, corporations, and organizations working to transform urban space into an entertaining site for the visual consumption of international cultures and identities. As I show, the history of world's fairs in New Orleans is a history of conflict and antagonism as elite groups and interests have struggled to project a conflict-free image of New Orleans while grassroots organizations have attempted to use expositions as political venues to challenge inequalities. Thus, New Orleans's experience with world's fairs reveals the deep fault lines of race and class and provides insight into how opposing constituencies have attempted to articulate and legitimate differing conceptions of an "authentic" New Orleans.

In chapters 4 and 5, I chart the historical development of New Orleans's tourism sector during the early twentieth century up through the 1960s. As I show, the development of the city's modern tourism sector coincides with the institutionalization of racial discrimination in all major facets of social life and culture in the city. The first half of the century is notable for the establishment of the New Orleans Association of Commerce to attract tourism investment and promote the convention trade. In chapter 4, I investigate the competition between New Orleans and San Francisco to attract the 1915 World's Fair, the growth of racial segregation in tourism, and the development of new strategies to promote Mardi Gras as a major tourist attraction. As I point out in chapter 5, the 1960s are a turning point in the historical development of New Orleans tourism. Rise of the civil rights movement combined with spreading urban disinvestment and suburbanization motivated political and economic elites to devise new tourism strategies to revitalize the city. In 1960, local leaders formed the Greater New Orleans Tourist and Convention Commission (GNOTCC), a forerunner to the current New Orleans Metropolitan Convention and Visitors Bureau (NOMCVB), to rationalize the process of tourism promotion and development. The GNOTCC is a major organization that, beginning in the 1960s, connects the above processes of commodification and rationalization with the below forces of grassroots cultural invention and improvisation to link New Orleans with a fledgling global tourism industry. Broadly, I show that new tourism networks, organizations, and financing helped stimulate a major growth in the number of tourist attractions while simultaneously generating new conflicts and struggles over meanings of local culture and authenticity.

The period after the 1970s inaugurates a new era of local and state government efforts to promote tourism, the formation of specialized tourism organizations, and the development of new tourism networks and marketing strategies (branding). This period also reflects the growth of grassroots cultural organizations and historic preservation groups such as the Arts Council of New Orleans, the Community Arts Center, the Jazz and Heritage Foundation, Save Our Cemeteries, and the Preservation Resource Center, among many others, dedicated to raising awareness of local culture and heritage. I first examine the planning and staging of the 1984 Louisiana World Exposition in New Orleans, the last world's fair held in the United States. On the one hand, this exposition set in motion the development of new tourism organizations and public-private networks to attract corporate hotel chains and entertainment corporations. On the other hand, the exposition helped spawn a powerful network of grassroots art groups and cultural organizations committed to nourishing and building a tourism from below. I then discuss the rise of urban branding as a major promotional strategy used by powerful tourism organizations to transform urban culture into an abstract sign to entertain visitors and build attractions. Urban branding is a process of transforming otherwise mundane and ordinary symbols, images, and experiences into evocative signs of place distinctiveness to expand the number of visitors and generate local support for tourism investment. In New Orleans, this narrative of distinction or brand strategy is constructed around three themes—history, music, and food—that constitute the "holy trinity" of New Orleans tourism. As I show, since the 1960s, broad sociocultural transformations have blurred the distinction between tourism and other institutions and cultural practices, a development I refer to as a shift from a "culture of tourism" to a "touristic culture." Today, a touristic culture denotes a process by which tourism discourses and practices increasingly frame meanings and assertions of local culture and authenticity.

In chapters 7 and 8, I use my field observations and interviews to highlight the conflicts and struggles over efforts to commercialize Mardi Gras and transform the French Quarter into an entertainment destination. As tourism has come to dominate more and more aspects of social life in New Orleans, both Mardi Gras and the French Quarter have become contested terrain, where various residents, business and property owners, and elected officials duel over competing meanings of the beloved neighborhood and the city's famous celebration. Disagreements over who speaks for the French Quarter, which groups should control land-use decisions, and how tourist development should proceed in the historic neighborhood define conflicts over tourism. I develop the concept "repertoire of authenticity" to refer to a loose set of themes and symbolic devices that French Quarter residents have cultivated and deployed to battle the growth of corporate entertainment chains, and legitimate their role as controllers of neighborhood redevelopment. In chapter 8, I draw on interviews with local residents and Carnival enthusiasts to explore the role of local actions and organizations in harnessing tourist images and representations to reinforce place distinctiveness and invent new Mardi Gras traditions and customs. As I show, Mardi Gras stands at the intersection of tourism from above and tourism from below. On the one hand, the extralocal forces of commodification, standardization, and rationalization are transforming the celebration. On the other hand, local groups and individuals are using tourism symbols and images to anchor Mardi Gras in place and create new Carnival traditions as a means of reinforcing the uniqueness of New Orleans's Carnival.

By way of conclusion, in chapter 9, I address the current moment, when a broad-based coalition of city leaders and tourism boosters are attempting to revitalize New Orleans in the aftermath of Katrina. Hurricane Katrina is an unprecedented disaster that has caused catastrophic human suffering, economic disruption, and physical destruction. In addition, the disaster has exposed to a global audience New Orleans's chronic poverty, strained race relations, and intense inequalities. Since the disaster, local elites have attempted to counter negative images of destruction and advertise New Orleans as a come-back city that is regaining its vibrancy, style, and confidence. At the same time, city leaders and tourism officials have clashed over the role tourism should play in the city rebuilding process. Moreover, the uncertainty and devastation unleashed by Hurricane Katrina has reinvigorated old debates and stimulated new arguments about meanings and definitions of local authenticity. New conflicts and struggles are emerging between local groups and neighborhoods over what constitutes authenticity, who should define what authenticity means, and how authenticity should be expressed. My goal is to explore how the destruction caused by Hurricane Katrina is leading to new assertions of "authenticity" and new interpretations of "New Orleans." Finally, I speculate on the future of metropolitan life, race and class relations, and tourism in the post-Katrina years.

2

Processions and Parades

Carnival Krewes and the Development of Modern Mardi Gras

It was the last day of carnival. . . . There was a grand procession parading in the streets, almost everyone dressed in the most grotesque attire, troops of them on horseback, some in open carriages, with bands of music, and in a variety of costumes. . . . All wore masks, and here and there in the crowd, or stationed in a balcony above, we saw persons armed with bags of flour, which they showered down copiously on any one who seemed particularly proud of his attire. The strangeness of the scene was not a little heightened by the blending of negroes, quadroons, and mulattos in the crowd; and we were amused by observing the ludicrous surprise, mixed with contempt, of several unmasked, stiff, grave Anglo-Americans from the North, who were witnessing, for the first time, what seemed to be so much mummery and tom-foolery. . . . The crowd seemed determined to allow nothing to disturb their good humor.
—Englishman Charles Lyell, recorded in a visit to New Orleans in 1846[1]

For over a century, Carnival and Mardi Gras have been tightly integrated into the social life of New Orleans and have always expressed the collective conscience and social antagonisms of the city. Traditionally, the Carnival season in New Orleans consists of a series of balls and parades from January 6 (Twelfth Night, or the Feast of the Epiphany) to Mardi Gras, or "Fat Tuesday," the day before Ash Wednesday and the beginning of Lent. Before the Civil War, Carnival and Mardi Gras developed as a relatively spontaneous and indigenous celebration for local residents that included public masking, masquerade balls, rambunctious street parades, and widespread frivolity. At various times during both the colonial and antebellum periods, city authorities prohibited masking and masquerade balls, though enforcement was often lax and uneven. The Civil War temporarily interrupted organized parading, and the years of Reconstruction (1866–1877) witnessed the growth of new Carnival clubs, organizations, and cultural traditions in the city. Railroad companies used Mardi Gras themes in their advertisements to stimulate travel, and by the 1880s and 1890s the local celebration had become nationally popular. By the end of the century, American and European travel writers advised readers that Mardi Gras in New Orleans was a lavish festival that expressed civic pride, community identity, and a local attitude of "Laissez Le Bon Temps Roule" (Let the Good Times Roll). As the twentieth century unfolded, the actual celebration and symbolic icon of Mardi Gras grew significantly larger as tens of thousands of tourists visited the city to participate in the annual festival. Through the century, the growth of media coverage, international publicity, and promotional campaigns helped create an enduring public image of Mardi Gras as the most extravagant celebration staged in any American city.[2] Today, although other cities around the world celebrate Mardi Gras, none have the intemperate and licentious reputation, long-standing cultural traditions, spectacular floats and parades, formal balls, and tourism infrastructure to accommodate the thousands of tourists that visit New Orleans each year.

Carnival and Mardi Gras in the Colonial and Antebellum Eras

> Great was the rejoicing in our fair city yesterday; from morn until midnight the gay-hearted youth, laying aside all cares, came forth in fanciful attire to celebrate the Mardi Gras. . . . Not only were the riders decked in fancy robes, but also their horses came in for a share of the decorations, and bore rich cloths round their necks and ornamental appendages to their tails. . . . When night came on, the city seemed all one masquerade. Groups of citizens in dresses, of every age and station, were wending their way to the various balls and theatres, and it seemed that mirth and laughter were the high priests that every one had sworn to worship.
> —Description of Mardi Gras from "The Carnival," 1855[3]

Evidence of a Carnival "season" of limited duration, with particular festivities and institutional forms, is sparse before the 1820s. Few newspapers noticed Carnival in a regular manner, and visitors to New Orleans reported little about concerted and formalized celebrations taking place. Across the city and region, public balls, concerts, plays, and street masking were frequent and widespread, and not restricted to a delimited season. During the colonial era, a rich tradition of black holidays and festivities flourished in New Orleans from January until March, a condition that caused city leaders to segregate and confine black celebrations to specific areas of the city, including Congo Square (today called Louis Armstrong Park), the only legal gathering place permitted for African slaves. By the first decade of the nineteenth century, Congo Square had acquired a reputation as a festive space of dance and revelry where blacks celebrated on Sundays and Ash Wednesday, engaging in sophisticated rituals that had no connection to Christian religious meanings.[4] Black Carnival celebrations at Congo Square and in other places in New Orleans during the colonial and antebellum eras paralleled the growth of a series of semisegregated private, subscription, and public balls. During the period of Spanish rule (1763–1803), public masked balls emerged as an important component of the cultural life of New Orleans but were later suppressed in 1781 due to fears among Spanish rulers that cavorting among the different classes, races, and ethnic groups at the balls would encourage revolt and lead to criminal behavior.[5] In 1805, after the United States assumed control of Louisiana, the New Orleans City Council banned public masked balls and outlawed masking in all streets, balls, and public places.[6] Broadly, up to the 1820s, there were no specific institutional forms or organized activities that defined Carnival or demarcated a Carnival season as distinct from other seasons.[7]

It is during the 1820s and 1830s that we see the growth of a rich ensemble of Carnival celebrations, public and private masked balls, and spontaneous street parades in New Orleans. In the early 1820s, the New Orleans City Council lifted its ban on public masked balls, marking the end of restrictions against masking and heralding the beginning of a new era of *bals masque,* masquerade balls held from the Feast of the Epiphany or Twelfth Night to Ash Wednesday.[8] Masquerade balls are the major institutional development that begins to distinguish Carnival balls from ordinary public balls that are held year-round.

Nineteenth-century travel accounts mention masquerade balls in New Orleans. In his travels through New Orleans in the 1820s, Benjamin Latrobe reported that "it is now the Carnival, every evening is closed with a ball, or a play." Karl Bernard, Duke of Saxe-Weimar Eisenbach, noted in 1825 that masked balls were "held every evening during the carnival" and on Mardi Gras day "all the ball-rooms in the city were opened." Later, actor Louis Tasistro observed that during Carnival

> New Orleans was one vast waltzing and galloping hall. The commingled sounds of fiddles and piano-fortes could be heard at every corner of the street throughout the livelong night. There was no thought of, no occupation, no interest in anything but dancing. Indeed, from the very commencement of Carnival, dancing, and nothing but dancing, had been the order of the day.

According to Tasistro, who observed the Mardi Gras celebration in 1841, "people seemed to have nothing else to do but to amuse themselves—to drown their senses in forgetfulness—to make their *Saturnalia* last as long as possible . . . by a round of brainless, valueless, and exaggerated enjoyments." Five years later, in 1846, Englishman Charles Lyell recorded in a visit to New Orleans that

> it was the last day of Carnival. . . . There was a grand procession parading in the streets, almost everyone dressed in the most grotesque attire, troops of them on horseback, some in open carriages, with bands of music, and in a variety of costumes. . . . All wore masks.[9]

Another defining feature of the antebellum Carnival was the plethora of informal parades and spontaneous street celebrations that local residents held annually from the 1830s onward.[10] The first newspaper account of an organized Carnival parade was in 1837 when the *New Orleans Picayune* noted in a February 8 article, "A lot of masqueraders were parading through our streets yesterday, and excited considerable speculation as to who they were, what were their motives, and what upon earth could induce them to turn out in such grotesque and outlandish habiliments."[11] A year later, the *New Orleans Commercial Bulletin* noted that "the European custom of celebrating the last day of Carnival by a procession of masqued figures through the public streets was introduced here yesterday, very much to the amusement of our citizens. . . . The exhibition surpassed any thing of the kind ever before witnessed here."[12] The actor Louis Tasistro described the Mardi Gras celebration in 1841 as "composed of two and three hundred of the first gentlemen of the city" with "every balcony and window, as far as the eye could reach . . . filled with anxious spectators, watching for the approach of the cavalcade."[13] The festive night concluded with a costume ball, a custom that would eventually become a permanent Carnival tradition in the ensuing decades.[14] During the 1830s and 1840s, almost all the street processions were small, unorganized, irregular, and relatively spontaneous celebrations. Grand processions like the kind described by Tasistro, Lyell, and others took place periodically but were not an institutionalized cultural practice. While local residents celebrated Mardi Gras through street marching, masking, and costume balls, these were neither centrally controlled nor rationally planned by formal organizations.

The unique features of New Orleans including its dominant French language, its prevailing Catholicism, and distinctive mix of African and Caribbean ethnic groups and European settlers spawned an urban culture and way of life that differed dramatically from other cities in the United States. In 1810, New Orleans registered a total population of 17,242 residents making it the seventh largest city in the United States. By 1830, the city population had more than doubled to 46,082 residents. A decade later, in 1840, New Orleans was the third largest city with 102,193 people, behind New York City with 312,710 residents and Baltimore with 102,313 residents. On the eve of the Civil War, in 1860, the population of New Orleans had mushroomed to 168,675 with much of this growth coming from a surge of European immigration.[15] Massive waves of Irish and German immigrants inundated New Orleans during the 1830s through 1860s adding to the city's already rich diversity of French, Spanish, British, and Caribbean ethnic groups. By 1850, there were approximately 20,000 Irish; 11,425 Germans; 7,522 French; and 2,670 English and Scottish residents living in New Orleans, according to the U.S. Census Bureau. Adding to New Orleans's ethnic gumbo was a community of free people of color that numbered almost 20,000 in 1840, a figure that made the city the home to the largest population of free black men and women of any city in the United States.[16] Historians have noted that the light complexions of some Africans attested to intimate contact with Europeans and reflect a plurality of ethnic and cultural relations and fluid identities in antebellum New

Orleans, a unique situation in U.S. cities at the time.[17] The city's subtropical climate with its abundant rainfall and frequent flooding meant that living space was confined to higher ground along the Mississippi River. As a result, various racial and ethnic groups migrating into the city were forced to settle together in densely packed neighborhoods, thus encouraging close contact and intermingling.

The combination of ethnic and cultural diversity, a large community of free people of color, and a variety of African and Caribbean peoples moving into the restless city hindered the establishment and maintenance of segregated neighborhoods and entertainment spaces. On the one hand, from the colonial days on, local authorities attempted to exclude free people of color and slaves from white accommodations and racially segregate major institutions, including hospitals, schools, public parks, theaters, bars and taverns, and government events.[18] In addition, during the 1820s through the 1840s, the New Orleans City Council adopted several laws to regulate and control public masked malls and impose racial segregation, laws that were unevenly enforced. On the other hand, segregationist laws did not automatically translate into a rigid system of racial exclusion or segregation within the celebration of Carnival. Indeed, racial and ethnic mixing in the streets, parades, and public balls was the rule rather than the exception during the celebration.

One major institutional factor frustrating the enforcement of segregation ordinances was the political division of New Orleans into three separate municipalities, an unusual and distinct division that lasted from 1836 to 1852.[19] Each of the three municipalities—two dominated by French creoles and the other controlled by Anglo-Americans—had its own separate courts, schools, language (French and English), and legal system.[20] This decentralization and fragmentation of local government made it difficult to create and maintain an organized legal system for reinforcing racial segregation in Carnival and other cultural spheres. In short, the combination of ethnic movement and in-migration, the lack of rigid racial residential segregation, and a politically fragmented government and legal system all worked in tandem to frustrate attempts to impose racial distinctions and divisions. Despite the oppressiveness of slavery and an overarching system of legal discrimination, class and racial interaction in the streets, public balls, and parades dominated the celebration of Carnival during the antebellum era.

By the 1850s, industrial expansion and population growth were transforming New Orleans, creating a volatile situation of rising wealth juxtaposed with increasing labor strife. The labor struggles intensified during the 1850s as dockworkers struck for higher wages and attacked strikebreakers for attempting to cross the picket lines in 1850, 1852, and 1854. State efforts to curtain labor struggles and keep unions off the docks led to the passage of a 1858 ordinance that made it illegal for workers to picket on the wharves or on ships.[21] Broadly, by the middle of the century, New Orleans was facing an influx of transient paupers and vagrants, the "dangerous classes," or the lumpenproletariat in Karl Marx's famous description in volume 1 of *Capital*.[22] While exact figures are obscure, the problem of pauperism can be seen in the passage of antivagrant laws in 1852, 1857, 1866, 1870, and 1879 aimed at discouraging poor vagrants from staying in the city.[23] Changing demographic and social conditions were destabilizing the city, projecting an image of social unrest, and, more important, leading to lamentations about the demise of Carnival. The *Daily Delta* newspaper, on March 4, 1851, observed:

> We can remember when the processions used to extend several squares, and embraced a great multitude and variety of oddities, all the duly marshaled and commanded. But alas! The world grows every day more practical, less sportive and imaginative—and more indifferent to the customs and institutions of the past. Mardi Gras, with all its laughter-moving tomfooleries, must go the way of all our other ancient institutions, and reposing on its past glory, may content itself with sneering at the hard realities of the present locomotive, telegraphic age.[24]

Two years later, on Ash Wednesday, February 8, 1853, the *Daily Crescent* deplored Carnival, asserting:

> In the early days of our city, when it was peopled by a Catholic community, who understood and could appreciate the observances of the Day, Mardi Gras was a season of striking and memorable peculiarities. . . . But now the aspect of things has changed. Our population is not what it was. The old regime is no more. It has fallen into the list of forgotten things, and sway over manners has passed to the swine-eating Saxon.

The same day, the French-language newspaper, the *New Orleans Bee* editorialized that "in olden time," Mardi Gras was observed with "outdoor processions of masques and other saturnalia, in order to give due effect to the last day of the Carnival. But all this has vanished, now, and people enjoy themselves more soberly." Three years later, in 1856, the *New Orleans Daily Delta* proclaimed Carnival as a dying tradition: "The good old Creole customs are rapidly falling into disuse, as the people of the [French Quarter] go down before the men of Maine and Massachusetts, who have succeeded in controlling the 'business' of the city to a great extent."[25]

These cynical news reports tell a nostalgic story of an "authentic" Carnival held together by venerable traditions and enriching customs whose coherence is eroding in the face of immigration and industrial transformation. On the one hand, the *Daily Delta*'s somber reflection on the "hard realities of the present locomotive, telegraphic age" evokes the desperate pace and frantic rhythm that railroad building and commercial trade are adding to life in antebellum New Orleans. On the other hand, the news reports represent a selective interpretation and ideological framing of Carnival that connects nostalgia for the past with the decline and loss of cultural heritage. In New Orleans, the propitious story of the Mardi Gras of old emerged as a powerful narrative of stigmatization to scapegoat the newly arriving Anglo-American immigrants. The diatribe against the "swine-eating Saxon" and "men of Maine and Massachusetts" implied an exogenous and threatening outgroup. In addition, the referents of "Catholic community" and "good old Creole customs" aimed to construct a sense of community authenticity and identity (e.g., "us" versus "them"). More important, the subjective quality of "creole" gave it a certain elasticity as newspapers like the *Daily Delta,* the *Daily Crescent,* and the *Bee* helped fashion a discourse of fading grandeur. Decades later, the notion of an aesthetically rich and fragile French creole culture gradually losing out to an Anglo-Saxon world of soulless materialism and cold rationalization would be incorporated into tourism guides and other promotional pieces to construct a nostalgic image of an authentic New Orleans of old.

Sociologists of culture have long examined nostalgia as an important component of people's constructions of place identity and community solidarity. Fred Davis's analysis of nostalgia, Melinda Milligan's examination of past memories and place attachment, David Hummon's study of commonplaces, and Herbert Gans's classic investigation of displacement in Boston's West End all represent efforts to understand how narratives of the past shape the identity of a place and the people who use it.[26] Narratives about the past do not simply "represent" a bygone era but fabricate a past and construct a sense of place and membership. In New Orleans, nostalgia functioned as an important cultural construction technique and cultural delegitimizing device, a mechanism for creating in-group and out-group boundaries. The image of a "golden age" was a useful resource in the collective quest by newspapers to create a sense of community authenticity in the face of rapid industrial and societal transformation.

The illustrative power of the symbol "creole" resided in the fact that it was an ambiguous referent, open to interpretation and waiting to be filled with meaning. As an evocative symbol of New Orleans, creole blended together cultural material from different component group traditions to become a master signifier of local culture. Creole and nostalgia operated not merely as cultural tools in the construction of a putative common history but as symbolic vocabulary to establish membership criteria. Constructions of Anglo-Saxons and other immigrants as threatening newcomers were important culture-building techniques that combined into a symbolic system for defining grievances and providing a blueprint for authenticity. At the same time, ethnic tensions and conflict surrounding the articulation of a community authenticity made constructions of commonality deeply problematic. Over the course of the next century, different groups would draw on similar strands of New Orleans history and culture, but in conflicting and opposing ways. By recasting the material of the past in innovative ways, in the service of new political agendas, local groups would (re)forge their own culture and history and reinvent themselves.

Carnival Krewes and the Rationalization of Mardi Gras

> Today is Mardi Gras day and is celebrated by people dressing themselves up and making fools of themselves generally.
> —Letter from a Union soldier in New Orleans, 1863[27]

Mardi Gras 1857 is a turning point in the history of New Orleans's Carnival. On this day, the Mystick Krewe of Comus, an organized group of

Fig. 2.1. The inaugural Krewe of Comus parade of 1857 from *Illustrated London*. Before 1857, a variety of cultural practices—including masquerade balls, public celebrations, and spontaneous street masking—dominated the celebration of Carnival. The Krewe of Comus introduced several new Carnival customs, including the krewe system (formal organizations that plan and stage parades), themed parades, and exclusive tableaux balls. More important, the establishment of a krewe system represented a new cultural form that rationalized the production of Carnival by establishing preplanned and scripted parades that separated spectators from krewe paraders. Over the course of the nineteenth and twentieth centuries, the Carnival krewe would become a major cultural institution to enhance the tourist appeal of Mardi Gras. (Reproduced by permission of Tulane University, Howard-Tilton Memorial Library, Special Collections)

several dozen social elites, staged their first themed parade and tableaux ball, a development that represented a new and distinctive form of elite cultural production (fig. 2.1). Costume balls and street parades had long been a cultural fixture of Carnival. Yet the members of Comus introduced several cultural innovations that would come to redefine Mardi Gras and create a more rationalized and "bourgeois" Carnival.[28]

First, the members of Comus established an exclusive social club to plan and stage Carnival parades and balls. Shortly after their first Carnival parade, they created the Pickwick Club, a private and secretive club that would be the formal organization for Comus. Later Carnival organizations adopted this formula of a private club and henceforth called themselves "krewes," thereby creating a new tradition of Carnival organizations using mythological namesake and iconology. The combination of a clearly defined leadership structure, committee system, and secret rites of passage helped promote and ensure rational administration and control over Carnival festivities, a development that is the antithesis of the spontaneity and unorganized nature of the antebellum Carnival. Second, Comus processions were nighttime, themed parades that contained floats. These themes included Demon Actors in Milton's Paradise Lost, for its first parade in 1857; Classic Pantheon in 1858; English Holidays in 1859; and Missing Links to Darwin's Origin of Species in 1873. Later Carnival krewes would follow Comus's lead and draw their themes from literary classics using marching bands, costumed and grotesque figures, and military divisions to parade through the city. Third, Comus staged an invitation-only tableaux ball at the end of their parade where only members of the krewe were in mask and costume.[29]

During these years, elites in the city created the Twelfth Night Revelers (formed in 1871), the Krewe of Momus (1872), the Krewe of Rex (1872), and the Krewe of Proteus (1882). What united these otherwise different parades was that each adopted the model of the exclusive social club or formal organization (à la Rex), staged a themed parade with floats, and held a tableaux ball for guests. Social elites in New Orleans borrowed from a rich and long tradition of Carnival balls and street celebrations, the local cultural "tool kit" in sociologist Ann Swidler's conception, to create a new cultural form, the Carnival krewe, to organize parades and private balls.[30] A major cultural innovation of Comus, Momus, Proteus, and Rex, the elite or "old-line" krewes, as they later became known, was to create organized parades and balls that constituted people not as active participants but as spectators.

Before Comus, Momus, Proteus, and Rex, almost all street masking and parading in New Orleans was relatively ad hoc and unorganized. Ragtag groups of revelers would create loosely structured and ephemeral processions through their spontaneous actions. Those who wanted to organize a street procession would designate a route and publicly invite all interested maskers to meet at a specific time to march. By restricting participation and developing planned tableaux and costumes, the old-line krewes aimed to eliminate the aura of spontaneity and promote order through a controlled procession. By the last quarter of the nineteenth century, the old-line krewes had established a new form of social differentiation between the "public" and "private" spheres of Carnival, separating activities open to the public (organized parades) from those limited to the private krewes and their guests (invitation-only tableaux balls).[31]

Harnessing Carnival to Attract Tourists

My own dear wife . . . my office has been invaded off and on all day by idlers who wished to look out my windows, and by the incessant noise and din on the streets. . . . It was a great jam during the whole day, and I think the numbers of strangers is much greater than at any year before. . . . At 3:00, the King of Carnival found his procession and marched up and down the streets. . . . After these followed a cavalcade in masks and after these followed innumerable pedestrians in mask many of them very grotesque. . . . I never saw such a crowd in New Orleans. . . . The day has been a great success, by far the finest Show ever seen here even in Antebellum times, what a pity that they have not the same energy for real work that they display in getting up amusements.

—Description of Mardi Gras, 1872, from an anonymous writer to his wife[32]

The emergence of the Carnival krewe and the rationalized parade reflects larger social transformations in New Orleans, including the decline of the longstanding Francophone culture and political influence in the city and the rise of a powerful Anglo-Saxon bourgeoisie. While the English-language newspapers in the city praised the first Comus parade and ball, the French-language newspaper, the *New Orleans Bee,* downplayed the celebration and commented mockingly that the parade was a close copy of a similar one staged in Mobile, Alabama, by a group called the Cowbellions during New Year's eve. Many historians have noted that the names of the first Comus members were prominent businessmen with Anglo-Saxon names.[33] An article in the *New Orleans Daily Crescent* described the Mardi Gras celebration of 1861 and observed that Comus "is an entirely secret organization; but yet it is well understood to be composed of gentlemen of wealth and of the first respectability in the city."[34]

Historian Joseph Roach maintains that the early founders of Comus were steamboat agents, accountants, lawyers, produce wholesalers, merchants, bankers, and other professionals.[35] Other members who later joined Comus included John Burside, a wealthy sugar planter; Edmond J. Forstall, a banker and agent for the Baring Brothers of London and Hope and Company of Amsterdam, two of the leading international commercial firms of the nineteenth century; James Robb, a prominent businessman and president of the New Orleans, Jackson, and Great

Northern Railroad; R. W. Adams, a wholesale grocer; and George W. Race, a lawyer for Fellows and Company.[36] In discussing the "Northern roots" of the Krewe of Rex, Carnival historian Errol Laborde maintains that two of the founding members of Rex, E. C. Hancock and C. T. Howard, were from Philadelphia. While other founders of the Krewe of Rex were originally from the North, all members came from wealthy backgrounds, including banking and finance, publishing, and administrative activities.[37]

The elite men of New Orleans who were involved in reinventing Carnival before and after the Civil War were helping to create new cultural institutions and lifestyles that would publicly proclaim their patrician taste and style. In his book *Fantasy City,* sociologist John Hannigan notes that the establishment of social clubs was one expression of America's newly emerging industrial elite who made their fortunes in steel, railroads, and banking.[38] For elite males in the antebellum era, membership in an exclusive social club was a symbol of class status—a cultural institution that defined upward mobility and status attainment. By linking the Carnival krewe with an exclusive men's social club, the leaders of Comus, Momus, Rex, and Proteus were able to launch a new formula for managing Carnival while providing a cultural avenue for advancing their own class interests. Drawn from the city's most elite gentlemen's clubs and the wealthiest families, the founders and members of the old-line krewes excluded all others who could not afford to socialize with them. As a result, Carnival krewes and their elite social clubs provided high-status "niches" for an otherwise fragmented or disorganized social elite, helping to forge a class unity among the wealthy and affluent. These clubs and their krewes also became cultural entry points for newly arriving wealthy entrepreneurs who wished to invest in New Orleans and assimilate themselves into elite society. To quote Emile Durkheim, who wrote that ceremonies are collective representations that serve to "sustain the vitality of beliefs," it can be said that the performance of Carnival for the old-line krewes expressed upper-class beliefs, reaffirmed their status as the social elite, and "revivif[ied] the most essential elements of [their] collective consciousness."[39] In the insular space of the social club and Carnival krewe, social elites could articulate, typify, and orient their experiences to make them meaningful. The construction of meaning, in turn, could provide a basis for strategic collective action and generate a rationale for political mobilization.

The process of rationalizing Carnival was closely linked to elite efforts to adapt the celebration to attract tourists to New Orleans. Social elites conceived of tourism as a vehicle of place promotion to raise business interest in New Orleans as a site of profitable investment and commercial growth. Through the promotional efforts of the elite Carnival krewes, local elites participated in a strategic campaign to commodify New Orleans and make the city seem safe and available to a prosperous business class. Early on, newspapers championed the use of Carnival as a tourist attraction. In a February 22, 1871, article, for example, the *New Orleans Commercial Bulletin* praised the economic windfall Mardi Gras would have on the city, estimating that the Comus parade itself attracted 100,000 spectators. "All these visitors," the newspaper noted, "are consumers." Three years later, a February 8, 1874, editorial in the *New Orleans Daily Picayune* commented that, "apart from the question of amusement and popular rejoicing, the splendor and magnificence of our Carnival are business matters."[40]

One important motivation for creating the Krewe of Rex in 1872 was to lure visitors and capital to New Orleans in an effort to revive the local economy that had been devastated by the Civil War. A report in the *New Orleans Republican* newspaper of February 11, 1872, two days before Mardi Gras, lavished praise on the maiden parade of the Krewe of Rex, commenting that "our foremost consideration . . . is to make our city attractive, not entirely for citizens, but principally for visitors. . . . Public attention has been drawn to New Orleans. This will bring hither no less than 15,000 people, and they will on a low average, expend $50 each, thus bringing capital to our city." Mardi Gras, according to the *Republican,* could be a means to lure tourists to the city, and "every visitor, on returning home, will give his less fortunate neighbors a pleasant or glowing account of the wonders of the Crescent City. Next year, the number of visitors will be doubled; and so our city will be benefitted. For this reason, residents should make the celebration as attractive as possible and Rex has pursued the right course." Thus, newspaper accounts lauding the economic multipliers of tourism suggest the deep historical roots in New Orleans of using tourism as a strategy of economic development and urban boosterism.[41]

For the elite krewes like Rex, preplanned and scripted parades offered uniformity, orderliness, and predictability, thereby offering assurances to prospective visitors that Carnival would be a safe and enjoyable event worth seeing. J. Curtis Waldo, a founding member of Rex, wrote about the establishment of the krewe in a 1882 tourist guide published by the Chicago, St. Louis, and New Orleans Railroad. As Waldo remembered, "the fame of the magnificent pageants of the Mystic [*sic*] Krewe of Comus, having spread throughout the length and breadth of the land, drew to our city such multitudes of strangers that they were unable to accommodate even the more distinguished of our visitors." The problem, according to Waldo, was that visitors "were unable to obtain invitations" to the tableaux balls; "as the years rolled on, the number of visitors increased, and the demand for cards to the evening entertainment grew more and more numerous, and the number who returned home disappointed was consequently larger each year." For Waldo, what was distinctive about the Krewe of Rex was the creation of a parade and ball for "strangers," or elite tourists, to enliven the tourist aspects of Carnival and promote the economic development of New Orleans. Such a story found its way into numerous travel brochures, including one published by the Southern Pacific Lines in 1917, which noted that "commercial instincts" among "a few public-spirited men" made them aware "that Carnival bought visitors to New Orleans, and that these visitors, when they returned home, usually carried empty purses. . . . The opportunity was too good to be lost, and straightway inspired by patriotism, business and social ambition," these men "acted with commendable vigor and enthusiasm" to create "the good Rex."[42]

Railroad guidebooks played a major role in raising the profile of the Mardi Gras celebration, while local efforts to attract tourists to the city reflected elite interests in converting Carnival to the demands and opportunities of tourism promotion. George Soule, one of the founders of the Krewe of Rex and the King of Rex in 1887, commented that "the Rex organization and other Carnival associations attract visitors to the city, all of whom spend some money in hotels, shops, stores, etc." Going further, Soule reported that Carnival "has proved a positive benefit to New Orleans in the past, and is now the city's greatest advertising asset for winter travel, and the best means of increasing friendship and patriotism among the American people."[43]

In short, the combination of social clubs, themed parades, and tableaux balls became important parts of the cultural repertoire of the old-line krewes to refashion Mardi Gras as a national event for visitors rather than just a local celebration for residents. The Krewe of Rex introduced several cultural innovations, including a permanent organization for planning Carnival, and the establishment of financial arrangements with local merchants and bankers to fund the Krewe's activities. Other cultural innovations by the Krewe of Rex included incorporating itself as the School of Design in 1874; selecting the official Carnival colors of purple, green, and gold; creating a Mardi Gras flag; and adopting the song "If Ever I Cease to Love" as the Carnival anthem.[44] Despite organized parades and evening festivities, Mardi Gras day was still not considered a local holiday until Rex chose to parade on that day, thereby expanding the celebration and establishing Fat Tuesday as a local holiday.[45] While Mardi Gras remained a celebration staged for both locals and guests, what is new in the 1860s and later is the efforts by elite Carnival krewes and city leaders to specifically promote Carnival as an extralocal celebration.

Race and Carnival in the Reconstruction Years

> [Mardi Gras] is a thing that could hardly exist in the practical North. . . . For the soul of it is the romantic, not the funny and the grotesque. Take away the romantic mysteries, the kings and knights and big-sounding titles, and Mardi Gras would die, down there in the South.
> —Mark Twain, *Life on the Mississippi*[46]

Elite efforts to rationalize Carnival to attract tourists reflected shifting race relations during the 1860s and 1870s. Before the 1850s, a unique three-tier system of whites, free people of color, and slaves defined race and ethnic relations in New Orleans.[47] By the 1850s, however, this three-tier ethnoracial system was eroding and being supplanted by a rigid racial dualism of white against black, the result of an immense wave of Anglo American immigration and local and state government efforts to segregate the races. In 1852, local leaders and elites eliminated the system of three separate municipalities, a major political development that coincided with the transferring of enforcement of racial restrictions from local to state authorities. In 1855, the State of Louisiana barred the incorporation of any new religious, charitable, scientific, or literary society composed of free people of color.[48] In 1857, the U.S. Supreme Court ruled in *Dred Scott v. Sandford* that neither free nor en-

slaved blacks had constitutional rights, a decision that effectively eliminated black freedoms everywhere. The economic and social upheavals
of the Civil War and the Reconstruction years (1866–1877) transformed
New Orleans, empowering previously impoverished slaves and creating
new bases of social conflict and political struggle. In 1860, Orleans Parish was home to about 11,000 free people of color; within ten years, the
number of free people of color increased almost five times to 50,456.
The white population dropped by 8,140 residents, from 149,063 in
1860 to 140,923 in 1870. During this time the percentage of free people
of color rose from 6 percent of the aggregate population to 26 percent,
while the percentage of whites dropped from 85 percent to 73 percent
of the aggregate population.[49] The decline in white population from
1860 to 1870 is noteworthy, given that the white population of Orleans
Parish had been increasing every decade since 1830.

Enfranchised free people of color and freed slaves rapidly assumed
positions of political power and leadership in the city, a movement that
generated intense protest and mobilization on the part of white elites.
On July 30, 1866, more than 100 persons were injured and 34 blacks
were killed when former confederate soldiers and local police clashed
with blacks during the attempt to reassemble the Louisiana Constitutional Convention (formed in 1864) in New Orleans, a riot that was
dubbed the "New Orleans Massacre."[50] A year later, in 1867, a massive
demonstration by blacks led to the desegregation of the city's streetcars.[51] Black representatives from New Orleans to the Constitutional
Convention of 1867–1868 wrote the state laws that led to the desegregation of public accommodations and public schools. These actions but-
tressed federal desegregation efforts, including in 1868 ratification of
the Fourteenth Amendment that entitled all persons born or naturalized
in the United States to citizenship and equal protection under U.S. laws,
a movement described by W. E. B Dubois in his classic book, *Black
Reconstruction in America, 1860–1880.*[52] In 1870, the Louisiana legislation removed the ban against interracial marriage and desegregated
schools a year later in 1871. From 1871 to 1877, New Orleans enjoyed
a brief period of racial desegregation where blacks could attend previously all-white public schools, eat in white restaurants, and congregate
in white pubs and saloons. This desegregation campaign ground to a
halt when the federal government recalled troops from Louisiana, and
Democratic leaders seized control of the state legislature. After 1877,
state leaders refused to intervene in local racial matters and embraced a

policy of de facto racial segregation and tacit support for discrimination. Later, the U.S. Supreme Court declared unconstitutional the Civil Rights Act of 1875 that had provided blacks with the right to equal treatment in public places and transportation.[53]

Carnival in the Reconstruction years and later became a cultural vehicle for displaying racial ideology, constructing racial identity, and reinforcing social exclusion through parades and balls. Several scholars have noted that the memberships of Comus, Momus, Rex, and the Twelfth Night Revelers overlapped with that of the Crescent City White League, a white supremacist organization formed in 1874 to establish a "white man's government" and suppress "the insolent and barbarous African."[54] On September 14, 1874, some 3,500 armed members of the White League led by Fred Nash Ogden (a member of the Pickwick Club and Comus) staged a bloody coup against the Republican administration of Governor William Pitt Kellogg, killing 38 and wounding 79 people. The "Battle of Liberty Place," as the insurrection became known, forced U.S. President Ulysses Grant to send federal troops to New Orleans to recapture city hall, all the police stations, the statehouse, and the arsenals that the White League had seized.[55] More than 100 members of Comus participated in this battle, including Edward Douglas Wright, later chief justice of the U.S. Supreme Court and proponent of the "separate but equal" doctrine that he voted for in the *Plessy v. Ferguson* (1896) decision. Years later, Perry Young, the official historian of the Mystick Krewe of Comus, quoted a Comus captain as remembering, "It is safe to say that every member . . . capable of bearing arms, participated" in the Battle of Liberty Place.[56] In celebration of their centennial anniversary, a 1956 Comus pamphlet noted that the 1874 coup was important because "many Comus maskers took part in the battle."[57]

The interlocking membership rolls of the White League and the old-line krewes established a formidable racial alliance dedicated to combating black enfranchisement. Throughout the 1870s and 1880s, the old-line Carnival krewes of Comus, Momus, Proteus, and Rex staged satirical parades that mocked the Republican administration and portrayed blacks as inferior to whites, infusing racial imagery with acrimonious content (fig. 2.2). At Mardi Gras in 1877, for example, the theme for the Krewe of Comus parade and ball was the "Aryan Race," a celebration that chronicled the so-called accomplishments of European males in the development of Western civilization.

A   B   C

Fig. 2.2. In 1873, Comus's theme of Missing Links to Darwin's Origins of Species derided both the carpetbag Republican administration and the new evolutionary theory of Charles Darwin. This parade and ball presented (A) President Ulysses S. Grant as an annoying insect, (B) Charles Darwin as a sagacious jackass, and (C) a gorilla playing the banjo as the "Missing Link." These satirical images inaugurate a long tradition of Carnival krewes using sarcasm and irony to criticize local and national political leaders, popular culture, and current events. (Reproduced by permission of Tulane University, Howard-Tilton Memorial Library, Special Collections)

Reinventing Carnival, Constructing Authenticity

> The celebration of Carnival in New Orleans has attained world-wide celebrity. Nowhere else have the festivities that grace this season been organized on a system of such thorough completeness and gorgeous magnificence. [New Orleans] mold[s] the festivities of Carnival into a grand and comprehensive system, and to present for the enjoyment of people, without fee or reward, public spectacles and pageants as splendid, brilliant, and beautiful as the genius and skill of man and the lavish expenditure of money could make them, and their fame has gone out among the nations.
>
> —Augustin Advertising and Information Bureau, 1908[58]

By the 1870s and 1880s, the Krewes of Comus, Momus, Rex, and Proteus were appropriating a rich tradition of diverse cultural practices to create new lines of hierarchy and racial division in the celebration of Carnival. As social tensions mounted before the Civil War and during the Reconstruction years and later, social elites struggled to protect their racial and class interests by establishing new Carnival traditions and rituals that were separate and autonomous from the longstanding indige-nous Carnival customs of grassroots street celebrations and informal parading. In addition, the Carnival balls of the old-line krewes sufficed as a cultural venue for reinforcing racial and class distance, establishing an insulated space for the wealthy and affluent to engage in ceremonies to affirm their prestige while minimizing social contact with those of lesser class status. At the same time, elite attempts to impose racial and class boundaries, and to establish a segregative and rationalized Mardi Gras of formal parades and exclusive balls, did not go unopposed. Dur-ing the 1870s and 1880s, local residents decried the routinized charac-ter of the krewe parades. Interestingly, the *New Orleans Republican* newspaper, which had initially supported the idea of the Rex parade in a February 11, 1872, article, condemned the controlled nature of the procession several days later in a February 14 article. According to the *Republican,*

> The matter with this procession is simply this: There was too much order about it. Confusion, disorder and discord, both of colors and sounds, is the great beauty of a Carnival procession, which does not in-tend to represent a single idea, nor to tell a single story, but means to play and make fun. Every crowd should have gone on its own hook. Just as chance had brought them together in the world of mimic, so it should part them asunder. . . . To control a Carnival procession by gen-eral orders defeats the object of the day. Hence the procession yesterday was a disappointment. The slow order of the march, the frequent halts, the system of arrangement, afforded opportunity for a close examina-tion and cheap display of criticism.[59]

Nine years later, an editorial in the March 6, 1881, edition of the *New Orleans Times* reinforced this critical view of the old-line krewes, la-menting that "before Rex . . . our thoroughfares swarmed with merry maskers from one dawn till almost the next, and their license was not always tempered by even a consideration of their sex." The problem, according to the *Times,* was that "Rex came and converted them from free citizens of the Carnival to his own subjects to follow in his train." Commenting on the erosion of the "democratic field" of Carnival, "wherein all ages and conditions enjoyed equal rights on Carnival day," the *Times* noted that Rex "straightway enforces his own rule, usurps the field as his own realm, compels attention to himself and to his staid

. . . [and] virtually abolishes the old buoyant Carnival of simple jests and pranks." Like the comments from the *Republican* newspaper in 1872, the *Times* expressed remorse at the decline of the "riotous quality" of Carnival and assailed the Rex parade as a "stern procession" of "splendor but no humor." Rex "refines the old fashioned Carnival even unto its death." As the *Times* editorial concluded:

> The old, robust laugh and the old, wild license have gone out of the Carnival of New Orleans. This laugh and license were, we believe, the vital conditions of its maintenance. How long the new Carnival will survive the old cannot, of course be determined with accuracy, but the change is not unlike a slow petrification from boisterous humor to the severe, classic decorum of sculpture.[60]

These cynical interpretations resonate with the gloomy appraisals echoed in the 1850s about the "loss" and "decline" of Carnival. The newspaper accounts intimate Carnival krewes as threatening and destabilizing forces that are usurping the "democratic field" of Mardi Gras, provoking intense fears about the future and integrity of the celebration. The concerns expressed by the *New Orleans Times* on efforts to "refine the old-fashioned Carnival" and abolish "old buoyant Carnival" suggest a growing anxiety that the Krewe of Rex is undermining the authenticity of Carnival as an indigenous festival. Like the newspaper reports from the 1850s, the accounts from the 1870s and later deploy themes of nostalgia and sentimentality to construct a notion of an "authentic" New Orleans to counter the growth of new cultural practices and activities in the celebration of Mardi Gras. Nostalgia was a useful symbolic device to orient intentions, set moods, and devalue the krewe system as perverse and inauthentic. Images and themes of nostalgia in the authenticity work of New Orleans's newspapers invoked the past to make sense of the present in an age of rapid change. As such, the nostalgic reading of the past reflected larger political and cultural transformations in the city, including the erosion of the spontaneity and free license of the antebellum Carnival and the creation of new forms of social order and control in the celebration.

Both opponents and proponents of the elite Carnival krewes drew on past images and representations of New Orleans to construct conceptions of urban authenticity to contest rival arguments and reinforce particular interpretations of the present and past. Here the past emerged as a fertile cultural resource that could be mined for a variety of different themes, resonant symbols and motifs, and other persuasive devices to legitimate different actors as cultural authorities. The elite Carnival krewes, for example, positioned themselves as agents of cultural "reform" and elaborated a set of beliefs about Mardi Gras that they used in their authenticity work to underwrite a new conception of Carnival tradition. The "official story" of Mardi Gras, for example, one passed down through the generations in magazines and local newspaper editorials, maintained that the antebellum Carnival was marked by rampant lawlessness, violence, and disorder. In response, enlightened citizens formed the elite Carnival krewes to bring order to this chaotic world, tame the unsavory past, and establish a more civil and humane Carnival for the enjoyment of all. According to a 1885 Rand, McNally, and Company tour guidebook,

> Years ago, maskers appeared on the streets in every conceivable costume, and, on several occasions, processions of quite an imposing character paraded the streets. Boys went around with sacks of flour and lime, covering those they met, and these "practical jokes" descended into such ruffianism that for a time the people discouraged the observance of the day. It was not, however, until the year 1857 that the day received its crowning glory, which has since made it a festival, talked of all over the continent.[61]

As explained in a February 1893 article in *Harpers New Monthly Magazine*,

> For many years [Carnival in New Orleans] was entirely popular and promiscuous in the sense that it was unordered and without either head or programme. The Mistick Krewe of Comus brought order and form into the first night parade in 1857, and [later] the Rex Society . . . made it possible and advantageous to do away with the promiscuous masking and merrymaking, attendant upon which had been the throwing of lime and flour, the drunkenness, and the usual disorder, which must everywhere characterize a loosely managed festival of the sort. Since then . . . there has never been a serious affray.[62]

In sum, the rise of modern Carnival emanated from the efforts of social elites to impose new forms of social exclusion, segregation, and rationalization over the celebration as expedients to attracting tourists to New Orleans. By segmenting people into riders and spectators, the rationalized parades of the old-line Carnival krewes of Comus, Momus, Proteus, and Rex provided symbolic ordering and continuity to an otherwise fragmented, chaotic, and discontinuous world. Guidebooks and advertisements henceforth would celebrate Carnival for its ability to deliver fun and entertainment in a rationally controlled and predictable fashion, conditions that are the opposite of the festive release, insubordination, and transgression of the pre-modern Carnival described by Russian literary theorist Mikhail Bakhtin.[63] By the late nineteenth century, the Carnival krewe had become authenticated as a customary practice and organizational structure that other groups were constrained to adopt to parade and participate in Carnival. Street celebrations, loosely organized marching clubs, informal parading, and other cultural practices would continue during Carnival in New Orleans. But the significance of the Carnival krewe was that it provided a source of cultural meaning, a focus of identification, and a system of relations for constructing and deploying meanings of local authenticity.

Over the course of the nineteenth and twentieth centuries, the Carnival krewe would become the anchoring institution of New Orleans's Mardi Gras celebration and serve as a cultural forum for reinforcing and contesting social inequalities and divisions. During the same time, we see the emergence of a variety of marching clubs, female krewes, and other organizations that do not parade on the main thoroughfares of the city. In 1890, workingclass men formed the Jefferson City Buzzards, the first of many walking clubs in the city. Six years later, local women founded the first all female Krewe of Les Mystrieus. In 1909, black residents established the Tramps Social Aid and Pleasure Club, an organization forced to parade through the back streets of New Orleans, as parading on the major streets was illegal for black krewes. Seven years later, the Tramps changed their name to the Zulu Social Aid and Pleasure Club. These new traditions and customs reflect local efforts to combat the rationalization of Carnival, affirm the authenticity of Carnival as a local festival for local residents, and create new expressions of Mardi Gras that are separate from the elite krewes. Over the twentieth century, the rise of mass tourism would interconnect with the formation of new collective representations of Carnival to shape and constrain constructions of culture and authenticity in New Orleans, inciting new social conflicts and struggles.

3

"Of Incomprehensible Magnitude and Bewildering Variety"

The 1884 World's Industrial and Cotton Centennial Exposition

Every quarter of the globe from the blazing rim of the equator to the frozen barriers of Siberia has contributed to swell the tremendous array of the world's productions and resources. In the Main Building the bulk of the visitors daily wander about amid the beauties and the luxuries collected there. Every aisle and passage way presents something grand, unique, and new. All the nations, civilized, semi-civilized, and barbarous, have poured the wealth of their possessions into the monster lap of the Exposition. . . . This Exposition has built itself up into the largest that has ever been seen, and contains more that is useful and grand, wonderful and beautiful than has ever been gathered together before in the history of the universe. It stretches out with its machine-shops, engine-rooms, States' collections, stock stables, poultry shows, cooking utensils, cocooneries, silk manufactures, dry goods establishments, agricultural implements, art and scientific exhibits, like a city swarming with all the life and mercantile transactions incident to a season and age of golden prosperity. . . . It has been a Napoleonic undertaking and achievement of the age. . . . Its success as an Exposition has been phenomenal. . . . To enter its portals is to improve the taste and refine the intellect. To walk among its wonderful treasures is to expand the mind and enlighten it with a universal knowledge of the generation.

—*New Orleans Times-Democrat*, January 19, 1885[1]

New Orleans was the host city for the 1884 World's Industrial and Cotton Centennial Exposition, an extravagant spectacle that helped raise the international profile of the city while encouraging the growth of new business networks and cultural organizations to bolster tourism. International expositions, or world's fairs, are large-scale, short-term events that express in concentrated form the social conditions of the modern metropolis—"the swift and continuous shift of external and internal stimuli . . . rapid telescoping of changing images . . . and the unexpectedness of violent stimuli," as described by Georg Simmel.[2] For New Orleans, the 1884 Exposition reflected and reinforced the city's growing reputation as a place of paradox and irony. On the one hand, the quote above from the *Times-Democrat* expressed an incipient form of urban boosterism centered around the promotion of New Orleans as an oasis of cosmopolitanism, a place of irresistible charm, and a fabulous mecca of wealth and abundance. On the other hand, the 1884 Exposition was plagued with financial difficulties, few foreign countries sent exhibits to New Orleans, and the exposition suffered from low attendance. Of the originally predicted 4 million visitors, only 1,158,840 attended the 1884 Exposition in New Orleans, a minuscule number compared with the 32,350,000 people who attended the Paris Exposition in 1889 and the 27,529,000 who attended the Chicago Exposition in 1893 (table 3.1).

Historians generally have given the exposition a mix of praise and criticism. Thomas D. Watson assailed the exposition's organizers for poor planning, mismanagement, and fraud.[3] Samuel C. Shepherd argued that while the exposition was a financial failure, it did offer "a glimmer of hope" that the future would be reconciliation between the North and South, economic revival for New Orleans, and improved racial and class relations.[4] Joy Jackson maintained that the exposition symbolized New Orleans's rebirth as a city of industrial growth and profitable investment.[5] More broadly, the exposition reinforced and extended the ideology of the "New South," an interrelated set of ideas and slogans that stressed sectional reconciliation and patriotic sentiment as expedients to attracting northern investors.

Condemned and celebrated, the 1884 Industrial and Cotton Centennial Exposition was the largest world's fair of its time and was the first exposition marketed and promoted by railroads, hotels, and other industries to stimulate travel and advertise cities as exotic locales and tourist attractions. In addition, the 1884 Exposition was the first world's fair whose buildings and grounds were lighted by electricity, a major invention that allowed for the manufacturing of the five tons of ice that were needed daily to preserve fruits, fish, and flowers displayed at the

TABLE 3.1
International Expositions or World's Fairs (1851–1900)

Site and year	Size (acres)	Attendance
London 1851	19	6,039,000 (paid)
Dublin 1853	2.5	1,156,000 (total)
New York 1853–1854	4	1,150,000 (total)
Paris 1855	29	5,162,000 (paid)
London 1862	23.5	6,211,000 (total)
Dublin 1865	17	956,000 (paid)
Paris 1867	215	9,063,000 (paid)
London 1871–1874	100	2,754,000 (total)
Vienna 1873	280	7,250,000 (total)
Philadelphia 1876	285	9,789,000 (total)
Paris 1878	185	16,032,000 (total)
Sydney 1879–1880	24	1,117,000 (total)
Melbourne 1880–1881	21	1,459,000 (total)
Atlanta 1881	19	290,000 (total)
Amsterdam 1883	62	1,439,000 (total)
Boston 1883–1884	3	300,000 (total)
Calcutta 1883–1884	22	1,000,000 (total)
Louisville 1883	45	971,000 (total)
New Orleans 1884–1885	249	1,159,000 (total)
Antwerp 1885	54.3	3,500,000 (total)
Edinburgh 1886	25	2,770,000 (total)
London 1886	24	5,551,000 (total)
Adelaide 1887–1888	18	767,000 (total)
Barcelona 1888	115	2,240,000 (total)
Glasgow 1888	70	5,748,000 (total)
Melbourne 1888–1889	35	2,200,000 (total)
Paris 1889	228	32,350,000 (total)
Dunedin 1889–1890	12.5	625,000 (total)
Kingston 1891	23	303,000 (total)
Chicago 1893	686	27,529,000 (total)
Antwerp 1894	86.5	3,000,000 (total)
San Francisco 1894	160	1,356,000 (total)
Hobart 1894–1895	11	290,000 (total)
Atlanta 1895	189	780,000 (paid)
Brussels 1897	148	6,000,000 (total)
Guatemala City 1897	800	Not available
Nashville 1897	200	1,167,000 (paid)
Stockholm 1897	514	Not Available
Omaha 1898	200	2,614,000 (total)
Paris 1900	553	50,861,000 (total)

SOURCE: John E. Findling and Kimberly D. Pelle (eds.), 1990, *Historical Dictionary of World's Fairs and Expositions, 1851–1988* (New York: Greenwood).

fair.[6] U.S. President Chester Arthur described the exposition on its opening day as "a colossal international exposition of incomprehensible magnitude and bewildering variety."[7] The *New Orleans Times-Democrat*, a newspaper owned by Edward Austin Burke, the director general of the exposition, proclaimed "this Exposition has built itself up into the largest that has ever been seen" and "contains more that is useful and grand, wonderful and beautiful than has ever been gathered together before in the history of the universe."[8] For S. D. McEntry, governor of Louisiana, "This Exposition marks a new epoch in the history of this country, and we may say in the history of the world, for it has passed beyond the line of locality and is international. . . . The whole world is here in generous competition and friendly intercourse."[9] Importantly, the exposition was the first concerted and highly organized attempt by diverse industries and actors to represent New Orleans as a site of rich history, delicious cuisine, and distinctive authenticity. In this sense, the 1884 Exposition played an important role in helping to construct a New Orleans iconography while serving as a spectacular site for introducing local people to a variety of cultures and products from around the world.

The mobilization of political and economic elites to plan and stage the World's Industrial and Cotton Centennial Exposition in New Orleans during 1884 and 1885 was a significant undertaking and represents as major turning point in the history of New Orleans as a tourist destination. Tourism and leisure travel did not exist in New Orleans before the Civil War. The high cost of a journey to a far away place prohibited most Americans from traveling far from home. For the few that did travel, transportation was chaotic and vexing due to imprecise railroad schedules, unpredictable timetables, and unsafe rail travel. Even when people traveled to New Orleans and other cities, they did not encounter specific tourism spaces or specialized tourist attractions. "Sightseeing" was not yet a cultural practice that people demarcated from other social activities. New Orleans's first guidebook, *Norman's New Orleans and Environs,* published by Benjamin Moore Norman in 1845, made no mention of specific tourist sites and provided a broad overview of the city's geography, climate, public buildings and churches, historical development, hospitals, theaters, and hotels, among a variety of subjects. Guidebooks such as Norman's did not cater solely to transients and the information provided was comprehensive and exhaustive rather than selective and differential. Thus, the subtitle of Norman's 223-page book told readers that it contained a "historical sketch of the Territory and State of Louisiana and the City of New Orleans, from the earliest period to the present time: presenting a complete guide."[10] After the Civil War, the expansion of railroads accelerated transportation and opened up remote places for people to travel. In addition, the invention of photography in the 1840s and the handheld camera in the 1880s enabled travelers to transcribe reality visually, thus providing a motivation for people to visit exotic places and capture images and experiences on film.[11]

Planning and Staging the 1884 Exposition

> The conception of the World's Fair at New Orleans and the vast effort to bring it to a successful issue are worthy of the highest commendation, and its fruits must be of national advantage. It will not be easy to divert public attention from that city for the next few months. A great magnet has been seen set up there, and the current of sight-seers, pleasure-seekers, and those on more utilitarian purposes will pour in increasing volume into the Crescent City.
>
> —*New Orleans Times-Democrat,* January 14, 1885[12]

The initial reason for staging the 1884 Exposition was to commemorate the 100th anniversary of the first shipment of cotton from the United States to Europe in 1784. Cotton production and distribution had been a mainstay of the New Orleans and Louisiana economy from the eighteenth century forward. The Civil War transformed the economy of cotton manufacturing, replacing the slave-based economy of the antebellum period with wage-labor and factory production. "Whoever says Industrial Revolution says cotton," remarked Eric Hobsbawm in his famous book *Industry and Empire,* that detailed the impact of industrialization on Europe. Cotton manufacturing was "the pacemaker of industrial changes" which "expressed a new form of society, industrial capitalism."[13]

The formation of the New Orleans Cotton Exchange during 1871–1880 ushered in a new era of industrial development for the city and region. By 1880, the Exchange had set up a futures market and established itself as a leading international cotton market. Despite being a center of trade and commerce, New Orleans never did develop a high wage manufacturing sector or textile industry. Most of the city's industrial activity was limited to cotton production and trade, sugar refineries, tobacco factories, coffee, and businesses catering to the local market.[14] Legislation passed in the 1870s and 1880s facilitated the building of new railroad lines, and, by 1880, five major railroads traveled through New Orleans. In 1883, the Southern Pacific established rail travel from California and New Orleans, heralding the beginning of long-range transport and trade between the Crescent City and other regions. More broadly, railroads were important not only for speeding up travel but also for establishing a set of four uniform time zones in the United States in 1884, an invention that encouraged the growth of tourism by standardizing travel schedules.[15]

Early mobilization for an international exposition came from the collaboration of three men: F. C. Morehead, president of the Nation Cotton Planters Association; Edmund Richardson, a major industrialist and cotton planter; and Edward Austin Burke, treasurer of the State of Louisiana and editor of the *New Orleans Times-Democrat* newspaper. In 1882, the National Cotton Planter's Association endorsed the idea of holding an exposition, and, in 1883, the U.S. Congress passed an act officially creating "The World's Industrial and Cotton Centennial Exposition." The congressional act placed the exposition under the joint auspices of the federal government, the National Cotton Planters' Association, and the City of New Orleans.

The planners of the 1884 World's Industrial and Cotton Centennial Exposition drew on preexisting organizations and an international network of institutions to stage the World's Fair in New Orleans. From the first Crystal Palace Exposition in 1851 in London, every decade had several fairs, with each city attempting to make their exposition more spectacular than the one before. International expositions developed through systematized planning, sophisticated financial arrangements, systems of fund-raising, and networks of skilled personnel. Planning for the Boston (1883), Louisville (1883), Atlanta (1881), and New Orleans Expositions did not take place in vacuum. Each exposition planning board researched and studied the expositions that preceded them and sent delegations of experts to the fairs before their own.[16] Exposition leaders in New Orleans organized auxiliary committees across the country, in many states, and every parish of Louisiana to collect materials and prepare exhibits of the resources of the United States and the state of Louisiana.[17] In addition, leaders of the 1884 Exposition visited various U.S. states, territories, and foreign countries to promote New Orleans and to build international support. In December 1882, Morehead ventured to Cincinnati and Baltimore "to see what those cities are doing in regard to the exposition." Later, in October 1883, Morehead traveled

Fig. 3.1. Aerial view of the 1884 World's Industrial and Cotton Centennial Exposition showing the principal buildings, including the prominent Main Building, the Agricultural Hall and Government Building (*far right*), Art Gallery (*in front of the Main Building*), and the Horticultural Hall (*bottom*) near the Mississippi River. U.S. President Chester Arthur described the exposition on its opening day as "a colossal international exposition of incomprehensible magnitude and bewildering variety." Although the exposition closed in June 1885, a smaller exposition, the North Central and South American Exposition (November 10, 1885, to March 31, 1886) used the same buildings. In the 1890s, all the buildings, except Horticultural Hall, were demolished, and the site was developed as Audubon Park; Horticultural Hall was destroyed by a hurricane in September 1915. The Audubon Zoo now occupies acreage where the structure once stood. (Reproduced by permission of Tulane University, Howard-Tilton Memorial Library, Special Collections)

to several states and foreign nations to "assist in organizing collective exhibits."[18]

During the spring and summer of 1884, construction of the exposition preceded on a 249-acre site in what was as then called Upper City Park (now called Audubon Park) (fig. 3.1). The principal buildings were the Main Building, the Government Building, the Horticultural Hall, and the Art Gallery. As reported by the *New York Times,* the Main Building, built entirely of wood, covered over 30 acres and was the largest wooden building ever constructed at the time (fig. 3.2). The Horticultural Hall covered over 3 acres, contained plants, fruits, and flowers, and was the largest conservatory in the world at the time[19] (table 3.2).

Fig. 3.2. The Main Building measured 1,378 feet by 905 feet and was the largest wooden structure in the world, covering 33 acres of floor space. The building contained Foreign Government,
Foreign and Domestic Industry, and Machinery exhibits, as well as a Music Hall, which could
seat more than 10,000 people and a stage that could accommodate 600 musicians. The Liberty
Bell traveled from Philadelphia and was prominently displayed. The building was illuminated by
800 arc and 3,600 incandescent lights, installed by the Edison Electric Co., and contained 18
elevators, 25 miles of walkways, and a glass roof. (Reproduced by permission of Tulane University, Howard-Tilton Memorial Library, Special Collections)

A number of other buildings were reserved for restaurants and public
accommodations and for special private exhibitions. Throughout 1884,
exhibits arrived from various foreign countries, and while not all governments participated officially, many were represented by private companies.[20] Every U.S. state and territory was represented at the exposition
except for Utah. The Liberty Bell traveled from Philadelphia and was
displayed in the Main Building. "Commodity monuments," including a
replica of the not yet erected Statue of Liberty, were a popular design
element of state and commercial pavilions. Anticipating future developments in the production of simulacra at twentieth-century theme parks,
the 1884 Exposition contained displays of simulated swamp scenes
in Louisiana and simulated fisheries in Massachusetts. Although plans
called for opening the exposition on December 1, 1884, cost overruns
and construction delays pushed the opening date to later in the month.[21]
The exposition opened on December 16 and closed on June 1, 1885.

Exposition organizers displayed goods from around the world for
people to visually consume, thus making it possible for the first time
for local residents to see strange and extraordinary places, cultures,

and customs and to imagine what it would be like to visit these places. A guidebook to the exposition (published by the Illinois Central Railroad) declared that the "Exposition places before you a picture of the universe" and the federal government "spreads before you a picture of the commerce of the whole world, and the share therein enjoyed by the United States. Each nation appears under her own flag and displays for

TABLE 3.2

Buildings and Exhibitions at the 1884 World's Industrial and Cotton Centennial Exposition

Buildings	Area (Acres)	Building Coverage (Sq. Feet)	Construction Dates	Exhibition
Main Building	33	1.7 million	3/1–9/3/84	General Exhibits, Foreign Exhibits, Machinery, Agricultural Exhibits, Music Hall
Art Gallery	1.25	25,000	9/20–10/31/84	Art and Cultural Exhibits
Factories and Mills	1.25	NA	9/25–10/31/84	Heavy machinery, construction tools, manufacturing technologies; cotton
Government Building	12	616,400	8/2–10/15/84	Federal government departments and State government exhibits
Horticultural Hall	3.5	69,600	3/1–9/1/84	Plants, fruits, flowers; tropical greenhouse
Other Buildings	15			Boiler house, Machinery extension, Saw mill building, Livestock barns (6); Iron, tile, and brick building, Wagon building, Banker's building, Furnituer pavilion, Terra-cotta exhibit building, Public comfort stations (2); Mexican Commission and Headquarters building, Mineral exhibit building (Mexico), Police buildings (3); other buildings (10)
Principal building coverage	66			
Total building coverage	81			

SOURCE: World's Fair and Exposition Information and Reference Guide, "1884 World's Industrial and Cotton Centennial Exposition," at http://www.earthstation9.com/1884_new.htm (accessed December 12, 2006); *Visitors Guide to the Worlds Industrial and Cotton Centennial Exposition, and New Orleans* (Louisville, Ky.: Courier-Journal, Job Printing Company, 1884).

your inspection her products, manufactures, and methods of transportation."[22] In the Main Building, according to the *Times-Democrat,* "the bulk of the visitors daily wander about amid the beauties and the luxuries collected there. Every aisle and passage way presents something grand, unique, and new."[23]

The overwhelming and spectacular experience of visiting the Exposition was captured not only in the quantity and concentration of displayed objects but the quantity and concentration of visitors in a single space. On the eve of the opening day, on December 16, for example, approximately 25,000 "strangers," including exhibitors and employees, had made it to New Orleans, a figure that represented more than 10 percent of the city's population.[24] Amid the concentration of visitors and merchandise, the 1884 Exposition gave visible form and legitimacy to the emerging leisure practice of "people-watching." According to one journalist, "the visitors themselves are as well worth seeing as the show. To sit on a bench on one of the broad aisles of the Main Building, or better still beneath the spreading arms of the great live-oaks on the grounds, and observe the passing throng, is to my mind, the best part of the sight-seeing at the fair."[25] Just as one's curiosity was constantly aroused by each new display, one could be amused by gazing at different visitors, a situation that reflected and expressed the ephemerality and temporariness of the exposition itself.

The organizers of the exposition unambiguously organized the fairgrounds along commercial lines, creating what Georg Simmel termed "the shop-window quality of things," with the exhibits projecting a feeling of amusement. For Simmel, the significance of international expositions is that "in the face of the richness and diversity of what is offered, the only unifying and colorful factor is that of amusement." A city that hosts an exposition enters into the "totality of cultural production" because merchandise from around the world has "attained a conclusive form and become part of a single whole" in the rationalized space of the exposition grounds.[26] In New Orleans, exposition planners and organizers designed the particular displays of artifacts and exotic peoples to have an "enchanting," "thrilling," and "wondrous" character. The territory of Dakota sent an exhibit of a wigwam of a Sioux Indian Chief, who sat on display every day with his wife and child.[27] In a pamphlet titled, "What Jean and Joe Saw at the New Orleans Exposition," author Anne C. Goater noted, "In the main building, they found the different foreign governments here had their exhibits; while business firms, representing various cities of this country, displayed their wares in the most tempting manner, to lure the passers-by to pause and examine their goods. Almost one half of the vast building had been given over to machinery and mechanical inventions of all kinds."[28] As a model for the rationalization of leisure, the 1884 Exposition allowed visitors to easily view the exhibits and impressed upon them the idea that places and cultures should be seen as objects of visual display.

Constructing Local Culture

> There is no reason why the New Orleans Exhibition, which opened yesterday, should not fairly rival the Philadelphia show of 1876 in interest and attendance. . . . The city is a quaint and curious one, resembling a town in the South of Europe rather than anything American, and so, apart from what is to be seen in the Exhibition buildings, every visitor will find the city itself a show well worth seeing.
> —*New York Commercial Advisor,* December 22, 1884[29]

For New Orleans, the 1884 World's Industrial and Cotton Exposition was the first large-scale public display of local artifacts, foods, and traditions and customs to a worldwide audience. The inclusion of the word "world" in the title of the exposition identified New Orleans not simply as an important point of river trade and commerce but as a cosmopolitan and international metropolis of industrial growth and abundance. The 1884 Exposition was significant because it reflected local attempts to capitalize on the tourist trade by constructing local culture and authenticity as consumable products.

The major social forces shaping the construction of knowledge about local culture took several forms in New Orleans. First, in 1885, a series of local books—a cookbook, an architectural guidebook, and a collection of local stories—were published for sale at the exposition, purporting to present New Orleans's authentic culture in all its diversity. These books included William H. Coleman and Lafcadio Hearn's *La Cuisine Creole: A Collection of Culinary Recipes*; Hearns's *Gombo Zhedes: A Little Dictionary of Creole Proverbs*; and Coleman's 324-page guidebook, *Historical Sketch Book and Guide to New Orleans and Environs*. Among other things, these books contained descriptions of the city; identified a variety of local myths; celebrated the city's cultural expressions, customs, and traditions; and included songs, recipes, and collective memories. These books not only selectively described the city but also gave the appearance of undeviating candor and credibility. According to the introduction to Coleman's 1885 guidebook,

> Many persons who visit New Orleans find difficulty in knowing where to go and what to see, and after the places have been determined upon they lose considerable pleasure by not knowing the traditions, legends, and incidents surrounding such scenes. New Orleans—by its cosmopolitan character, and having been so far removed in its earlier history from the rest of the colonies, and during its occupancy by the Spanish and French—took to itself usages, customs, and even a patois of its own, the story of which has furnished material for romance equaled by few other cities in this country.[30]

We can view Coleman and other iconoclastic journalists like him as civic boosters actively engaged in the construction and production of a touristic mode of local "authenticity." Central to this process of authenticity construction was the development of an urban iconography about New Orleans that could act as an attraction for potential tourists and a cultural framework for validating their experience once they arrived in the city. The ingredients of this New Orleans iconography included French and Spanish architecture, the Vieux Carre (French Quarter), Mardi Gras, Les Coulisses (French Opera), beautiful oak trees, spanish moss, voudouism, cities of the dead (cemeteries), and scenes of romance and mystery. In the years he was in New Orleans, from 1877 to 1888, Lafcadio Hearn published hundreds of descriptions of New Orleans that appeared in the *New Orleans Daily Item, New Orleans Times-Democrat, Harper's Weekly,* and *Scribner's Magazine.* The prolific writings of Hearn complemented a plethora of stories about New Orleans written by George Washington Cable that were published nationwide in the *Century Magazine* and *Scribner's Magazine.*[31] Coleman and Hearn's laudatory reports on the 1884 Exposition focused international attention on the Crescent City and helped disseminate and popularize an image of New Orleans as a city of romance, creole culture, and famous architecture, images that over time would become "the exemplar of nostalgic manuals," according to urban scholar M. Christine Boyer.[32] Cable, Coleman, and Hearn did not give people a representative account of New Orleans but a cursory and perfunctory reading of the present and past. Before the late nineteenth century, very few writers presented literary images and colorful writings on the region's political, ethnic, and cultural life. The global visibility of the 1884 Exposition raised the cultural profile of New Orleans and legitimated the signifying work of Cable, Coleman, and Hearn. These journalists helped "construct" New Orleans while visitors to New Orleans participated in "consuming" representations of the modern metropolis itself.

In addition, the Women's Department generally and the Louisiana Women's Exhibit specifically played major roles in displaying local culture at the exposition. For example, the Women's Department staged exhibits celebrating women's achievements in an array of fields, including masculine-dominated fields such as science, engineering, and architecture, among others. While not all states sponsored a women's exhibit, many states, including Louisiana, assembled large and impressive exhibits that contained miniatures, jewelry, laces, documents, and old furniture.[33] Broadly, the women's exhibits operated as information disseminators, transmitting knowledge and information about New Orleans and the exposition to communities around the United States. More than 100 women served as reporters for newspapers and magazines, and hundreds of female school teachers attended the Fair.[34] Local women working through the Louisiana Women's Exhibit were able to focus global attention on New Orleans's cultural artifacts and historical memorabilia. One effect of the Women' Exhibit, according to local writer Grace Elizabeth King, was the "opening of the past history of the city, not only to strangers, but to the citizens themselves"[35] These exhibits allowed local women to showcase their achievements in the arts and crafts, an opportunity that reflected and helped reinforce a constellation of groups and individuals working to cultivate an appreciation for the arts among local women. Such an effort later spearheaded the development of the distinctive "Newcomb Style" of pottery making, a cultural innovation that would become a major tourist attraction and focal point of community identity in the twentieth century.

Records of the 1884 World's Industrial and Cotton Centennial Exposition suggest that the fair helped nurture the growth of new strategies of place promotion, new conceptions of urban culture, and new business networks to advertise the city on a global scale. By the advent of the exposition, there were nine railroads, twenty-four steamship and steamboat lines, and at least thirteen hotels serving New Orleans (table 3.3). The growth of this tourism infrastructure did not happen by

TABLE 3.3
New Orleans's Transportation and Hotels, 1884

Railroads	Steamship Lines	Steamboat Lines
Louisville & Nashville	Cromwell	Red River
Illinois Central	Morgan	Lower Coast
Mississippi Valley	Florida Steamship	Upper Coast
N.O. & Northeastern	French Commerce	Anchor
Morgan's La. & Texas	Mexican Gulf	Bayou Sara
New Orleans Pacific	N.O. & Central American	Vicksburgh
N.O., Spanish Ft. & Lake	N.O. & Guatemala	Washington & Atchafalaya
Ponchartrain Road	Campa A.L. DeValores	Ouachita River
West End	Belize Royal Mall	Bayou Teche
	Oteri Pioneer Line	Ohio River
	Mexican Transatlantic	Mandeville & Covington
	N.Y. & Rotterdam	
	Austrian Mall Morgan	

Hotels	Number of Rooms	Capacity
Royal	250	1,000
St. Charles	275	1,000
City	137	450
Vonderblank	45	200
Waverley	62	150
Cassidy's	40	100
Chalmette	50	150
Stock Dealer's	50	100
Denechaud's	60	150
Strange's	75	150
Lalley's	50	100
Lee House	100	200
Continental	200	500

SOURCE: *Visitors' Guide to the World's Industrial and Cotton Centennial Exposition, and New Orleans* (Louisville, Ky.: Courier-Journal, Job Printing Company, 1884).

accident but was cultivated and developed through concerted and rational planning.

To accommodate visitors, the exposition organizers established a Bureau of Information to "aid visitors in securing suitable accommodations at moderate rates." As reported by the *New York Times*, the bureau was "open day and night" with "28 branch offices" that provided listings of all hotels and boarding and lodging houses in New Orleans. The bureau was also the advertising arm of local hotels, directing visitors to the hotels, and establishing "the rates that many charged according to fixed tariff."[36] Throughout 1884 and 1885, an Accommodations Bureau augmented the efforts of the Information Bureau by securing rooms for people coming to the city for the Mardi Gras celebration.

During the first month of the exposition, a *New York Times* article noted that "preparations for the Mardi Gras reception of visitors have already been inaugurated, and it is confidently asserted by the Accommodation Bureau that the regular tribute of 100,000 visitors will hardly inconvenience them."[37]

A Rand, McNally, and Company Guidebook published for the 1884 Exposition told visitors that "Mardi Gras, and the festivals occurring, have made New Orleans the centre of attraction to pleasure-seekers, during the winter season."[38] One promotional booklet published for the 1884 Exposition declared, "The carnival pageants occurring about the middle of the Exposition period will be the most elaborate and brilliant of this world-wide famed festival."[39] A guidebook published by the Illinois Central Railroad emphasized that Mardi Gras of 1885 would "eclipse in grandeur and magnificence of all former carnivals."[40]

To generate sales and build mass support for their emerging industries, railroads, steamboats, and hotels published visitors guides containing detailed instructions educating people on why they should travel, what they should see, and how they should sightsee. Exposition guidebooks published by Rand, McNally, and Company, the Illinois Railroad, the Richmond and Danville Railroad, and many other hotel and railroad companies contained a variety of descriptive essays and whimsical pieces purportedly describing New Orleans as a crucible of cultural diversity and creativity. Showing enthusiasm for the city and its history, these guidebooks erased the line between fiction and nonfiction with accounts that reduced the city to a set of aesthetic and literary images, a process that would continue into the twentieth century. Railroad companies, hotels, and guidebook publishers cultivated an organized alliance, using print media and other technologies to construct New Orleans as unique place with an individuality and authenticity of its own.

Urban culture did not refer to some objective or a priori conception of group identity but was a blend of diverse symbols and motifs that these firms strategically deployed to stimulate consumer demand to travel. Central to this promotional strategy was the effort to imbue New Orleans with pleasurable meanings—for example, the "Paris of America" and the "City of Progress, Beauty, Charm, and Romance"—and present the city as an amalgam of understandable and consumable images.[41] Broadly, the exposition helped legitimate the emerging social practice of viewing urban culture as a collage of stylized images and staged scenes.

Fig. 3.3. The 1884 Industrial and Cotton Centennial Exposition was the first U.S. World's Fair aggressively promoted by railroads, hotels, and other industries to encourage people to travel and view cities as places of amusement, leisure, and exoticism. In the guidebooks published for the exposition, New Orleans appeared as an exceptional place among U.S. cities through a combination of architecture, cuisine, and characteristics of the local population. One strategy used by tourism interests to stimulate travel was to project an image of leisure time as separate and autonomous from work time, a division that would become more pronounced by the early twentieth century with the rise of large corporations and the rationalization of industrial work. Guidebooks published for the exposition constructed New Orleans as a place of rest and relaxation, to reinforce in the minds of readers a sharp distinction between "a time of labor" and a "time for recreation." (Reproduced by permission of Tulane University, Howard-Tilton Memorial Library, Special Collections).

Descriptions and representations of New Orleans found in advertisements, public statements, and guidebooks published for the exposition constructed and defined the city as a melange of cultural objects and tourist attractions, thereby lending credence to the custom of seeing cities as sites of amusement and spectacle (fig. 3.3).

Race and the Colored People's Exhibit

A strong effort has been made to bring out a full exhibit of everything pertaining to the industry by our colored population, whether relating

to art, mechanics, agriculture, or the home, which will display the progress made by the negroes since emancipation. A handsome sum was sub-
scribed from the exchequer of the Exposition for the purpose, and every
encouragement held out. A great deal of interest has been aroused.
—Rand, McNally and Company, *The World's Industrial and Cotton
Centennial Exposition at New Orleans*[42]

The 1884 Industrial and Cotton Centennial Exposition was the first major exposition to use racial themes and images, including stereotypes of
whiteness and blackness, to project an image of white supremacy while
delegitimizing the cultural creations of blacks. Interestingly, throughout
most of the nineteenth century, manifestations of racial discrimination
existed within an uneven, partial, and incomplete system of racial segregation in New Orleans. While high levels of black in-migration, discriminatory hiring, and prejudicial behavior of whites affected black
life, these factors did not generate clearly defined segregation patterns.
Even during and after the Reconstruction Years, when racial discrimination began to intensify, whites and blacks mixed in a variety of institutional settings, even as builders and spectators at the exposition fairgrounds. On the eve of the exposition's opening, the *Cleveland Gazette*
newspaper reported that "hundreds of workingmen of all colors and
races are busy putting on the finishing touches to the massive buildings."[43] One exposition commissioner, Blanche Kelso Bruce, told a
Washington audience that "there is no color line, and that is a great feature of the Exposition. The colored people are treated like the whites,
and there certainly can be no complaint that discrimination is shown."[44]
  Other reports suggest that blacks and whites could interact freely and
that blacks did not face rampant discrimination at the fair. One reporter
for *Harper's Magazine* commented that on "Louisiana Day" at the exposition, the "colored citizens took their full share of the parade and
the honors. Their societies marched with the others, and the races mingled in the grounds in unconscious equality of privileges." "In New Orleans," according to this article, "the street cars are free to all colors; at
the Exposition white and colored people mingled freely, talking and
looking at what was of common interest."[45] This pattern of racial mixing was not uncommon in New Orleans. From the 1870s through the
1890s, hotels, restaurants, dance halls, music houses, saloons, and other
places of leisure and entertainment experienced some racial mixing, albeit in an uneven fashion.[46] Lax enforcement of segregation laws meant

that whites and blacks could cavort together in a variety of entertainment spaces. Yet the pattern of racial mixing was not an indicator of lessening racial inequality but a legacy of slavery times, the outcome of the races having lived close together despite formal relations of racial exploitation.

The 1884 Industrial and Cotton Centennial Exposition provides insight into the incorporation of race into tourist modes of visualization, discourse, and commodity display during the late nineteenth century. One unique feature of the exposition was the role the Colored Department played in organizing and displaying some 16,000 products, inventions, and other achievements by blacks from all over the United States. Excluded from the Philadelphia Exposition in 1876, black exhibitors rejoiced at the opportunity to participate in a world's fair. In an opening ceremony for the 1884 Exposition, Bishop Henry A. Turner remarked that Colored Department "was so unexpected, so marvelous, so Utopian, that we could scarcely believe it was true."[47] Blanche Kelso Bruce, the chief commissioner of the Colored Department, maintained that the Colored Exhibits of each state allowed blacks a collective voice and major venue "to show their advancement and deny the assertion so often made that freedom has not developed in them higher aims and better accomplishments all citizens should have."[48]

Messages circulating through the Colored Exhibit and tour guides and magazines commented that whites were giving blacks an "opportunity" to proclaim their "progress" from the barbaric days of slavery to the emancipation. Yet themes of racial progress and rising opportunity that dominated the 1884 Exposition were pretentious, patronizing, and disingenuous. The inclusion of the word "colored" in the title of the Colored Department and Exhibit identified blacks as the "other" and people of color more generally as the antithesis of white. Major Burke noted that the Colored Department "was designed by mangers of the Exposition . . . to reach out our hand to our brother in black; and shed upon that unfortunate race the sunlight of science and invention, and implant in him the desire to come out of the slough of ignorance and make a manly effort to occupy with us the improved farm, the workshop, and the factory."[49] One magazine noted that the exposition would show the "magnitude of the Negro problem" and help bring sympathy to this "ignorant mass, slowly coming to moral consciousness."[50] Another magazine article noted that blacks "inherit from slavery one great blessing—the habit of industry," but "the higher attainments of civilization . . . [are] traceable to either contact with the white race or to the admixture of white blood."[51]

At the same time, magazines and guides made clear that black contributions were either inauthentic or inferior in comparison with the accomplishments of whites. One account assailed the Colored Department as a sham because it did not represent the achievements of "the pure-blooded negro." "It would be more correct to call it the Somewhat Colored Department," according to Eugene Smalley, a reporter for *Century* magazine. As Smalley noted:

> The woman who comes forward to explain the Kentucky exhibits has blue eyes and brown hair. The maker of an assortment of tools . . . displays unmistakable Caucasian features. And so it goes throughout the whole display. Even the chief of the department . . . is three-fourths white. . . . We must imagine that black blood in the mixed race to have greater potency than the white to develop its own race tendencies, and insist that in an ethnological sense the old barbarous rule of slavery was correct, and that the smallest admixture of the African taint makes the man a negro. Or course, the truth is on the opposite side of the proposition: the white blood is the more powerful, and the man who carries a preponderance of it in his veins is not a negro, and must be classed with the white race.[52]

We can interpret Smalley's statement as part of a broader racial discourse running through the exposition to authenticate "whiteness" as a signifier of cultural and political superiority. Stigmatizing the Colored Exhibit as inauthentic or second-rate was a political strategy to champion white culture and to denigrate other nonwhite inventions, products, and displays. Several decades later, local historian John Smith Kendall argued that the Colored Exhibit "did not in any sense represent the achievements of the negro race in its purity, for in practically every instance of distinguished merit the exhibitor was found to be a descendent of a superior race."[53] Later expositions in Chicago (1893) and St. Louis (1904) and other cities embraced this racial discourse to link technological and national progress with scientific racism and international conquest.[54]

To be sure, depictions of blacks and meanings of race on display at the 1884 Exposition were deeply contested. Indeed, the Colored Department sufficed as a political vehicle for black agitation for social justice. In a speech at the exposition, black attorney David A. Straker of North Carolina called for radical change, remarking that "we need an education of heart, of brains, and of hands" in addition to educating blacks to be laborers.[55] *Century* magazine reported that "on a 'Historical Chart of the Colored Race' displayed in the Colored Department is this motto: 'We must unite; we must acquire wealth; we must educate, or we will perish.'"[56] The American Missionary Association noted that the Colored Department provides evidence that "the negro race can enter every profession and calling in which the white man is found. No trade or occupation should be closed against them. Open doors should welcome to honorable competition, white and black alike."[57]

Such opportunities for social emancipation would prove fleeting, however, and by the 1890s, the specter of Jim Crow segregation and anti-black prejudice was beginning to engulf the major institutions of New Orleans. During this time, we see the passage of state laws mandating segregated railroad cars, railroad stations, streetcars, schools, and public accommodations.[58] Violence between striking black and white dockworkers in 1894 fueled pro-segregation sentiment, and the infamous *Plessy v. Ferguson* decision endorsing "separate but equal" facilities was a Louisiana case that made it to the U.S. Supreme Court in 1896. The *Plessy* decision had rippling effects throughout Louisiana and the rest of the nation as state and local governments moved to harden the color line. In 1898, the state of Louisiana amended the state constitution to remove blacks from voter registration rolls. In 1888, more than 128,000 blacks were registered to vote. By 1900, under the new state constitution, black voters numbered only 5,320.[59] Tensions between whites and blacks escalated in 1900 when rioting broke out during the pursuit of a black fugitive, Robert Charles. Twelve persons were killed, including five blacks, and two schools were destroyed by fire.[60] The Teamsters, the Knights of Labor, and the American Federation of Labor rose to prominence during the 1880s and helped forge interracial ties among New Orleans laborers, leading to a three-day general strike in 1892 involving over 20,000 workers, the first interracial strike in U.S. history to enlist both skilled and unskilled laborers. Yet racial cooperation in labor ended later in the decade with the spread of segregationist laws that disenfranchised blacks and mandated racially segregated public institutions.[61] By the end of the first decade of the twentieth century, rigid racial segregation established the pattern for black-white relations for the next half century.

Vestiges of the 1884 Exposition

> The Exposition places before you a picture of the universe. Europe in
> her royal robes, with the fruit of her proud civilization in her hands,
> Asia hoary with the frost of centuries, gorgeous in her investments, and
> blazing with jewels, Africa, as represented by her daughters Egypt and
> Liberia, the Islands of the Ocean, the Republic of the New World. . . .
> Stolid must he be who will not concede that it is worth a temporary ex-
> ile from home, worth the journey of a few hundred miles, and a moder-
> ate outlay of time and cash, to look upon their August faces. Under
> other circumstances you would sail over the oceans, cross deserts, climb
> mountains, and face dangers seen and unseen, to fund the treasures
> which are *laid at your feet.*
>
> —Illinois Central Railroad, "Will It Pay to Visit the
> World's Exposition?"[62]

It would be a mistake to view the 1884 World's Industrial and Cotton Centennial Exposition as an ephemeral and insignificant spectacle
that had little long-lasting effect on New Orleans. While the exposition
lasted only six months, it played a major role in raising public interest
in local culture and focusing international attention on New Orleans as
a place of leisure and exoticism. More broadly, the exposition influ-
enced the cultural and economic development of New Orleans by helping to establish a series of connections among a loose network of groups
with interests in promoting urban tourism. Persuading large numbers of
people to travel was a shared interest of diverse industries, including the
rising railroad industry, hotel firms, and guidebook publishers. Writers
such as George Washington Cable, Lafcadio Hearn, and William H.
Coleman constructed New Orleans as a place of mystery, romance,
beauty, and rich history to captivate and attract visitors to the city.
Cable's and Hearn's fictional writings, in particular, imparted a stereotypical image of New Orleans as a place of frivolity, naughtiness, and
endless partying, images that over time would become part of people's
everyday consciousness and impressions about the city. Later writers in
the twentieth century elaborated on these resonate themes and amplified
them to build a veritable cornucopia of culture materials to lure tourists
to the city. In the nineteenth century, the advertising work of railroad
companies and guidebook publishers complemented and embellished
the place-making work of Cable, Hearn, and Coleman to frame social

conditions, assign meaning to New Orleans, and thereby organize tourist experience. Over time, a variety of literary images and slogans applied to New Orleans became commodified and were incorporated in movies, advertising, and other video and print media.

Railroad advertising and other promotional efforts organized for the 1884 Exposition played a major part in broadcasting and championing the elite Carnival krewes of Comus, Momus, Proteus, and Rex as the cultural leaders and the dominant signifiers of the "authentic" Mardi Gras. Local newspaper stories, national magazine articles, and railroad advertisements carried stories about the old-line Carnival krewes and their elite balls beyond the exposition grounds to an international audience. At the same time, journalists and editors devoted little coverage to street celebrations, marching clubs, and other grassroots aspects of Carnival. By the 1880s and 1890s, national magazines and newspapers were sending reporters to New Orleans to cover Mardi Gras. A February 19, 1890, article from the *New York Times* observed that New Orleans's streets contained "at times tens of thousands of people, a good proportion of whom were visitors from the North and West." Three years later, the *New York Times* of February 12, 1893, reported that "New Orleans is filled with visitors, most of the welcome guests hailing from the Northwest. Many names prominent in financial and commercial circles and in Chicago and other influential marts of the great Northwest are written on the hotel registers." James B. Townsend, a reporter for *Illustrated American,* commented at the Mardi Gras celebration of 1896 that "many New York visitors for the most part occupied seats on the stand outside the Boston Club [the social club of the Krewe of Rex], and were favored with an especially good view of the procession." According to Townsend, "The distinctly social side of the Carnival . . . and in fact the most attractive to Northern visitors was the balls of Proteus and Comus," whose "entertainments were so distinctively novel and enjoyable as to interest and amuse the visitor from beginning to end."[63]

By the turn of the century, materials printed by railroad companies, hotels, and guidebook publishers all contained descriptions of Carnival, including histories of the celebration, with illustrations of the elite Carnival krewes. Illinois Central Railroad produced an illustrated book titled *New Orleans for the Tourist,* while the Louisville and Nashville Railroad published a pamphlet called "New Orleans and Her Carnival," and the Southern Pacific Company published a twenty-eight-page guide in 1899 titled "Winter in New Orleans: Carnival, Racing, French Opera."[64]

Furthermore, the exposition helped legitimate an emerging conception of urban culture as an object of visual consumption, a conception that reflected broader transformations in the political economy of consumer capitalism. One distinguishing characteristic of nineteenth-century world's fairs, including the New Orleans Exposition, was the growing emphasis placed on commodity display, entertainment, and amusement as central components of urban life. In *Land of Desire*, William Leach described the rise of consumer capitalism during the late nineteenth century and early twentieth century as a "future-oriented culture of desire that confused the good life with goods." By the end of the nineteenth century, according to Leach, the "cardinal features" of the rising consumer culture were "acquisition and consumption as the means of achieving happiness; the cult of the new; the democratization of desire, and money value as the predominant measure of all value in society."[65]

Like other international expositions, the New Orleans Exposition played a key role in generating and supporting the development of mass consumption by presenting culture, traditions, and customs as spectacles. The images of New Orleans presented at the exposition expressed what Walter Benjamin called "the age of mechanical reproduction."[66] As a controlled space of leisure, expositions enclosed spectators within the fairgrounds, regulated their movements and pleasures, and focused their gaze on exotic objects and images. Advertisements of New Orleans "culture," "history," "Carnival," and so on were hypostatized descriptions that reflected profiteering motives, including a desire to celebrate travel and transform diverse images about the city into a homogeneous set of picturesque scenes for tourists to recognize, understand, and consume. As an enchanted world for the display of exotic goods, the exposition implied a world of amusement and fascination that offered the possibility of exciting people's desires to travel and consume.

Finally, we can view the 1884 Exposition and the early development of tourism in New Orleans as embodying a combination of local and extralocal influences, a process captured by the heuristic tourism from above and below. During the nineteenth and early twentieth centuries, tourism comprised a multidimensional mix of industrial growth, the rise of mass culture, new connections between the federal and local governments, and new communication and transportation technologies to stimulate travel. Before the 1880s, a tourist wishing to travel to New

Orleans or any other city would have found it difficult to purchase a ticket that showed the specific railroad with a clear departure and arrival time. The lack of a uniform system of time meant that it was difficult to organize and coordinate travel connections and to establish regularized travel operations across time and space. The development of the telegraph in the 1840s facilitated the adoption of standard time by allowing people to communicate with one another in distant places, thus enabling the instantaneous synchronization of one local time with another one far away. The standardization of time was given a major push by the consolidation of the railroad industry and the adoption of four times zones in the United States in the 1880s.[67]

As mentioned, early corporations including railroad firms, exposition planners, hotels, guidebook publishers and other travel interests were guided by a logic of bureaucratic rationalization, standardization, and commodification to enhance the efficiency and predictability of traveling. At the same time, local groups and individuals attempted to construct a sense of local authenticity by harnessing local traditions, histories, and identities to persuade people that New Orleans was a unique and distinctive place. The interaction of tourism from above and below manifested in the formation of new networks and organizations to construct and transmit images and symbols of "authentic" New Orleans to bolster profit making and build tourism and travel markets. Local writers, cultural organizations, and other groups sufficed as constructors and inventors of an array of cultural themes, symbols, and motifs. At the same time, early hotels, railroads, and other travel interests became communication networks and channels of cultural transmission.

As I point out in the next chapter, representations of "authentic" New Orleans become increasingly commodified as tourism develops into a mass industry. Localized cultural practices that once existed outside the logic of commerce and market exchange now enter the ring of commodification, marketed for outsiders. This commodification is aided by the rationalization of image production and an emerging racial discourse that links culture and authenticity/inauthenticity with specific racial groups. New expert culture makers emerge to reformulate New Orleans's urban iconography to exclude particular groups of people from the discourse of culture and tourism. As I show, the interaction between dominant narratives and counternarratives of New Orleans become organizational strategies for political mobilization to both reinforce and challenge social inequalities.

4

Authenticity in Black and White
The Rise of Tourism in the Twentieth Century

I desire to call the Board's attention to the far reaching importance
of nation wide publicity your Association of Commerce continues
to secure for New Orleans. In one way or another, the fact that the
"new" New Orleans is being developed through the application of
the science of industrial and commercial economy is driven home
in every article sent out or inspired. Hence the very favorable
opinion the leading businessmen of the United States now have
of New Orleans. As a result, editors all over the country, in increasing numbers, are asking us for articles about New Orleans.
The *National Geographic Magazine* has just asked for fifty photographs of New Orleans. The editor of the *Annals of the American
Academy of Political and Social Science* has asked for an article.
This proves that we have made New Orleans, through the highest
form of exploitation, appeal to the highest class of publishers in
the country.
—Monthly Report of the General Manager to the President and
Board of Directors of the New Orleans Association of
Commerce, September 8, 1916[1]

Contrary to the opinion prevailing in the minds of many of our
citizens and businessmen, conventions simply do not gravitate nat-
urally to New Orleans because our city is popular and desirable.
We are one favorite convention center of the nation among some
forty or more others in this country, competing with other foreign
capitals. . . . The campaign demands to secure conventions are
insistent that the Bureau and its executive staff be constantly alert
and active in behalf of maintaining the position and desires of New
Orleans before the influential spirits of convention organizations
which are prospects for the City. You all know the story of convention development. Some groups must be followed for years before
they are ripened to the point of becoming New Orleans conscious.

All must be sought from one to thee years before they are secured. A lapse of an interval often breaks the chain and throws years of effort and expense to the winds.

—Annual Report of the Convention and Visitors' Bureau, November 30, 1937[2]

The 1884 World's Industrial and Cotton Centennial Exposition set the stage for a new era of tourism development supported by new business organizations, corporate networks, and marketing strategies to bolster New Orleans as an attractive place for investment and leisure. As reflected in the quotes above, the promotion of tourism was part of a larger process of urban place building that aimed to aestheticize space and culture and to make both residents and visitors "New Orleans conscious." At the heart of this aestheticization was the application of corporate rationalization and commodification to transform the signifiers and markers of New Orleans authenticity into consumable objects and consumption-based entertainment experiences. By the late nineteenth century, the growth of urban commercial spaces such as department stores, restaurants, theaters, hotels, and amusement parks welcomed visitors to a bustling and colorful city of picturesque sights and architectural splendor (fig. 4.1).

Commercial development and the expansion of urban rail transportation helped nurture the growth of a new public scenery of streetcar boulevards and retail corridors that provided the setting for displays of wealth and commodities. The street railway mileage in New Orleans grew from 125 miles in 1880 to 177.2 miles in 1900, and it peaked at 222.1 miles in 1920.[3] By the early twentieth century, St. Charles Avenue and Canal Street had become the major boulevards for the old-line Carnival parades, with the former housing the mansions of the elite and the later containing a variety of specialty shops and small commercial businesses. Shopping spaces along Canal Street and in other areas embodied innovations in the mass production of consumer goods and strategies of display that became commonplace in U.S. cities, a development described by Mark Gottdiener, Sharon Zukin, and William Leach.[4] The promise of industrial expansion and abundance became a spectacle itself, expressed in the New Orleans's gigantic railroad yards, sport system, monumental buildings, and the French Opera. At the same time,

Fig. 4.1.The rise of railroads and the growth in size and specialization of New Orleans's hotels were central forces in the development of tourism during the second half of the nineteenth century. Before the 1880s, hotels in New Orleans were primarily known as local commercial centers that served both residents and travelers. By the end of the century, New Orleans and other major cities were experiencing a hotel building boom as aggressive business owners adapted their accommodations to attract new kinds of patrons, especially conventioneers, trade associations, and professional bodies. Hotel development was part of a larger rationalization of work that reflected the application of scientific techniques to enhance worker productivity and profitability. According to one tourist brochure, "New Orleans hotels are scientifically designed, equipped and operated under trained management to give you the security, privacy, and creature comforts that are worth far more to your mental and physical well being than the price you pay at the cashier upon leaving." (Reproduced by permission of Tulane University, Howard-Tilton Memorial Library, Special Collections)

the building of the Fair Grounds racetrack and parks along Lake Ponchartrain drew both residents and visitors to pursue leisure at baseball games, gambling houses, and amusement gardens. The emergence of jazz music, the increased popularity of voodoo ceremonies and gaming,

Fig. 4.2. During the Antebellum era, Canal Street was the major dividing line separating the French Quarter of Creole society and culture from the American Sector dominated by Anglo-Saxon business and finance. By the 1880s, Canal Street had become a major commercial strip and boulevard for the old-line Carnival parades, including the Krewe of Rex, shown here during the 1950s. Shopping spaces along Canal Street and in other areas embodied innovations in the mass production of consumer goods and strategies of display that became commonplace in U.S. cities during the twentieth century. (Reproduced by permission of the New Orleans Public Library, Louisiana Division and the City Archives)

and the indelible Mardi Gras celebration contributed to projecting an image of New Orleans as a unique place with a distinctive culture and irresistible charm (fig. 4.2).[5]

The public spaces of New Orleans during the decades after Reconstruction were subject to a series of profound transformations linked to the dominance of the commodification process and new relations of sexual exploitation. By the end of the nineteenth century, New Orleans was increasingly associated with two contrasting yet interconnected gendered images: New Orleans as a city of love and romance and New Orleans as a place of unrestrained and promiscuous sexual pleasure. The image of "Romantic New Orleans" had long been cultivated and elaborated by urban sketch writers such as Lafcadio Hearn and disseminated to a national audience through magazines, railroad advertisements, and other tourist guides.[6] During the late nineteenth century, this benign motif began to be juxtaposed with an image of New Orleans as a city of vice and prostitution, the Sodom and Gomorrah of the urban South. In 1880, New Orleans had 365 houses of prostitution located in various parts of the city.[7]

In 1897, the city government created a special red light district, "Storyville," to segregate and regulate the prostitution trade in the city. Named for Sidney Story, the councilman who introduced the original ordinance to concentrate vice, Storyville employed hundreds of prostitutes and became a major tourist attraction until its closing in 1917 by request of Secretary of the Navy Josephus Daniels. Historian Alecia Long argues that the commodifiction of sex and the segregation of prostitution in Storyville was a critical factor in defining New Orleans as sexualized city and as a major pleasure destination for male travelers.[8] Tourism promoters devised a different kind of advertising for these visitors than they did for tourists who came to attend the Mardi Gras balls and other attractions. In 1895, for example, promoters published and circulated 20,000 red light district directories to interested tourists. In *All on a Mardi Gras Day,* historian Reid Mitchell notes that in 1906, the *Sunday Sun,* a gentlemen's magazine, printed a special Carnival edition for visitors with advertisements of a variety of brothels.[9] In light of the rationalization and commodifiction of urban space, Storyville came to serve as a metaphor for the growing presence of the commodity form. The increasingly commodified urban area was charged with a poignant sexualization that made Storyville a tourist spectacle, enticing travelers who were interested in indulging New Orleans's reputation as a haven for sexual gratification.

More generally, the emergence of New Orleans as a major tourist destination was not something that developed by fortuity, accident, or happenstance. Guidebooks and promotional material had long pointed locals and tourists to places of recreation and entertainment activities in the city. By the late nineteenth century, the promotional material of business leaders not only advertised New Orleans as a progressive city but also implied an evolving form of civic boosterism centered on attracting tourists and remaking the city into a landscape of consumption. In 1894, several hundred businessmen formed the Young Men's Business League for the purpose of bringing "to the notice of the business world the material wealth of our city and its advantages for business, manufactures and residences."[10] By the turn of the century, more local businesses joined to create the New Orleans Progressive Union, an organization to entertain distinguished visitors to New Orleans. In 1913, the Progressive Union and the Young Men's Business League merged with several other associations to form the New Orleans Association of Commerce.[11] A year later, the Association of Commerce joined the Chamber of Commerce of the United States.

The Association of Commerce was the first organized group of business leaders in New Orleans to create a tourism and convention bureau and promote the city on a widespread scale using rational organization and mass media. Early New Orleans writers—such as Grace King, Kate Chopin, Lafcadio Hearn, Robert Tallant, George Washington Cable, William Coleman, Lyle Saxon, and others—facilitated the creation of a collective memory of New Orleans culture with deep historical roots in an amalgam of different people and groups. Yet it was the Association of Commerce that supplied the organizational structures, marketing strategies, and promotional efforts to disseminate this image on an international scale and link New Orleans with a fledgling mass tourism industry. The members of the committees of the Association of Commerce were urban imagineers—signifying agents—who gave substance and imagery to New Orleans and worked diligently to influence the presentation of the city to locals, businesses, and tourists. Broadly, it was the Association of Commerce's quasi-bureaucratic form, flexible division of labor, and several-layered authority system that helped rationalize the process of symbol production while identifying and creating new opportunities for advertising New Orleans on a global scale.[12]

The image building of urban writers and the Association of Commerce reflected and supported an emerging system of urban promotion led by magazines, music, silent films, motion pictures, radio, and, later, television (fig. 4.3). Bruce Raeburn has noted that theaters served as a training ground for New Orleans's early jazz musicians in the years after World War I. Theaters allowed local players to gain national exposure, and the advent of silent films made theaters into a steady source of union employment. Recording and radio made it possible to project music over time and space and introduce people around the world to New Orleans jazz.[13] The transmission of cultural images and symbols about the city received an added boost with the development of silent films. In 1912, George Klein, Samuel Long, and Frank Morton founded the Kalem Company and began to produce silent films using New Or-

A   B   C

Fig. 4.3. Early-twentieth-century visitors' guides were forms of urban impression management to influence perceptions about cities: (A) *Tourists' Guide to New Orleans* by the New Orleans Railway and Light Company; (B) *Tourist' Guide to New Orleans* by the New Orleans Railways Company; (C) *Impressions of a Visit to Historic New Orleans, "The Paris of America,"* from the St. Charles Hotel. As constructions of local culture, visitor guides simplified and reduced the nuance and complexity of local culture to a few resonate themes and images. As information disseminators, these guides coached visitors on what to see, what to do, and how they should experience the city. For early tourism boosters, New Orleans's rich history and iconography serviced as an inexhaustible resource for extracting and constructing a plethora of symbols, motifs, and mnemonic devices to stimulate travel and to guide visitors to particular markers of distinction. Images of architectural splendor, creole cuisine, jazz music, beautiful parks, unique cemeteries, charming neighborhoods, prosperous economy, and warm climate predominate in early-twentieth-century visitors' guides. (Reproduced by permission of Tulane University, Howard-Tilton Memorial Library, Special Collections)

leans as a setting. During its first year, the company produced *The Bell of New Orleans, Girl Strikers, The Pilgrimage, Mardi Gras Mix-Up, Bucktown Romance,* and the *Darling of the C.S.A.*[14] Later, the advent of television and motion pictures encouraged the theatrical stereotyping of New Orleans, creating a symbolic reality colored by the selective interpretations of producers and writers. Cinema, motion pictures, and television superimposed a "visual city" on the "built city," creating a narrative map of familiarity and coherence in place of complexity and variety. Movies like *Streetcar Named Desire* with Marlon Brando, *Louisiana Purchase* with Bob Hope, *King Creole* with Elvis Presley, and many others, presented slices of authenticity to reinforce and accentuate certain stereotypes while creating for each viewer a private impression of New Orleans.[15]

Business Mobilization and the 1915 Panama-Pacific Exposition

We claim that for a world's exposition . . . New Orleans is the only city that fulfills every requirement. . . . From the financial standpoint the New Orleans proposition is every whit as good as that of San Francisco. From the geographical standpoint the situation in New Orleans is ideal; from the same standpoint the situation of San Francisco is impossible. In essential considerations of location and relation to our own country and to the outside world, New Orleans, of all the considerable cities of the United States, offers without a doubt the best site; San Francisco incontestably the worst. This proposition is undebatable.

—W. B. Thompson, on behalf of locating the 1915
Panama Exposition in New Orleans[16]

During the late nineteenth century and early twentieth century, the growing challenges of urbanization and industrialization spearheaded the mobilization of New Orleans business elites to form new organizations and develop strategies to promote travel to the city. Exemplary of this growing interest was the decision to launch an organized campaign in 1910 to obtain the 1915 World's Panama Exposition, celebrating the opening of the Panama Canal. Indeed, the financial failure of the 1884 World's Industrial and Cotton Centennial Exposition did not stop local elites from mobilizing to secure another world's fair.

Early planning for the exposition came in February 1910 when a delegation of fifty New Orleans businessmen, led by Louisiana Governor Jared Y. Sanders and New Orleans Mayor Martin Behrman, traveled to Washington, D.C., to lobby President William Howard Taft and the U.S. House Committee on Industrial Arts and Expositions to designate New Orleans as the exposition city. Business leaders in other cities soon followed in pressing the federal government to choose their cities as locations for the fair. Over the next several months, the urban campaign developed into a major lobbying struggle between San Francisco and New Orleans.[17] San Francisco businessmen were successful in getting a resolution introduced in the U.S. House Committee on Industrial Arts and Exposition authorizing the U.S. president to invite foreign nations to the exposition in San Francisco. New Orleans businessmen countered by having a similar resolution introduced in the Committee on Foreign Affairs. Businessmen in New Orleans associated with the Progressive Union formed the World's Panama Exposition Company to secure private and public funds, lobby government officials, and obtain the endorsement of commercial organizations throughout the country for the exposition.[18] During this time, businessmen in San Francisco launched a major civic effort to pave the city's streets, improve the waterfront, and beautify the city.[19] An intensive publicity campaign by the city of San Francisco combined with a massive lobbying effort by Union Pacific, Sante Fe, and other national railroad companies overshadowed New Orleans's promotional efforts. In the end, the U.S. House of Representatives voted 188–159 in favor of San Francisco, and the World's Panama-Pacific Exposition opened in 1915.

The struggle between San Francisco and New Orleans reflects the emergence of new forms of urban competition and resultant negative publicity developed by urban boosters to stigmatize rival cities and attract flows of capital and people to build tourism. Throughout the campaign to attract the exposition, businessmen in San Francisco published advertisements and brochures trumpeting the advantages of their city, and arguing that New Orleans was facing lackluster commercial expansion and poor population growth. One highly critical and iconoclastic booklet published out of San Francisco maintained that New Orleans was a poor site because of the lack of "hotel accommodations, fit drinking water, sanitary conditions, or any of the other necessary requisites to make it an Exposition City to afford convenience and comfort of a world crowd." This booklet claimed to "present arguments in cold figures with a touch of humor, which prove without question that New Orleans is physically unable to cope with the responsibilities of an International Exposition." These "cold figures" included comparisons with average monthly temperature and rainfall for each city and proclamations such as "New Orleans has not the climate, the money or the facilities. People will not visit her during the vacation months. This was proven by lack of attendance during her Exposition in 1884."

Even more important was the reference to New Orleans's growing "big negro population" and San Francisco's "steady growth in population, with at least 98 percent white" as an argument for locating the fair in San Francisco (fig. 4.4). "Bear in mind," according to this booklet, that "color counts" as an "indication of poverty and inability to keep up the local support of an exposition." In describing New Orleans's population growth over the preceding ten years, the booklet noted that the supposed "tendency of negroes to live in the town has increased" and that "negroes in New Orleans today must be practically counted

Fig. 4.4. The mobilization of political and economic elites in San Francisco and New Orleans to attract the 1915 World's Fair symbolized the emergence of a new era of place promotion organized around the strategic deployment of racial imagery and inflammatory rhetoric. In this print of the 1915 Panama-Pacific Exposition, urban boosters in San Francisco castigated New Orleans as a commercially weak city whose past experience with the 1884 Industrial and Cotton Centennial Exposition was symptomatic of a "repetition of failure." The cartoon frames New Orleans as a financial liability and an unattractive place, while other advertisements pointed to San Francisco's "practically all white" population as a major indicator of its ability to "keep up local support of an exposition." (Reproduced by permission of Tulane University, Howard-Tilton Memorial Library, Special Collections)

out of the population as supporters of the fair." The booklet stigmatized New Orleans as having "no recognized metropolitan area. Back of it are swamps, bayous, small villages and plantations, the population being small and black."[20]

These examples reveal an emerging strategy of place promotion organized around the cultivation and deployment of racial imagery for urban place building and authenticity construction. San Francisco's urban boosters used racial language and categories as a major selling tool and promotional device to obtain the exposition. Race was not an ancillary category or a peripheral concern in San Francisco's promotional literature. The use of race was strategic and methodical, and advertising and promotions advanced a conception of urban authenticity based on white racial identity. Elites in San Francisco attempted to build support for the city both through the symbolic construction of "the other" (New Orleans) and through the actual condemnation of blacks. Here blackness emerged as a symbol of urban decline, physical deterioration, deepening poverty, and cultural decay. The realm of racial ideas, discriminatory policies, and segregation practices in the late nineteenth and early twentieth centuries—from the "separate but equal" Supreme Court decision in *Plessy v. Ferguson* (1896) to the spread of Jim Crow —symbolized the entrenchment of white supremacy. Broadly, urban boosters circulated ideas of white superiority to champion the economic and social advantages of San Francisco, stigmatize blacks as obstacles to a profitable exposition, and associate urban prosperity and cosmopolitanism with whiteness.

San Francisco's deployment of race to stigmatize New Orleans connects with larger sociocultural changes in the United States, including the racialization of European ethnic groups during the turn of the century. Several scholars have used the term "racialization" to explain the construction and extension of racial images, symbols, and meanings to nonracial practices and activities.[21] Michele Lamont and colleagues on the cultural construction of racial boundaries, Matthew Frye Jacobson on the emergence of whiteness as a pan-ethnic category, and Daniel Bernardi on racial discrimination and the rise of mass cinema draw attention to the centrality of racialization in institutionalizing white supremacy in the fields of law, politics, and mass culture.[22] Central to these and other studies is the emphasis on how early-twentieth-century racial discourse merged race, culture, and social class to the extent that "American" and "white" became interchangeable and encompassing. This diverse scholarship suggests that the formation and meaning of "white" as a racial category emerged through social conflicts and struggles over access to and control over political and economic resources, including land ownership and labor market position.[23] In San Francisco, exposition boosters used race rhetoric to homogenize a variety of European ethnic populations into a single "race," especially to distinguish them from the diverse people of New Orleans, who were supposedly not equal to the predominantly white population of San Francisco. In short, the competition to obtain the exposition highlights transformations in the meaning and content of race and draws attention to the growing salience of whiteness as an ideological category used by cities in their struggles to promote commercial growth.

Racial Politics of Authenticity Construction

> The entire trend in the handling of the different races has been one of segregation. Along these lines peace and amity and working together have been the result. But, almost invariably in our civic life where there has been impingement by the negro in white sections or by whites in negro sections turmoil and trouble have been the result.
>
> —Executive Committee of the New Orleans
> Association of Commerce, 1930[24]

The production of tourism both reflected and reinforced trends toward the intensification of racial discrimination and segregation that defined New Orleans in the decades after 1920. During the first two decades of the twentieth century, New Orleans began to adopt racial segregation ordinances to disempower blacks.[25] Despite a large amount of interracial labor protest and activity in New Orleans during the turn of the century, by the 1930s, the city government had passed several statutes stipulating that only certified voters could be employed on the docks.[26] The state of Louisiana gradually instituted a series of procedures to restrict blacks from voting, and by 1930, of the 117,347 registered voters in New Orleans, only 2,128 were black.[27] In 1924, the Louisiana legislature granted cities with a population of 25,000 or more the power to enact racial segregation ordinances. The New Orleans City Council voted unanimously to enact a segregation statute, and city leaders appointed a special attorney to prosecute violations.[28] More generally, from the early twentieth century through the 1960s, an explicit endorsement of racial discrimination and exclusion defined the policies and everyday practices of the all public bodies, cultural institutions, and business firms. Blacks were excluded from "white" public spaces, including schools, parks, and museums. In addition to the docks and port industry, blacks experienced rampant segregation in all major sectors of employment and were not allowed to become public servants.

Up through the middle 1960s, blacks were not permitted to be members of the Association of Commerce, and at least one department, the Young Men's Department, had passed a resolution that "membership in the organization shall be open to all white males."[29] In 1926, the Association of Commerce voiced dissent when local black leaders attempted to form a "colored auxiliary" of the association. According to minutes of a meeting of the Executive Committee, members were adamant that a colored auxiliary "was not to be tolerated." While "there is a field of usefulness for colored people in civic up building," according to the Executive Committee, blacks are not permitted to be members of the association, and thus "a separate and distinct individuality would be more desirable for them." As a result, the Executive Committee implored black leaders to "give particular thought to the selection of a name of their organization so that it will not be confused with our organization or any of the white civic organizations in the city."[30]

The increasing salience of the black-white racial divide manifested within the realm of tourism and culture in several ways. First, local elites racially segregated all entertainment venues and public places devoted to recreation, conventions, and tourism. In February 1930, the Auditorium Commission of the Association of Commerce became embroiled in a controversy over whether to "grant permits for the holding of colored conventions in the Auditorium." According to minutes of a meeting of the Executive Committee, the Auditorium Commission was divided on this issue because, on the one hand, members hesitated to give a permit due to the fact that "a good portion of the revenue will come from social functions of the white citizens of New Orleans." The rationale for racial exclusion was that whites would be less likely to patronize the auditorium if blacks and whites were allowed to co-mingle. On the other hand, the commission felt that they could not restrict "colored people [from] the use of some part of the Auditorium for their conventions as they are tax payers as well as we are." To remedy this problem, the Executive Committee instructed the Auditorium Commission to "go to the City with the idea that some portion of [the Auditorium] should be used by the colored people for their functions without permitting them the use of the Auditorium proper," a condition that meant "having separate entrances and certain sections" for blacks.[31]

In April 1940, the Convention and Visitors Bureau (CVB) and the Auditorium Commission of the Association of Commerce carried on a "long discussion of the problem of bringing the National Conference of Social Workers [NCSW] to New Orleans" because this organization "embraces the racial question"—"allowing negroes equal privileges in the auditorium and hotels" as whites. The point of controversy involved "whether the invitation from New Orleans should be extended on the basis of segregation of negroes or without restrictions." The national secretary of the NCSW, Howard Knight, informed the CVB that Oklahoma City "had no objection to permitting negroes equal privileges of attending meetings in [their] auditorium . . . [and that] the extension of the invitation with segregation would militate against acceptance of New Orleans' invitation." According to minutes of a meeting, the CVB authorized its chairman to meet with the Auditorium Commission "with a view to working out the negro angle in the public auditorium" and to extend an invitation to the NCSW "with the specification that segregation would probably have to apply."[32]

During the 1930s and later, local authorities and elites justified racial segregation on the belief that black presence would lead to property devaluation and disinvestment and would negatively affect residential areas. In April 1930, the Executive Committee expressed regret on the opening of the Crescent Theater "exclusively for the negroes": "It is not a question of legal right," nor is it "a question of catering to the amusement of a certain class of our population," according to a press release contained in minutes of a meeting. The real problem is "taking a section of the city and ingrafting upon it a center for the entertainment of our colored population that is going to be against the general sentiment of our people." "Catering to that class we fear . . . [will cause] a deterioration of that neighborhood and bring about conditions that will be of detriment to the negro in one instant and to the white as well."[33] In 1946, the Civic Affairs Committee of the Association of Commerce reported on efforts to "bring about for the colored population . . . a recreational park, an educational and moral training program [and] adequate playgrounds and bathing beaches." The motivation for these efforts was not altruism or benevolence but the maintenance of the racial color line. According to minutes of a meeting, the Civic Affairs Committee "recognizes the gravity of the negro problem in New Orleans and has been working for some time toward the end of having needed recreational facilities provided for Negroes which will serve to curb the ever growing tendency on their part to encroach on white facilities."[34]

Second, the image of New Orleans as a unique place of rich history, ethnic diversity, and unforgettable charm was built on the erasure of blacks from tourist images and local promotional campaigns. During the later half of the nineteenth century and continuing through the twentieth century, tourist advertisements and other promotional campaigns played up the rich ethnic and cultural diversity of New Orleans while completely ignoring the racial dynamics of the city. On the one hand, even though nonwhites formed a major segment of the local population, they remained invisible in tourist advertisements from the nineteenth century forward. On the other hand, when blacks did appear in tourist guides, they were typically shown as domestic servants, mammies, and wage laborers but never as potential tourists who might want to visit New Orleans. Tourist advertisements presented ethnic and racial minorities as caricatures. There were no accounts that celebrated black history or the contribution of blacks to the development of New Orleans. Moreover, while tourist guides and other booklets might mention the population of the city, few mentioned changes in population or facts about the city that did not fit the dominant tourism image. One tourist guide noted that New Orleans is "one of the healthiest cities in the Union. Average resident white death rate is less than 15 percent," without mentioning the extraordinarily high death rate among blacks, which was more than double that of whites.[35]

The selective and strategic implantation of white-friendly images of New Orleans into a large number of magazines, newspapers, and other outlets constituted the city as a desirable destination for whites and helped encourage the building of a segregated tourist industry. It is also important to note that advertising and promotion were about creating public "knowledge" about New Orleans. Such efforts were a critical form of power in which the ability to put into circulation certain images of New Orleans occurred with little or no substantive input from local residents who were absent or featured in these images. While local architecture, history, and cuisine might be celebrated in tourism advertisements, the contributions of black workingmen and women were not. In short, exclusionary racial practices within the sphere of tourism not only applied to conventions and entertainment spaces but also occurred within advertising and media. Racial discrimination within tourism fit into the larger institutional apparatus of racially segregative public and private actions that formed an effective system of racial subordination.

Third, the development of tourism was closely associated with the transposition of culture as race and race as culture. During the early twentieth century, tourism advertisements and promotional efforts in New Orleans began to recast the language of culture in a racial discourse that conflated "creole" ethnicity with white culture. Before the late nineteenth century, "creole" meant indigenous to Louisiana or New

Orleans.[36] In a popular 1873 tour guide of the city, Edwin L. Jewell defined creole as "all who are born here . . . without reference to the birth place of their parents."[37] Within two decades after the Civil War, "creole" was being redefined "as white descendants of the French and Spanish settlers."[38] By this time, whites were appropriating the term to purposely exclude descendants of people of color or African ancestry.[39] On the one hand, the transformation in content of the term "creole" paralleled the rise of Jim Crow segregation and the intensification of racial discrimination in the decades after the end of Reconstruction. On the other hand, the fusion of whiteness with creole reveals larger shifts in the political economy of consumer capitalism, especially the rise of tourism, during the turn of the century and later. Advertising and promoting "creole" both reflected and reinforced an emerging public awareness of culture as a reified thing, an object that could be commodified and consumed. This understanding encouraged the consumption of culture as a major component of the emerging tourism industry. In New Orleans, "creole" came to stand in as a signifier of local authenticity, a term that could be applied to different historical contexts, experiences, and images. By the 1920s, the term had been incorporated into the orbits of profit-making, transposed onto a variety of enticements, consumption-based experiences, and saleable objects such as food, history, and areas of the city (the "Creole Quarter").

The racialization of creole, in short, reflected a reciprocal process of homogenization and diversification of social relations that defined the rise of modern tourism in New Orleans. As the social content of "creole" became conflated with white culture, tourism boosters and advertisers attached a variety of pleasurable experiences to the category as a means of exciting consumer demand to travel to the city. In the realm of tourism and place promotion, racialization was manifested in the institutionalization of racial discrimination, whereby racial prejudices, categories, and significations became a normal feature of tourism business practices and the production of tourist imagery. Racial and ethnic images and discourse had long been an important component of tourism advertising and promotion in New Orleans. Railroad companies, guidebook publishers, and hotels all attempted to transform racial and ethnic differences into saleable commodities to bolster profit making and support tourism industry building. What is new in the 1920s and later is that tourism became racialized so that a set of racial relations, segregationist ideology, and institutional tourism practices based on racial meanings and distinctions emerged and over time developed a life of its own. The political and economic elites of New Orleans, interacting and organizing through the Association of Commerce, were decisive agents in the racialized production and representation of New Orleans economy and culture. Members reacted to change, but they were also catalysts of change, working to build and legitimate an image of New Orleans as a racially exclusive destination for white tourists and conventioneers.

"The Old Quarter Is Our Greatest Tourist Asset"

We of New Orleans are fortunate in having with us today a link forming a continuity with the past. It is reassuring in this day of chancing concepts, of families dividing, of the tearing up of roots to be able to live beside history. It makes us proud of our heritage, it encourages us to live up to it and it bespeaks an earthly immortality in future generations. Few places in the United States can boast these steadying influences and no place can show a complete city of them. . . . The old city of New Orleans, popularly known as the French Quarter or the Vieux Carre, is indeed unique in the United States and should be preserved at any cost. . . . Basically, the French Quarter is being preserved by a small group of citizens who are the last to receive any consideration on the part of the City fathers. . . . They are people . . . [who] feel themselves in a group apart, bound in what appears to be a hopeless struggle for the survival of a part of the City much beloved by them.

    —Mary Morrison, "Problems of the Vieux Carre"[40]

The rise of organized tourism promotional campaigns were not only intertwined with presumptions about racial categorization but also reflected a growing awareness among elites that urban neighborhoods should be seen as tourist attractions and markers of local authenticity. The emergence of modern tourism in New Orleans coincides with the transformation of the Vieux Carre (French Quarter) into a tourist destination, a space for the generalized display and consumption of local culture and history. Before the turn of the century, the Vieux Carre contained a mixture of ethnic and class groups, as well as of commercial businesses that catered to local residents: gambling, factories, and expanding commercial department stores along Canal Street. During the years after World War I, the Vieux Carre began to acquire a reputation as a center for arts and crafts and a focus of culture and historic preservation.[41]

In 1919, local artists and socialites formed the Arts and Crafts Club of New Orleans and in 1922 opened a prominent gallery in the Vieux Carre to display, teach, and sell art. In the early 1920s, a group of local women activists established the Quartier Club, renamed Le Petite Salon in 1924, to host talks by artists, writers, and political activists. The 1920s also witnessed the growth of many tearooms, art galleries, bookshops, restaurants, clubs, and speakeasies. During this time, the Vieux Carre became known as a "bohemian sanctuary," a fashionable and affordable place for a heterogeneous population of artists and writers to live and work. In his guidebook entitled *Fabulous New Orleans,* local writer Lyle Saxon described the French Quarter as a neighborhood of artists, with every block having an artist studio.[42] In his foreword to *Sherwood Anderson and Other Famous Creoles: A Gallery of Contemporary New Orleans* (1926), William Faulkner "mused on the richness of our American life that permits forty people to spend day after day painting in a single area of six city blocks."[43] Later, more artists and writers, including Tennessee Williams, Ernest Hemmingway, and F. Scott Fitzgerald, were attracted to the area, contributing to the ambiance and prestige of the neighborhood's arts movement and culture.

During the 1920s and 1930s, the renovation and demolition of several famous buildings, combined with the escalating property values, inspired several protest movements to preserve the history and beloved architecture of the district. In 1925, the State of Louisiana created a Vieux Carre Commission to monitor development in the French Quarter. In 1936, residents and the Association of Commerce pushed for enabling legislation that gave the Vieux Carre Commission the power to enforce land-use regulations and property codes and to approve or reject architectural changes in the area. The concept—which later was adopted as a model for preservationists in many areas of the nation—was that of the "tout ensemble," which meant that the overall appearance and social integrity of the Vieux Carre was to be protected, not just individual buildings or blocks of the area. Two years later, property owners incorporated the Vieux Carre Property Owners Association as a nonprofit organization dedicated to the "preservation, beautification, and general betterment of the Vieux Carre." Later, the organization expanded its membership to include residents other than property owners. With its more inclusive membership, the organization dedicated itself to "awakening, fostering, and cultivating a feeling of civic pride among the residents and property owners" of the Vieux Carre.[44]

While the Vieux Carre Property Owners Association argued for the preservation of the French Quarter as an authentic and charming neighborhood, the Association of Commerce campaigned for the preservation of the historic area for its potential to generate exchange-values through tourism development. During the first decades of the twentieth century, the Association of Commerce established a "Vieux Carre Businessmen's Association" and a Retail Merchants Bureau to organize sightseeing tours through the neighborhood.[45] By the 1930s, Vieux Carre walking guides had become an institutionalized practice of the association in connection with its plans to bring conventions to the city. The "Old Quarter is our greatest tourist asset," according to minutes of a meeting in 1938.[46] During the 1940s and later, the Convention and Visitors Bureau (CVB) considered several proposals to create a corporation to finance the "preservation of the Vieux Carre as a tourist and convention attraction."[47] Throughout the decades, the Association of Commerce, city officials, and neighborhood leaders shared a view that the preservation of historic buildings and residential integrity were not only advantageous for attracting tourists but also necessary to preserve the local culture and authenticity of the city of New Orleans. On the one hand, tourism boosters and local elites developed and circulated an image of the Vieux Carre as a major locus of local authenticity and a focal point of New Orleans culture, an image that was disseminated to both residents and visitors. On the other hand, neighborhood organizations played a crucial role in protecting the residential basis and architecture heritage of the French Quarter, at the same time helping to create a veritable cornucopia of cultural resources that would fuel the expansion of corporate tourism in New Orleans in the decades after 1950 (fig. 4.5).

The above points draw our attention to the role of aesthetic networks, residential networks, and heritage networks in the construction of local authenticity to undergird and reinforce the tourism from below processes of localization and hybridization. Aesthetic networks composed of artists, novelists, and journalists served as generators and purveyors of cultural knowledge and information about New Orleans. Residential networks encompassing the Vieux Carre Property Owners Association played a major role in raising consciousness of the Vieux Carre as a unique place of distinctive charm and ambiance. The adoption of

Fig. 4.5. The Vieux Carre, or old French Quarter of New Orleans is probably one of the most famous historic districts in the United States. Established in 1718, the neighborhood consists of a mix of residential and commercial land uses within a rectangular grid of approximately 120 blocks along the Mississippi River. The Vieux Carre was first a French trading center and, later, after 1762, a Spanish colonial outpost. With the Louisiana Purchase in 1803, the United States inherited a thriving commercial center supported by river trade. In 1937, the neighborhood was designated as a historic district and remained the city's only landmark district until the 1970s. By the middle of the twentieth century, the Vieux Carre had acquired a reputation as a charming residential neighborhood with a unique historical background and architectural styles. Shown here are Jackson Square and the St. Louis Cathedral in the 1920s. (Reproduced by permission of the New Orleans Public Library, Louisiana Division and the City Archives)

the concept "tout ensemble" not only functioned as a planning instrument and physical design tool but also became a cultural symbol to unify residents as caretakers of a sui generis neighborhood. During the 1930s, aesthetic and heritage networks were supported by the federal government's Historic American Buildings Survey, which employed local writers, architects, draftsmen, and photographers to inventory French Quarter landmarks. The Works Progress Administration's (WPA) Federal Writers' Project under the direction of local writer Lyle Saxon produced the *New Orleans City Guide* in 1938 and *Gumbo Ya-Ya* in 1945, a collection of Louisiana folk tales and mysteries. Together, the Historic American Buildings Survey and the Federal Writers' Project incubated local cadres of cultural activists dedicated to expanding the content of New Orleans's urban iconography. The presence of cross-cutting networks of neighborhood leaders, residents, artists, and others operated as agents of place socialization, introducing newcomers and others to local cultural traditions, including histories about the city's cuisine, music, and heritage.

Broadly, the ensembles of different networks were crucibles of cultural invention, while the Association of Commerce served as a major conduit for cultural diffusion, spreading information about local culture through tourist advertising, film, and the mass media. Aesthetic, heritage, and neighborhood networks were not only sets of ties between individuals and associations but clusters of relationships that constructed and supplied a constellation of meanings and stories that people used to evaluate local authenticity and define New Orleans culturally. Through their diverse interactions, local artists, writers, neighborhood residents, historic preservationists, and others created networks in symbolically patterned ways. At the same time, the different network structures circulated cultural forms such as definitions of local authenticity, meanings of community identity and collective memory, and styles of group action. As agents of authenticity, the networks selected and excluded some elements of the present and past to define local culture and to coordinate action within and between the network forms. In this sense, authenticity was a site of struggle subject to the "authenticity projects" of networks and organizations engaged in mnemonic battles. From the standpoint of the first half of the twentieth century, "authentic" New Orleans was an invented category that occupied a temporal space connecting past and present. Representations of New Orleans evolved from the conflicts of the past while constraining the processes of meaning-making that followed.[48]

New Strategies for Promoting Mardi Gras

New Orleans is famed throughout the Nation, and this publicity has spread to some extent abroad, for its Mardi Gras. Aside from our Vieux Carre and its contents, the most outstanding thing about New Orleans is Mardi Gras. For years New Orleans has been building good will through the event, but unfortunately during the recent past, economic and other social conditions have contributed to a necessity for making that event less pretentious than in the past, therefore if it is the desire to use Mardi Gras as an attraction for influencing Americans to visit our city, then we must give thought to the ways and means for enhancing its glamour and appeal.

—Howard S. Greene, director, Convention and Visitors Bureau
of the Association of Commerce, May 30, 1933[49]

Another major component in the building of New Orleans's tourism industry entailed a series of organized efforts to enhance the tourist appeal of Mardi Gras. Local elites had long advertised and promoted Mardi Gras to attract tourists and market the city as a fun and entertaining place. What is different in the twentieth century is the use of new strategies of advertising and the formation of new alliances among local businesses to promote the celebration on a national and global scale. During the second decade of the twentieth century, the Convention and Visitors Bureau (CVB) and the Publicity Bureau of the Association of Commerce emerged as the major institutions for adapting Carnival for tourism. These two organizations attempted to rationalize the production and consumption of Mardi Gras by establishing new Carnival balls and parades for tourists, an idea that incited some conflict and division within the Association of Commerce.

In 1930, the CVB formed a "Committee on Carnival Visitors Ball" to "investigate the subject of the cost, and other factors concerned, with the presentation of a Carnival ball for visitors." According to minutes of a December 18, 1930 meeting, members felt that "hotels and others were considerably embarrassed by requests from Mardi Gras visitors for invitations to the various Carnival balls and that their reaction was unfavorably against New Orleans" when they could not gain admittance. One member, Jules J. Paglin, claimed that, since many visitors were unable to attend Carnival balls, "there was a growing tendency around the country to avoid New Orleans at Carnival time because of this situation." During the discussion, the main topic of debate centered on whether the CVB should assume the responsibility of acquiring funds to plan and develop a ball. While some members believed that a Carnival ball for visitors was necessary, others questioned whether the CVB could finance such an operation. As the meeting ensued, others wondered about the effect a Carnival ball for visitors would have on the authenticity of the celebration as a whole. According to the minutes of the meeting,

Mr. Clark then interjected a protest against what he termed the "commercializing" of New Orleans Carnival and the placing of a dollar sign on this historic celebration, which he declared was intended, he believed, from the plan embraced in the special committee Chairman's report, to develop support of the project by the selling of tickets, with the idea in view of realizing a profit there from.[50]

Mr. Clark's protest was a lone voice and did not reflect the sentiment of the majority of members of the CVB. Most members of the CVB were united around the idea of making Mardi Gras more hospitable to tourists but not necessarily through explicit commercialization and advertising. In the minutes of meetings of the association, members repeatedly conflate commercialization with overt advertising in parades and on floats. In 1938, the Publicity Committee castigated what it saw as the increased use of "Advertising Trucks" following the parades because these "inject an air of commercialization into the Mardi Gras celebration which must be guarded against."[51] According to the Publicity Bureau,

Mardi Gras differs from events in other cities in that it is distinctly a celebration and not a promotion. The fact that it has no inherent commercial features, that every thing is free or by invitation is well known nationally. This lack of commercialism gives it individuality and helps to maintain and increase its popularity.[52]

Despite the association's opposition to overt commercialization, members were not against more subtle forms of commercialization, including profit-oriented Carnival balls staged for visitors. Nor were members opposed to business-led efforts to create new parades to entice visitors to stay in New Orleans for longer periods of time. The debate over commercialization was a debate over who should define commercialization and control the process. In 1941, for example, the members of the Publicity Bureau voiced opposition to the growth of concessions along Canal Street during the parades because these merchants give "too much of a small-town Carnival commercial aspect to the Mardi Gras" and interfere "with the news reel cameramen and visiting photographers who are now limited in the shots which they can make because of the large number of signs advertising this or that soft drink or other product."[53] In short, the Association of Commerce opposed efforts by

small merchants who were not affiliated with the association to advertise and profit from the Mardi Gras celebration. At the same time,
members of the association established commercial linkages with hotels, railroads, and other tourism boosters to advertise and transmit images of Carnival to a global audience to motivate people to visit New
Orleans.[54]

By the 1930s and 1940s, the CVB was taking a proactive role in creating and organizing new parades and balls for tourists to bolster the
global appeal of Mardi Gras. In 1933, the CVB organized a subcommittee to "make a study and investigation of the feasibility of organizing a children's Carnival pageant" to be held on the Saturday before
Mardi Gras. Such a parade "would have the effect of bringing in people
from the surrounding territory and the retail merchants would capitalize there from." According to the initial proposal, the motivation for a
children's parade was not to enhance community well-being or self-
esteem but to "influence a good many people to remain over in New
Orleans for the week-end, if not through Carnival." As the proposal
noted, the parade "would provide a much needed event in our Mardi
Gras program, for as it now stands when Momus comes out on Thurs-
day the program remains blank and uninteresting until Monday night.
This is a subject of a great deal of criticism encountered from visitors to
New Orleans, tourists and transportation interests in the North and
East."[55] A year later and for several years thereafter, a children's parade,
named the Krewe of NOR (an acroynm for "New Orleans Romance")
marched through the streets of New Orleans, a parade that was "conceived, developed, produced, and staged by the Convention and Visitors' Bureau," according to a 1934 report of the CVB.[56] In 1937, local
businessmen established the Krewe of Hermes as "the patron of the visitor." Hermes paraded on Friday night and was organized in response
to "insistent demands that visitors have a chance to attend at least one
Carnival Ball."[57] The Krewe issued a limited number of invitations to
visitors to its parade and ball and, like the Krewe of NOR, was explicitly staged by businessmen to make Carnival more entertaining for visitors to the city.

Generally, the diverse attempts by the CVB and the Publicity Bureau
to advertise and promote Carnival and establish new Carnival balls
and parades reflect a broad effort to rationalize the production of Carnival and make the celebration more hospitable for tourists. On the one
hand, members of the Association of Commerce were cultural entrepre-

neurs in a literal sense, seeking to adapt Mardi Gras for instrumental purposes, especially profitmaking and commercial development. On the other hand, attempts to accommodate Mardi Gras to please tourists generated considerable conflict among local residents, who decried attempts to commercialize the celebration for economic gain. Some local residents reacted negatively to the Krewe of NOR children's parade during the 1930s, dismissing the parades as ugly and generic. Carnival historian Perry Young slighted the NOR parades as unoriginal and lacking in culturally redeeming qualities: "They had just as well be built in Los Angeles or Terre Haute."[58] Others contested the racially segregative nature of Mardi Gras and elite efforts to use the celebration to project racially biased and prejudiced views of local culture. In 1934, the Krewe of NOR debuted with a parade containing themes drawn from Louisiana history. The African American newspaper, the *Louisiana Weekly*, chastised the segregative nature of the parade, which refused to admit black children and compelled white children to paint themselves black "in order to represent Negro life during the early days of Louisiana's rise to statehood."[59] Five years later, in 1939, the Krewe of NOR adopted the theme "Peoples of New Orleans" to celebrate the history of New Orleans and the contribution of different ethnic groups to U.S. history. The parade included images of Greenlanders, Persians, and Siamese but no Africans. For social elites, the Krewe of NOR was a grand and authentic expression of New Orleans's cultural and ethnic heritage that promised to enliven the commercial prospects of the city. For African Americans, the various themes the Krewe displayed reflected a narrow and partial view of the city that was racist and devoid of authenticity. Against a backdrop of racial protest and conflict, the Krewe of NOR disbanded in 1949.

Finally, like other realms of New Orleans society and culture, the production of Mardi Gras was a racialized affair that reflected the increasing salience of the black-white racial divide in the construction of local authenticity. Racial segregation and class exclusion had been a hallmark of Carnival since the Reconstruction years when the old-line krewes instituted rationalized and exclusive parades and balls. What is different in the twentieth century is the emergence of new challenges to the segregative nature of Carnival, combined with the growth of new forms of racial marginalization. One dimension of racial marginalization was the exclusion of new African American parades, balls, street celebrations, and other Carnival inventions from the discourse of tourism promotion and advertising. During the late nineteenth and early twentieth centuries, African Americans organized a plethora of new street parades, informal celebrations, and Carnival krewes such as the Krewe of Zulu, the Jolly Boys, and others. Up until the 1980s, few African American cultural contributions and innovations ever appeared in tourism brochures, travel guides, and promotions. Through the realm of tourism promotion and advertising, social elites communicated a subtle but clear message: the "authentic" Mardi Gras was a white celebration, and blacks were to be segregated and excluded from public space.

Another dimension of racial marginalization was manifest in the emergence of new struggles over the control of urban space by working class people and women. The period after World War I witnessed the formation of the Krewe of Venus, a major women's Carnival krewe, and later, the Krewe of Orleanians, a parade of several dozen individual truck floats. While Comus, Momus, Proteus, and Rex excluded women and non-elites in their parades, the Krewe of Venus and the Krewe of Orleanians included new classes and categories of people that heretofore had been positioned as spectators and nonparticipants by the dominance of the elite krewes. Yet these new krewes explicitly excluded black New Orleanians from participating in their parades, thereby reinforcing the racially segregative nature of Carnival. Even as late as 1965, the registration form for the Krewe of Orleanians contained the statement: "The Benevolent and Protective Order of Elks being a strictly white organization, participation is restricted to those of the Caucasian (white) race."[60] In short, new krewes appropriated Carnival space for white men and women while denying it to blacks, thereby legitimizing racial exclusion as a basis for urban place making and authenticity construction in the twentieth century.

5

Boosting the Big Easy
New Orleans Goes Global

The Federal Government, which keeps a close eye on the tourist
industry and publishes its findings frequently, says that "no matter
how you slice it, the tourist business is big business. But it is not
a 'closed' business. Your community can get its share if it does
something about it." This is the challenge of New Orleans, which
is one of the most popular tourist areas in the United States, but
which amazingly enough has not done enough about it in the
past. . . . The fascination which the name "New Orleans" holds
in the minds of so many Americans has nurtured a business
which has been taken for granted by far too many of the people
in our city.

— Tourist Planning Committee, 1960[1]

By the 1950s, New Orleans could boast the development of
a tourism infrastructure composed of hotels and motels; amusement
parks; sightseeing tours, carriage rides, taxi and bus guides; travel bureaus and tourist information centers; and museums.[2] Several decades of
commercial investment and place promotion had transformed tourism
from a relatively ad hoc and uncoordinated set of activities into an increasingly specialized and rationalized industry. A central element of
this tourism building process was the development of a series of place
marketing strategies to attract visitors and commercial investment to
the city.

First, tourism advertising and promotions reduced the complexity of
urban culture to several transparent themes that could be advertised on
a global scale. Here images of famous buildings, delicious cuisine, rich
history, and the Vieux Carre, among other symbols of the local, were
inserted into tour guides and promotional pieces as symbolic indicators

of New Orleans culture and authenticity A second strategy, the romanticization of the past, appeared in tourism advertisements, brochures, and other materials to conjure up emotionally satisfying themes of past times and invoke a mythical conflict-free past. Closely related to the theme of nostalgia was the idealization of the present and the cultivation of heroic imagery to project an image of an economically prosperous New Orleans community. As tourism evolved in New Orleans, commercial boosters linked nostalgia for the past with a message of commercial and industrial development. A final strategy, the aestheticization of space, implied the proliferation of scenic enclaves and the circulation of people to particular places to consume culture, history, nature, and otherness. Here pictorial imagery, pamphlets, and guidebooks played an important role in implanting knowledge and priming visitors on what to see in New Orleans, while Mardi Gras and sites such as the French Quarter were advertised to residents and visitors as expressions of local culture.

While tourism practices and place promotion campaigns were implemented by tourism boosters to attract visitors, they were also undertaken to construct and transmit a set of images, symbols, and motifs to fabricate a touristic conception of an "authentic" New Orleans. It is important to note that not all symbols, themes, or advertising strategies were equally potent and persuasive devices to attract visitors. Some had an advantage because their ideas and language connected with preexisting cultural beliefs and community sentiments. In the 1920s the Publicity Bureau of the Association of Commerce broadcast weekly slogans such as "New Orleans: The South's Greatest City," "New Orleans: America's Most Interesting City," "New Orleans: City of Progress," "New Orleans: City of Romance," and several dozen others.[3] In the 1930s and later, the Publicity Bureau prepared dozens of "canned" stories about New Orleans that it sent to magazine editors and newspapers around the world for their use. Declaring New Orleans as "one of the most outstanding 'story' cities in this country," the association produced stories such as "Historic New Orleans," "Port of New Orleans," "Modern New Orleans," and other topics covering cemeteries, antiques, recreation, courtyards, monuments, old homes, streets, museums, and other stories.[4]

Slogans attained their power as expressions of local culture because they resonated with longstanding cultural narrations contained in stories, myths, and folk tales. References to the "Big Easy" have their origin in the nineteenth century, as early jazz musicians often gave nicknames to different places and people. Over the years, the nickname became associated with New Orleans as more and more people used it to refer to the city with a slow, easy pace and a relaxed attitude toward life. Generally, the romanticization of the past, idealization of the present, and aestheticization of space provided a loose set of themes and symbolic cues to help residents and visitors locate and perceive the constituents of authenticity and use these to orient their experiences. By linking images of the past and present in the collective memory to tourist modes of visualization and discourse, referent images could make connections to disparate activities. In turn, people could assess the compatibility of the image with their established knowledge frameworks and accept the image or reject it accordingly.

The distinction between tourism from above and below contextualizes tourism development within a social and historical framework that points to novelties and continuities with the past. Such a perspective acknowledges the role of historical conjuncture and contingent events in embedding tourism flows in places and shaping conflicts over culture and authenticity. A major assumption of the tourism from above and below heuristic is that tourism discourses and practices are conditioned by and give rise to structures and networks shaped by local histories, cultural norms, indigenous concerns, and shared local experiences. On the one hand, tourism discourses and practices make up a loosely organized vocabulary for interpreting the past and present. They also provide a cultural information guide that some groups may use to frame social conditions, shape collective action, and evaluate meanings of community identity. On the other hand, tourism discourses and practices may undermine some longstanding cultural meanings, stabilize and give new meaning to others, and subject other elements of local culture to transformative pressures. Thus, an adequate conceptualization of the connections between local culture and tourism must recognize both the local and extralocal logics and trace historically their interrelationships.

One novel feature of the post–World War II era is the development of new federal, state, and local government policies to attract tourism investment and create delimited spaces to enhance tourist consumption.[5] Another feature is the increased power of new transportation technologies and international hotel chains in controlling and channeling tourism investment flows. Chain hotels are pioneers of standardized tourism that stamp homogeneity on otherwise idiosyncratic and heterogeneous places. In later decades, chain firms would eclipse small locally owned and controlled businesses and come to dominate the cruise ship industry, entertainment industry, and other leisure and tourism sectors. Planet-wide chains could offer reassuring sameness, comfortable familiarity, and confidence of security amid the bewildering variety and strangeness of different places. In addition, it is during the postwar era that we see the erosion of overt and legally sanctioned racial discrimination in leisure and tourism practices. Before the 1960s, racial discrimination in tourism provided legitimation for a racialized ideology that associated local culture with whiteness and racial segregation. The rise of the civil rights movement and the passage of civil rights legislation during the 1960s not only opened up new political opportunities for blacks but also set in motion a broad shift in New Orleans's social and political culture. The desegregation of hotels and other entertainment and leisure activities in the city signified the growing political power of African Americans while creating a discursive space for blacks to claim ownership over local culture and authenticity.

Finally, in the postwar era, new corporate networks, organizations, and modes of financing helped link New Orleans with an expanding global tourism industry while generating new conflicts and struggles over the effects of tourism in New Orleans. During these decades, "going global" became a common ideology in urban tourism planning to refer to the importance of harnessing global flows of tourism investment by emphasizing unique local attributes.[6] For New Orleans's tourism boosters and elites, going global meant developing world-class tourist attractions, cultural events, and arts facilities to accommodate tourists while marginalizing local communal needs, cultural values, and quality of life issues. Before the 1960s, few groups voiced opposition to elite efforts to build tourist attractions and create entertaining spectacles. The expansion of the tourism sector in New Orleans in the 1960s and later, however, coincides with the growth of new organizations and networks to challenge the disruptive impact of tourism development on residential space and life. As a result, by the 1980s, an infrastructure of grassroots cultural institutions and preservationist groups had taken root in the city, at the same time that the political agenda had been reoriented to accommodate more corporate forms of tourism.

Economic Crisis and Racial Conflict in the Postwar Era

Negro citizens of New Orleans will no longer tolerate the spoon feeding of their rights. We want our rights now. This city is not immune to the new temper and tensions that are being manifested everywhere. Perhaps demonstrations against racial inequality in this community would be the spark to free this city of its inertia and complacency in the area of human relations.
        —Dutch Morial, president of the NAACP Youth Council, 1963[7]

In the first two decades after World War II, New Orleans faced a situation of lackluster economic growth combined with new forms of racial conflict and protest against discrimination and inequality. During these years, political and economic elites reacted with alarm to the spread of urban blight, the increasing percentage of black residents living in New Orleans, and the movement of whites to newly developed suburban areas. From 1940 to 1960, the percentage of whites living in Orleans Parish declined from 69.7 percent to 62.6 percent, while the percentage of whites increased in all suburban parishes, including Jefferson Parish, St. Tammany Parish, and St. Bernard Parish. At the same time, the percentage of blacks living in Orleans parish increased from 30.3 percent to 37.2 percent. The increasing percentage of blacks in Orleans Parish paralleled declining percentages of blacks in the suburban parishes.[8] In 1959, members of the Executive Committee of the Chamber of Commerce bemoaned the "movement of the white population to outlying sections of the City . . . [and] the influx of negroes into the deteriorating and blighted areas in the center of the City." As the Executive Committee put it, the "deterioration of large areas" is a "grave situation" that is "retarding the growth of our economy" and "will result in further blighted areas [and] loss of needed revenue for the City." "It has become increasingly apparent," according to the chamber, "that we step up our promotional and other activities to improve conditions."[9]

In addition, the decades after World War II witnessed a major expansion of the U.S. hotel-motel industry and the beginnings of the internationalization of U.S. hotel chains, a development that portended a major transformation in the relationships between hotels, customers, and communities. In 1939, there were 41,508 hotels and motels containing 1.6 million rooms in the United States. By 1963, almost 74,000 hotels

and motels with about 2.5 million rooms dotted the American landscape.[10] This huge growth reflected the rise of large, hierarchically organized hotel chains that could promote economies of scale. Hotel chains
such as the Hilton Corporation, Howard Johnson, Holiday Inn, Hyatt
Corporation, Marriott Corporation, and others injected a new form of
competition into the hotel industry that threatened the longstanding
dominance of independent proprietors. Unlike locally based hotels,
chain hotels could offer visitors the assurance that their hotel's products
and services were the same in all locales. Hotel chains were guided by a
logic of standardization, rationalization, and homogenization, combined
with delivering a wide range of professional hospitality services. Before
the 1950s, the hotel business in New Orleans was dominated by a few
independently run businesses. These firms were characterized by flexible
management skills, heavy reliance on unskilled labor, and lack of specialized labor training. The dominance of the hotel market by a few
owners meant that they had little incentive to launch expensive capital
projects, including building new hotels or renovating and expanding old
ones. Moreover, lack of capital financing and low levels of tourism flows
discouraged large-scale tourism investment and development in the city.

During the 1940s and 1950s, political and economic elites viewed
new hotel building as a major growth strategy to attract conventions
and promote tourism.[11] Yet local hotel owners in New Orleans recognized that attracting new hotels meant catering to large, extralocal,
chain hotels. As a result, independent hotel owners were less than enthusiastic about expanding tourism in New Orleans because they lacked
the economic power to finance and control the industry expansion. In
1946, the Convention and Visitors Bureau (CVB) of the Chamber of
Commerce reported that it would "not work to bring any large conventions here in the immediate future . . . because the hotels, in view of
their overcrowded conditions, are not in position to handle them." Two
years later, in 1948, the Executive Committee of the Chamber referred
to "the congested hotel situation in New Orleans and to the desirability
of something being done to provide additional facilities to take care of
increased business which cannot be handled under present conditions."
According to minutes of a January 1948 meeting, however, "there does-
n't seem to be an inclination on the part of local hotel executives to get
anything started in the way or expansion or new building projects to
provide greatly needed additional hotel accommodations." As the Ex-

ecutive Committee lamented, "the scarcity of hotel accommodations, which is now a year-round situation, is not conducive to promoting business for New Orleans."[12] In 1955, Seymour Weiss, president of the Roosevelt Hotel and director of the CVB, commented at a July meeting that "the convention business was one of the greatest in the country and that competition for it was very keen among interested cities. . . . The local hotel business has been very unsatisfactory. . . . [There is] a definite need to strengthen our sales efforts."[13]

Another distinguishing feature of the post–World War II era is the rise of new challenges to racial inequality, challenges that created a sense of political crisis among social elites during the 1950s and 1960s. Throughout the 1940s, local civil rights groups staged numerous protests demanding an end to racial discrimination in employment, schools, and public accommodations. In 1949, when confronted with demands that blacks be hired as police officers, the Civic Affairs Committee of the Chamber of Commerce recommended that "Negro police should be placed on the force at New Orleans—not because they are Negroes, but for the reason that they would help to reduce crime in our city, particularly crime by and among Negroes."[14] According to the Civic Affairs Committee, "negro policemen [should] be confined to those areas in which negroes live and congregate . . . to stem agitation on the part of the radical negro element."[15]

As racial protest and agitation escalated in the 1950s and 1960s with the rise of the civil rights movement, the Chamber of Commerce adopted an official stance of "no position" in matters of segregation and desegregation due to intense internal opposition among business leaders over racial issues. In 1956, the Executive Committee refused to oppose Louisiana House Bill 1412 prohibiting interracial social and athletic activities. While some members feared that bill would hurt sports and tourism in New Orleans, others felt that "we can justify the case of segregation in the South."[16] During these years, the chamber's "no position" policy on segregation amounted to de facto support and implicit endorsement of racial segregation. Through the decades, the chamber refused to invite or accommodate conventions and business groups that did not practice racial discrimination and exclusion. According to minutes of a meeting of the Executive Committee in March 1959, "Efforts to increase the convention business are a potent business building factor. . . . [Yet] New Orleans is losing desirable conventions because of the race situation, which now means we have to concentrate on those who do not have colored members."[17] By the 1960s, this segregationist stance was proving difficult to defend in the context of the increasing racial insurgency and elite fears that New Orleans was losing tourism business to other cities.

In sum, postwar socioeconomic transformations, including mass suburbanization and urban disinvestment combined with spreading civil rights protests, created new social problems and imperiled the economic fortunes of business leaders. As noted by Morton Inger and Joseph Luders, tourism and downtown business activity in New Orleans plummeted with the escalation of black protest in the 1950s and 1960s.[18] A protracted controversy over school desegregation in 1960 fed into a larger wave of sit-ins, pickets, and boycotts of downtown merchants by civil rights activists. By the end of 1960, these protests reduced sales by 40 percent at department stores and 20 percent at hotels and restaurants, according to Inger. Prolonged sit-ins and picketing of Canal Street merchants by the Congress of Racial Equality (CORE) in 1961 intensified the financial turmoil and likely affected other tourism-oriented businesses near the downtown. Echoing a larger current of racial discontent simmering in the city, Dutch Morial, president of the NAACP Youth Council, proclaimed in 1963 that blacks would "no longer tolerate the spoon feeding of their rights" and warned city leaders that "demonstrations against racial inequality in this community" would be forthcoming if "complacency in the area of human relations" continued.[19]

Broadly, racial disruptions were magnified by increased interurban competition for tourism dollars brought on by national and international industry transformations. In the late 1940s, the International Association of Convention Bureaus (IACB) began devising the first "economic impact" surveys to determine the financial effect of a particular convention on a city. Throughout the nation, local tourism committees and convention and visitors bureaus began implementing these surveys to track visitor spending. In the mid-1950s, a number of cities, including Las Vegas, began using hotel room taxes to fund convention centers and CVBs.[20] By the late 1950s, the U.S. Department of Commerce was publishing a booklet, "Your Community Can Profit from the Tourist Business," that offered a listing of different special events and attractions cities could use to attract tourists."[21] In 1960, the Chamber of Commerce of the United States announced it was adopting tourism promotion as a major economic development strategy:

Tourist promotion is a key operation in any regional, state, or community development program. Basically, there are three ways in which to bring new money and business into any given area. These are agricultural development, industrial development, and tourist development. Tourist development is probably the quickest, least difficult method of the three.[22]

During this time, New Orleans found itself in a new competitive environment as cities throughout the United States adopted new initiatives to stimulate tourism and capitalize on the growing convention business. As the 1950s progressed, increased competition among U.S. cities for tourist dollars and intensifying civil rights protest created political and economic disruptions that threatened the convention and tourism trade. It was during these years that city officials and elites debated new tourism-oriented revitalization strategies and created new organizations and networks in an attempt to enhance the economic prosperity of the city and insulate the tourism decision making apparatus from racial challenge and protest.

Formation of the Greater New Orleans Tourist and Convention Commission

We are convinced that nothing of great value can be accomplished by way of increased tourist trade unless the people of New Orleans develop a *deep desire* for it; we are further convinced that the creation of such a desire depends upon more widespread appreciation by the public of the dollars-and-cents value of greater numbers of visitors to out city.
—Harry M. England, chairman, Tourist Planning Committee, 1960[23]

Formation of the Greater New Orleans Tourist and Convention Commission (GNOTCC) in 1960 was the culmination of several years of political struggle and conflict over the future direction of tourism development in the metropolitan area. Initial discussions to create a tourist and convention commission came in the early 1950s when owners and representatives of local restaurants and motels began to lobby Mayor deLesseps S. Morrison to create a city bureau that was independent of the Chamber of Commerce. In 1952, the Executive Committee of the chamber reacted negatively to the idea of an additional tourist bureau, arguing that "it has a very capable Convention and Visitors Bureau" and is "already performing the type of work proposed by the contemplated bureau."[24] Various tourism interest groups—including the Service Station Association, the Louisiana Restaurant Association, and the Greater New Orleans Motor Hotel Association—advocated the establishment of a separate tourist bureau that would promote the city to a diverse range of tourists rather than just conventioneers. These groups were joined by representatives from Delta Airlines, National Airlines, McDougall's Travel Service, Travel Consultants, Inc., American Express Company, and Illinois Central Railroad, among others, who supported the creation of a professional agency with full-time specialists. These national organizations also supplied information to proponents on other cities' experiences with organizing and financing an autonomous tourist bureau.[25]

Mayor Morrison emerged as a major cheerleader and proponent of a specialized tourist bureau, noting in an October 1954 letter to Lawrence A. Molony, president of the Chamber of Commerce, "Many cities, with much less appeal for the individual tourist than New Orleans, have brought thousands and thousands of new dollars to their communities through Tourist Commissions. They have created such commissions because of the fact that the promotion of tourist business is a highly competitive specialized function."[26] While not all tourism groups supported the creation of a separate and autonomous tourist bureau, all the major interests agreed that new approaches and financing were needed to promote New Orleans and expand tourism. There were disagreements over administrative and financial issues but not basic policy goals.

In April 1960, after a year of planning and debate, political and economic leaders formed the GNOTCC to "establish and maintain the city of New Orleans as the premier tourist center of the world."[27] Over the next few months, the staff and functions of the CVB of the Chamber of Commerce were consolidated into the GNOTCC.[28] The charter to establish the GNOTCC called for the creation of a board of directors with several dozen members, a group of officers, a year-round staff of professional sales people, and dues-paying members. In 1960, the average budget for local CVBs in the United States was $124,399, with Los Angeles leading at $954,000 and New Orleans at the bottom, with an annual CVB budget of $38,547 (table 5.1). By 1961, the annual budget of the GNOTCC stood at $125,000, a huge increase from the year before.

TABLE 5.1
Budgets and Organization of Convention and Visitor Bureaus (CVBs)
in the United States, 1960

| City | CVB Budget | Type of Convention and Visitor Bureau | | |
		Independent	Department of a Chamber of Commerce	Department of a Municipal Government
Los Angeles	$954,000	Yes		
New York	580,000	Yes		
San Diego	300,000			Yes
Washington, D.C.	200,000		Yes	
Chicago	183,000	Yes		
Philadelphia	170,000		Yes	
Denver	153,577	Yes		
Atlantic City	150,000	Yes		
San Francisco	139,420	Yes		
Las Vegas	130,000			Yes
Cleveland	124,767	Yes		
Jacksonville	104,781	Yes		
Miami Beach	100,000			Yes
Detroit	98,066	Yes		
St. Louis	93,186	Yes		
Milwaukee	91,000		Yes	
Pittsburgh	85,000	Yes		
Boston	82,000		Yes	
Indianapolis	80,031	Yes		
Dallas	75,000		Yes	
Cincinnati	69,500	Yes		
Seattle	58,000		Yes	
Miami	55,039			Yes
Omaha	53,470		Yes	
Atlanta	45,787	Yes		
Kansas City	44,700		Yes	
New Orleans	38,547		Yes	

SOURCE: Tourist Planning Committee, 1960, *Subcommittee #2 Report*, p. 4. Volume 98 (MSS 66. NOCC, UNO).

A combination of private subscriptions, public subsidies, civic contributions, and revenue-producing publications helped start the GNOTCC.[29]

We can view the GNOTCC as a major agent linking the tourism from above processes of commodification and bureaucratic rationalization with the tourism from below actions of local organizations and groups. As a specialized agency for promoting the city, the GNOTCC helped shape and influence the development of the tourism industry in New Orleans in several ways. First, the GNOTCC became a major organization for raising international interest in New Orleans through its promotional activities and connections with national organizations and government bodies. As an industry builder, the GNOTCC united diverse businesses—hotels and motels, restaurants, airlines, travel agencies, and so on—into a loosely organized network where actors could interact, identify goals, and engage in strategic planning. On the local and state levels, the GNOTCC provided industry coordination through its membership in the Louisiana Travel Promotion Association and the Hotel Sales Management Association. In addition, the GNOTCC extended local contacts and established new connections with national organizations and tourism interests through its memberships in the International Association of Convention Bureaus (IACB), the American Society of Travel Agents, the Society of American Travel Writers, the Discover America Travel Organization, the National Association of Exhibit Managers, the Professional Convention Management Association, and the National Tour Brokers Association.

Second, the GNOTCC played a major part in rationalizing convention and visitor services by establishing formal rules and procedures for long-range planning and coordination of convention meetings, the solicitation of bid proposals, and provision of logistical assistance to airlines, hotels, and other tourism organizations. The GNOTCC was the first major organization in the metropolitan area to begin collecting and maintaining systematic data on tourism investment in the city, tracking numbers and expenditures of domestic and international travelers, charting convention delegate spending and hotel growth, and monitoring the allocation government tax revenue created by visitor spending. As an information provider, the GNOTCC published tour guides and descriptive pieces to support local tourism businesses while attempting to persuade more businesses to become members of the GNOTCC. Through its News Bureau, the GNOTCC disseminated a constant stream of entertaining stories and spectacular photographs to travel editors, columnists, automobile clubs, magazines, and tourist information centers around the world.

A third strategy of tourism promotion involved the cultivation of a legitimating ideology that linked the production of tourism sites and images with a prosperous and progressive New Orleans community. Early leaders of the GNOTCC recognized that major advertising and promotional campaigns would be needed to build local support for tourist attractions. Thus, much of the advertising and promotion of tourism that takes place in the 1960s and later is aimed at convincing residents that the development of tourism was really being done on their behalf and, more important, that tourism was constitutive of civic life and local authenticity. In acknowledging the lack of public support for tourism, Harry M. England, one of the first leaders of the GNOTCC, noted in 1960, that "we are convinced that nothing of great value can be accomplished by way of increased tourist trade unless the people of New Orleans develop a *deep desire* for it."[30]

Over the next decade, the GNOTCC developed a major public relations campaign that was explicitly designed to create local demand for tourism expansion. "One of the best sales tools any convention bureau can have is the enthusiastic support of its members and the entire community," according to the GNOTCC's 1973–1974 Annual Report: "Your pride in your city will build New Orleans . . . and a strong convention industry."[31] Central to this promotional strategy involved the advancement of the GNOTCC as an unbiased information center and major interpreter of New Orleans culture, history, and authenticity. While planned and specialized promotional activities had long been a feature of the tourism activities of the Chamber of Commerce and its bureaus, what is different in the 1960s and later is that promotional activities directed at visitors and local residents become more specialized and methodical. Local elites and tourism boosters designed the GNOTCC to maximize the calculability, efficiency, and predictability of tourism promotion. Thus, the rationalization of tourism promotion through a large bureaucratic organization supplanted the informal, piecemeal, fragmented, and uncoordinated nature of convention and tourism promotion that existed before World War II. Over time, the GNOTCC came to serve as a focal point and umbrella organization of a diverse range of groups involved in producing and disseminating information about local culture, history, and entertainment venues.

By the end of the 1960s, a complex and sophisticated tourism infrastructure was emerging to supply products, services, and entertaining experiences to tourists coming to New Orleans. Before the 1950s, the dearth of specialized organizations and financing impeded large-scale growth and investment in tourism. In the 1950s and later, powerful travel companies—airlines, transnational hotels, tour operators, and so on—expand their operations internationally by promoting economies of scale, industrial concentration, and product differentiation. On the local level, state and local government actions helped encourage the growth of an interconnected network of specialized organizations that initiated a transition to a more rationalized form of tourism development dominated by large bureaucratic corporations. The growth of tourism in New Orleans in the 1960s and later is evident in the building of Rivergate Convention Center (opened in 1968), the Louisiana Superdome (1975), and dozens of hotels. In 1971, Marriott opened a forty-two-story, 1,000-room hotel on Canal Street; in 1973, International Hotels opened a seventeen-story, 375-room hotel nearby. Other hotels that opened in the early 1970s included the Chateau Le Moyne Hotel (166 rooms), French Quarter Inn (66 rooms), Le Pavillon Hotel (260 rooms), St. Louis Hotel (68 rooms), a Marriott hotel (956 rooms), and the Hyatt Regency (1,184 rooms).[32] According to figures from the GNOTCC, during the 1960s, convention bookings rose from $7.5 million in 1961 to $90 million in 1969. Convention attendance increased more than four times, rising from 68,000 delegates in 1960, to 232,000 in 1969, and to 263,000 delegates in 1971.[33]

The construction of the convention center combined with the building of hotels provided the institutional foundation for the expansion of other entertainment amenities, including sightseeing tours, restaurants, and other spectacular attractions to service tourists. Table 5.2 shows the growth of the metropolitan tourism industry in the twenty-five years after 1950, using data from New Orleans phone books. Huge increases in the number of hotels and motels parallel a massive expansion of sightseeing tours, travel agencies, museums, convention services, and other tourist attractions. Before 1955, there were no convention services listed in the phone book; five years later, twenty-one convention businesses had opened, offering an array of services, facilities, and other activities to the burgeoning convention sector in the city. These convention services included artists, car rental services, florists, consultants,

TABLE 5.2
Expansion of New Orleans's Tourism Industry, 1950–1975

Year	Hotels and Motels	Hotel/ Motel Supplies, Management, and Equipment	Sightseeing Tours, Tour Operators and Promoters	Travel Agencies, Bureaus, and Tourist Information Centers	Museums	Convention Services, Facilities, and Bureaus	Sights of Interest and Tourist Attractions
1950	157	0	11	15	4	0	0
1955	189	0	20	18	4	0	0
1960	250	7	23	20	4	21	1
1965	264	7	24	32	7	22	3
1970	275	8	24	49	7	57	10
1975	293	21	30	92	14	114	23

SOURCE: New Orleans phone books, 1950–1975.

decorators, audiovisual services, advertising services, caterers, photography and printing services, and security guards, among many other businesses. By the late 1970s, these convention services were being supplemented with a plethora of guided tours in the French Quarter, cruise ships, swamp tours, bus tours, plantation tours, home and garden tours, architecture tours, and other excursions.[34] Growth in the number of sightseeing tours and tourist attractions reflects the increasing differentiation and specialization of spectacular sites and sights.

Tourism Expansion and Conflict in the French Quarter

> The important point and one we believe is self-evident is simply this—a French Quarter without people living in it would cease to be the Vieux Carre. A French Quarter consisting entirely—or even largely—of commercial establishments, transients' lodging places, museums and bars, would soon lose its real vitality, its life and its value.
> —Leon Godchaux, chairman of the Central Area Committee of the Chamber of Commerce, 1963[35]

One of the major goals of tourism planning during the 1960s and later was the commitment by the GNOTCC and business groups to prevent the "deterioration of the historical and architectural quality of the French Quarter" and to "upgrade the appeal of the area to visitors in all respects."[36] In 1959, the Central Area Committee of the Chamber of Commerce commissioned the Real Estate Research Corporation of Chicago to conduct an "Economic Survey of the Central Area of New Orleans." The resulting report noted the popularity of the French Quarter and concluded that the city lacked the convention space and hotel rooms to attract large numbers of tourists.[37] This report recommended building a major convention center adjacent to the French Quarter, as well as an 800 to 1,200–room hotel.[38]

Local resident groups, neighborhood coalitions, and historic preservationists welcomed hotel construction and tourism development as a means to revitalize the city and promote economic growth and prosperity. William Long, president of the Vieux Carre Property Owners Association, appeared before the Chamber of Commerce in March 1959, commenting that the "Vieux Carre is a center of tourist interest" and appealing for cooperation and assistance from hotels and tourism boosters to make the neighborhood "more attractive to visitors."[39] In 1960, leaders of the Spring Fiesta Association, a group of French Quarter residents offering tours of historic homes, suggested that hotel building and convention solicitation "be recognized as the most fertile field for seeking tourists."[40] The *New Orleans Times-Picayune* and *States Item* newspapers were enthusiastic about the development of tourism, with editorials and stories championing hotels and conventions as vehicles of progress. Over the decade, fourteen new hotels opened in the French Quarter, adding more than 2,000 rooms to the residential district.

As the pace of hotel development increased during the 1960s, the sentiment of resident groups and preservationists began to shift from tacit support to active resistance and mobilization. While not all hotel developments generated protest and opposition, the planning and construction of the Royal Orleans (opened 1960; 351 rooms), the Inn on Bourbon (opened 1965; 196 rooms), the Bourbon Orleans (opened 1966; 211 rooms), and the Royal Sonesta (opened 1969; 500 rooms) all garnered scrutiny from resident groups and historic preservationists. In 1966, the Vieux Carre Property Owners passed a resolution demanding that city leaders launch an investigation to determine who was to blame for damage to homes by the Bourbon Orleans hotel construction in the 300 block of Bourbon Street. Jacob Morrison, attorney for property owners, argued that the damage was caused by "Texas entrepreneurs hell-bent on making a buck out of New Orleans' tourist trade."[41] During debate over the Bourbon Orleans hotel development in 1966, the hotel developer's attorney argued that hotels would increase residential property values and that commercial properties were a crucial component of residential life in the neighborhood.[42]

Historic preservationists and neighborhood groups led by the Vieux Carre Property Owners were skeptical, arguing that the vitality and charm of the French Quarter would be diminished as tourism-oriented establishments proliferated. As French Quarter resident Leon Godchaux maintained, "a French Quarter without people living in it would cease to be the Vieux Carre. A French Quarter consisting of . . . commercial establishments, transients' lodging places, museums and bars, would soon lose its real vitality, its life and its value."[43] Over the next few years, more groups mobilized to oppose hotel efforts to initiate zoning changes to expand commercial land uses in the French Quarter. These opposition groups included the Louisiana Landmarks Society, the Civic

Beautification Association of Garden Clubs, the French Quarter Residents Association, the French Quarter Parents Association, and the Jackson Square Residents Association.

Much of the increased opposition to hotel development was nurtured and supported by federal government policy reforms and local social movement organizations that were fighting a local expressway battle. Two developments were important. First, in 1966, the federal government passed the National Historic Preservation Act that established a national program to coordinate and support public and private efforts to identify, evaluate, and protect historic and archeological resources. The Preservation Act created the National Register of Historic Places, which encouraged the formation of state historic preservation societies and required an environmental review process to consider the effect of any federally funded project on local historic areas. That same year, local historic preservationists were successful in getting the French Quarter listed as a National Historic Landmark on the National Register of Historic Places. These developments motivated local groups to initiate several lawsuits to challenge the destabilizing effect of hotel development on the French Quarter.

Second, during the 1960s, neighborhood activists opposed to hotel building joined forces with a burgeoning national anti-expressway movement to battle government efforts to construct an elevated Elysian Fields Riverfront Expressway along the Mississippi River.[44] Networks of French Quarter activists, historic preservationists, and resident groups mobilized legal and material resources and supplied each other with information on expressway and preservation conflicts in other cities. As interrelated conflicts, the struggle against hotel building and the Riverfront Expressway spawned combative coalitions of resident groups and activists dedicated to empowering local residents by defining the battle over the French Quarter as a national issue. As the following quote suggests, anti-expressway opponents developed a strategy of defining the French Quarter as a unique place of incomparable significance, not only for local residents but also for the entire country—a "national" neighborhood worth saving for people everywhere. As one person told me,

> There were people all across the city who did nothing for years except to fight that highway. We literally had a strategy and campaign to make it a national issue. The initial kickoff that made it a national issue was when I got *Town and Country* magazine to do an article about it. The

author wanted to do a story about debutantes in New Orleans but became fascinated by the Riverfront Expressway controversy after I told him about it. He started interviewing everybody, even strippers in the French Quarter about what they thought about the highway. I was in New York City when the story came out and, Bam! that was it, *Newsweek* picked it up and other newspapers. We were well organized, we were small, and we were dedicated. And we were successful because we made it a national issue. We were able to go to Washington and obtain lawyers who had begun to make an impact on the federal government at a national level.[45]

Hotel opponents and anti-expressway activists formed a powerful alliance, with each attempting to mobilize opposition through increased public visibility for affected residents through demonstrations and direct action, as well as attendance at city council meetings and public hearings. An editorial in the *Vieux Carre Courier* newspaper proclaimed,

The Courier's editor and representatives of Quarter civic groups have attended endless meetings of the City Council and the Vieux Carre Commission shouting as loudly as we can that commercial interests are making a Coney Island of the Quarter, that too many hotels and motels are destroying its atmosphere, that pandering hot dogs and corn on the cob does not make a historic district.[46]

One French Quarter resident I interviewed recalled her experience with organizing people and the importance of external allies in helping to mobilize opposition:

I remember going to meetings at City Hall. We were active in preservation at that time. The idea behind the expressway was just miserable. Fortunately, for New Orleans there were enough people who were able to fight it. There was a lot of help from the Tulane University School of Architecture. There were many people who went to City Hall and fought it. The City did not care. They really didn't. There wouldn't be a French Quarter today if people hadn't come here from other places to save it.[47]

The preceding quotes provide insight into the emergence of the French Quarter as an activist neighborhood with networks and organizations extending outward to encompass supporting groups around the country. Expressway opponents, organizations representing French Quarter residents, historic preservationists and other supporters used both "catastrophizing" claims (to emphasize the severity and potential harmful consequences of hotel development and expressway building) and "victimizing" claims (to highlight the plight of ordinary people against powerful real estate developers and their allies at the city, state, and federal levels).

Another resonant theme deployed and transmitted by activists was that of nostalgia. Neighborhood organizations like the Vieux Carre Property Owners used nostalgia to connect the battle to preserve the French Quarter with a sentimental past and an uplifting neighborhood culture. In the context of anti-expressway protest and militancy, nostalgia became a useful mobilizing device to contest hotel expansion and to generate support for neighborhood preservation, bringing together otherwise diverse and unconnected groups, including neighborhood coalitions and environmental organizations, among others. Residential propinquity and shared historical experience of being part of a long tradition of preservationist causes in the French Quarter formed the basis of residents' claims that they had the cultural authenticity and authority to dictate and control what kind of commercial development should occur. Echoing a question posed by a 1968 report from the Real Estate Research Corporation of Chicago, the *Vieux Carre Courier* asserted, "the question is, how long can this (commercialization of the Vieux Carre) continue without destroying the character of the Quarter, which is the very reason for the success?" According to one popular trope at the time, "how long can you chew up the goose and expect her to lay the golden eggs?"[48] Such a symbol suggested that the residential base of the French Quarter was the source of its authentic charm and that the overbuilding of hotels would kill the neighborhood's tourist appeal.

As a result of the increasingly truculent opposition, in January 1969, the City Council imposed a moratorium on new motel and hotel building in the French Quarter. Several months later, in July, U.S. Secretary of Transportation John A. Volpe canceled the Riverfront Expressway amid the threat that it posed to the historic character of the neighborhood.[49] Yet these victories were pyrrhic, and several redevelopment efforts foreshadowed more intense conflicts and struggles in later years. In 1973, the Vieux Carre Property Owners and Associates successfully sued the City of New Orleans to halt city efforts to sponsor a French-produced "Sound and Light" show in Jackson Square. Co-sponsored with the GNOTCC, the computerized "Sound and Light" show was to convey the "mood of New Orleans" through an interplay of light, sounds, tape recordings, and other special effects. Proponents such as Mayor Moon Landrieu proclaimed the project "of great national significance," while critics such as the *Times-Picayune* newspaper editors deplored the "commercialized tourist-attraction project" and argued that the French Quarter "should be kept attractive for more substantial reasons than a passive-spectator show."[50]

In 1975, French Quarter residents mobilized against a $2.5 million dollar redevelopment of the French Market, one of the oldest public markets in the nation. Opposition was sparked when the city government reorganized the French Market Corporation as a de facto private corporation to promote commerce and entertainment in the French Quarter. The rationalization of the leasing structure and tenant mix, the construction of several parking lots, and the renovation of buildings focused on restaurants and shops frequented by tourists.[51] At this point in the market's history, as the website of the City of New Orleans mentions, "entertainment and tourism became primary aspects of market life."[52] While the French Market had been a public-private entity since the 1930s, privatization in the 1970s and later attempted to reconstitute the organization as a for-profit organization. Critics derided the renovation for transforming the French Market from a public market for residents into a suburban-style shopping mall for the benefit of tourists.[53]

Finally, the mid to late 1970s saw the building of Canal Place, a high-rise mixed-use retail development on the up-river side of the French Quarter. The planning and construction of Canal Place inflamed historic preservationists and French Quarter resident groups, who sued the developer for violating historic district regulations and blocking public access to the river. These actions resulted in some reduction in the scale of the project but did not halt the development.

New Orleans's strategy of going global is the major precipitant of the intense conflicts over tourism development in the French Quarter in the 1960s and later. For tourism boosters and elites, a prosperous New Orleans meant attracting corporate investment to enhance the appeal of the French Quarter as a tourist destination. French Quarter residents, historic preservationists, and members of other grassroots cultural organizations did not oppose tourism development en masse but the encroachment of corporate interests on residential meanings and uses of the French Quarter. For networks of historic preservationists and French Quarter resident groups, the entry of corporate hotel chains threatened to usurp their control over the authenticity of the French Quarter and New Orleans more generally.

In the chapters that follow, we see the expansion of New Orleans's going global strategy to attract the 1984 World's Fair and to further the commodification of the French Quarter and the Mardi Gras celebration. As I point out, local resident groups and grassroots organizations have opposed corporate-driven tourism by appealing to the historic "charm," "authenticity," and residential "identity" of the French Quarter neighborhood. Other symbols such as "neighborhood," local "character," and "community" contain a multiplicity of meanings that provide actors with a venue for argument, but one that leaves the specifics of the content ambiguous. Today, these symbols and themes combined with a range of collective action tactics (e.g., disruptive action and litigation) have become major components of the organizational and tactical repertoires of residential networks seeking to preserve neighborhood use-values as an expedient to bolstering the tourist appeal of the French Quarter. In this sense, we can view residential identity, neighborhood authenticity, and other touristic terms as a strategic vocabulary or set of cultural resources that groups wield more or less self-consciously in their social and political struggles to build and enhance place distinctiveness.

6

From a Culture of Tourism to a Touristic Culture

The 1984 Louisiana World Exposition and the Holy Trinity of New Orleans Tourism

The Council for a Better Louisiana urges your favorable consideration of a world exposition in New Orleans in 1980, or as soon as
thereafter possible. . . . In the judgement of the Council, a world
exposition would not only bring a badly needed economic boost to
Louisiana but it would also serve as a catalyst for securing many
needed permanent public facilities in the state and would be a
means of unifying the leadership of the state in programs for
advancement. In the economic outlook for Louisiana, a hard fact
is that the production of oil and gas which has supported much
business activity is on the downturn. Reserves are being depleted
and the state needs to promote other bases for economic growth
such as tourism.

> —Council for a Better Louisiana to the U.S. Secretary of
> Commerce, 1977[1]

One hundred years after hosting the World's Industrial and
Cotton Centennial Exposition in 1884, New Orleans was again the host
city for another international exposition, the 1984 Louisiana World Exposition, the last world's fair held in the United States. Initial discussions for hosting a major exposition came in the 1960s when a statewide coalition of business leaders formed the Council for a Better Louisiana (CABL) to remedy the state's lagging economic growth and attract
new sources of capital investment. Over the decade, CABL and the Louisiana Tourist Development Commission outlined an ambitious plan of
economic development that included the staging of an international ex-

Fig. 6.1. Aerial model of the proposed "master plan" showing the Louisiana World Exposition, Inc. (LWE's) vision of what the 1984 Exposition would look like along the Mississippi River. The Crescent City Connection bridge is at the bottom left. Also visible are the gondola ride and monorail that circled the exposition grounds every twelve minutes. The large structure with the "inverted V" roof elements served as the exposition's Great Hall. After the fair closed in November 1984, it was converted into Phase I of the Ernest N. Morial Convention Center. (Reproduced by permission of the New Orleans Public Library, Louisiana Division and the City Archives)

position. Economic and political elites, including Louisiana State Comptroller S. E. Vines, Governor Edwin Edwards, and New Orleans developer Lester Kabacoff supported CABL's plans for a world's fair that would rejuvenate the state economy. These individuals eventually formed the nonprofit Louisiana World Exposition, Inc. (LWE) to plan and finance the exposition through a public-private partnership between the state and local governments and the local business elite.

Fair organizers and planners chose to locate the Exposition on an eighty-two-acre site along the Mississippi River, adjacent to the Central Business District, and encompassing the historic Warehouse District. The major theme of the exposition, "Rivers of the World—Fresh Water as a Source of Life," reflected the United Nation's designation of the

1980s as the Decade of International Drinking Water and Sanitation (fig. 6.1). In June 1981, the Exposition received formal certification by the Bureau of International Expositions in Paris, and by the end of the year, planners and organizers were moving ahead with site acquisition, construction, and marketing to attract visitors to the fair. The exposition opened on May 12, 1984, to international acclaim and media fanfare, and it closed on November 11 under a shadow of negative publicity and financial trouble.

Like expositions in San Antonio (1968), Spokane (1974), and Knoxville (1982), the Louisiana World Exposition in New Orleans embraced a strategy of producing a single theme fair that would have residual effects: the construction of permanent tourism facilities and riverfront development to enhance the city long after the fair was gone. In 1981, the Reagan administration alerted exposition officials that it was willing to spend only $10 million on the U.S. Pavilion for exhibitions and other expenses, unlike the $20 million it had allocated for its Knoxville pavilion. Nevertheless, local architects and planners predicted that the exposition would transform the Mississippi riverfront "into a world of pavilions, lagoons, rides, watercourses, floats, exhibits, entertainment, cuisine and music."[2] A permanent $88 million Exhibition and Convention Center formed the centerpiece of the fairgrounds, and several corporations including Liggett and Meyers Tobacco and Chrysler erected major pavilions. Joining the United States with exhibits of the history, industry, and culture of the world of rivers were more than a dozen foreign nations, including Australia, Canada, Denmark, Egypt, France, Italy, Japan, Liberia, Mexico, China, Korea, Peru, England, and West Germany.

One of the major architectural features of the fair included the Wonderwall, a half-mile-long midway that featured a variety of architectural themes and historic motifs with shops, food booths, stages, video arcades, and rest areas. Other notable features included a ten-car, 146-passenger monorail that circled the exposition grounds every twelve minutes, and a gondola ride that took passengers on 2,200-foot cable trips across the Mississippi River.[3] Although local leaders invited President Ronald Reagan to attend opening ceremonies, he did not, and the 1984 Exposition failed to draw executive branch support and the usual federal largesse that past U.S. world's fairs had received. More than 7.3 million attended the fair from May 12 through November 11, a paltry amount in comparison with expositions held in Montreal (1967), San Antonio (1968), and Vancouver (1986) (table 6.1).

TABLE 6.1
North American International Expositions
(World's Fairs), 1962–1986

Site and year	Attendance
Seattle 1962	9,639,969
New York 1964–65	27,000,000 (in 1964);
	51,607,307 (in 1965)
Montreal 1967	50,000,000+
San Antonio 1968	64,000,000
Spokane 1974	5,249,130
Knoxville 1982	11,127,786
New Orleans 1984	7,335,279
Vancouver 1986	22,111,578

SOURCE: The World's Fair and Exposition Information and Reference Guide, http://www.earthstation9.com/worlds_2.htm, accessed April 15, 2006.

Similar to the 1884 Industrial and Cotton Centennial Exposition a century earlier, researchers and journalists have derided the 1984 Louisiana World Exposition as a financial debacle that siphoned public resources and bankrupted businesses and sponsors.[4] Echoing the condemnation of the 1884 Exposition, critics assailed the 1984 Exposition for its low attendance, lack of foreign participation, and poor corporate and federal support. Many blamed the low attendance on the fact that it was staged just two years after Knoxville's 1982 World's Fair only two states away. Other critics argued that the low attendance at the exposition signaled the societal irrelevance of world's fairs. "World's Fairs are passe," remarked Harry Greenberger, president of the French Quarter Business Association in November 1984; "You can go to Disney World. You can go to Epcot. What world expositions used to be were the leading edge of the newest ideas and the newest technologies. Now we see that everyday on television."[5] An international exposition used to be one of the most effective ways in which a country or company could sell its products, according to Paul W. Creighton, vice president of exposition operations; "Television has changed all of that. Nowadays people have a fair every day right in their own living room. A company doesn't have to come to a fair to sell its products."[6]

Despite its problems, the fair was fondly remembered by many New Orleans residents and was noteworthy architecturally for the Wonderwall designed by Charles Moore and William Turnball. In addition, throughout 1984, the *Times-Picayune* ran highly complimentary "Letters to the Editor" from people around the country who had been to

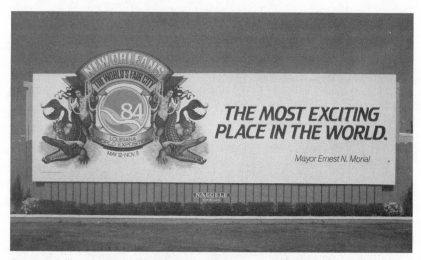

Fig. 6.2. A billboard with the official logo of the 1984 Louisiana World Exposition showing a stylized depiction of the Mississippi River with alligators and mermaids. (Reproduced by permission of the New Orleans Public Library, Louisiana Division and the City Archives)

other fairs and said that the Louisiana World Exposition was the best. Moreover, journalists and researchers have long maintained that the exposition helped encourage the economic revitalization of the historic Warehouse District, an area adjacent to the French Quarter that experienced a major wave of gentrification in the 1980s and later.[7] Interestingly, at the time, some people criticized the 1984 Exposition as a contrived tourist attraction that was devoid of local character and authenticity. A *New York Times* article, for example, assailed the New Orleans Exposition as "one of the strangest world's fairs in memory" that contains "essentially a collection of harsh and unappealing industrial buildings."[8] Years later, local journalists and residents would redefine and celebrate the exposition as an important source of community pride (fig. 6.2, fig. 6.3).[9]

Reviled and revered, the 1984 Louisiana World Exposition is a major turning point in the historical evolution of New Orleans as a major tourist destination and historic city. While the 1984 Exposition had the dubious distinction of being the only world's fair ever to declare bankruptcy, it did help spearhead the development of what I call a "touristic culture" in New Orleans. Whereas a "culture of tourism" is premised on the showcasing of local culture to attract tourists, a "touristic culture" refers to the blurring of boundaries between tourism and other major institutions and cultural practices. Specifically, touristic culture is a process by which tourist modes of staging, visualization, and experience increasingly frame meanings and assertions of local culture, authenticity, and collective memory.[10] A central element of touristic culture is the idea that claims about local culture and authenticity are bound up with and operate through an interlocking set of tourist discourses and practices. These discourses and practices are activated and set in motion through aesthetic, residential, heritage, and media networks, as well as specialized tourist institutions for cultural production. Claims and debates over local culture and authenticity become salient in particular group situations and are acted upon by identifiable and interested actors

Fig. 6.3. A major architectural feature of the 1984 Louisiana World Exposition was the Wonderwall, a half-mile-long, multihistoried midway featuring a variety of architectural motifs with shops, food stands, and rest areas. The Wonderall was designed by California architects Charles Moore and William Turnbull along with the fair's principle architects, Perez and Associates. Although news reports suggested that fair visitors enjoyed the Wonderwall, critics assailed the structure as postmodern bunk and "vacuous kitsch," a criticism that dovetailed with more general admonishments of the exposition as a simulated tourist spectacle. Years later, local journalists and residents would reinterpret the Wonderwall and the exposition as a major cultural expression of New Orleans's longstanding penchant for fairs and celebrations. (Reproduced by permission of Tulane University, Howard-Tilton Memorial Library, Special Collections)

who are embedded within social networks and institutions. The notion of touristic culture suggests that tourism discourses and practices provide different actors with the cultural tools and resources to cope with, understand, and make sense of the social problems, global-local processes, and institutional pressures that constrain their actions.

The development of a touristic culture reflects a long historical process and is evident in the planning and staging of the 1984 Exposition and later tourist attractions. On the one hand, the exposition reflected elite concerns in promoting a conflict-free image of New Orleans and legitimating corporate control over tourism revitalization and expansion. The privatized and bureaucratized nature of the LWE insulated the exposition planning apparatus from public debate and grassroots influence while enhancing the capacity for political and economic elites to leverage public resources and make costly investments to expand the city's tourism infrastructure. Proponents were quick to point to the so-called residual effects of the exposition, including an addition of 10,000 hotel rooms built for the fair by international firms such as Sheraton, Hotel Intercontinental, Hilton Riverside, the Westin, Winsor Court, and Holiday Inn. Adding to this tourism infrastructure was the completion of the first phase of a major convention center and the Riverwalk mall, a tourist-oriented shopping center, designed by the James W. Rouse company.[11] These developments are illustrative of tourism from above and reflect the establishment of new public-private networks for reinforcing and extending the commodification process and connecting New Orleans to an expanding global tourism industry.

On the other hand, the 1984 Exposition revealed the fault lines of race and class, mobilizing challenges against racial exclusion and generating new debates over meanings of local authenticity. Critics argued that the exposition's residual products—such as riverfront development and reinvestment in the Warehouse District—did little to address wider social problems, including neighborhood disinvestment and racial polarization.[12] For critics, exposition attractions and other tourism developments seemed increasingly divorced from the problems and concerns of the city's neighborhoods and working people. These concerns became even more poignant as reports surfaced during the 1980s documenting the poverty-level wages and paltry benefits that New Orleans's workers were receiving from working within the hotel sector, a nonunion industry.[13] At the same time, the exposition played a major role in mobilizing African American artists, historic preservationist organizations, and other groups to create new representations of local culture and expand the content of New Orleans's urban iconography. This latter process is a major element of tourism from below and reflects the growth of a network of grassroots cultural organizations working to invent new conceptions of authenticity and collective memory.

In the years after the exposition, government policies and public-private actions spurred the growth of arts districts, historic neighborhoods, schools of hotel and restaurant management, gambling, museums, and so on. By the 1990s, a proliferation of tourism attractions and entertaining spectacles meant New Orleans residents were now living in a metropolitan area reconfigured as interesting, entertaining, and attractive for tourists. This major expansion of tourism reflects the increased rationalization and commodification of space and culture, as well as the establishment of a constellation of diverse organizations working to continually construct and reconstruct a sense of identity, belonging, and authenticity for residents.

Racial Conflict and the 1984 Louisiana World Exposition

> The soul, spirit, and stomach of the World's Fair that started its six-month run in New Orleans a week ago is the city itself: brooding and flamboyant, raucous and urbane, devout and dissolute. The fair stirs together the razzmatazz of Mardi Gras, the harmony of New Orleans' elegant old buildings and the French-Spanish-African-Italian-Irish-German-Creole-Cajun gumbo gusto of its everyday, every-night street life. This is officially a World Exposition, on the scale of the one in Knoxville, Tenn., two years ago. Alongside that effort, New Orleans can hold its candle proudly, and with a raffish wink that few cities would wish to match.
> —*Time Magazine*, May 27, 1984[14]

Political and economic elites conceived the Louisiana World Exposition as a major spectacle to revitalize the city and imbue social consensus in an era defined by fiscal crisis, racial upheaval, and metropolitan transformation. Racially, New Orleans's public school system became majority African American in 1970, the result of a huge out-migration of whites from the central city to the suburbs. In 1978, Ernest (Dutch) Morial became the first African American mayor of the city, inaugurating an era of enhanced political power for black politicians and institutions. Demographically, massive losses in urban population in the decades after 1960 coincided with beginnings of a long-term erosion of the tax base of the city. Various studies and newspaper reports from the mid-1960s forward document the revenue problems of the city.[15] In the two decades after 1964, the distribution of property taxes for New Orleans dropped from 33.3 percent of total revenue to 9.8 percent. During the same time, the city became more reliant on sales tax revenue, with the distribution of sales taxes increasing from 33.5 percent of total revenue in 1964 to 57.3 percent in 1984.[16] The loss of revenue from property taxes and increased dependence on sales taxes reflected the passage of several statutes by the state of Louisiana during the 1970s that significantly reduced the ability of local governments in the state to raise revenue.[17] Fiscal constraints imposed by the state government combined with the suburbanization of people and businesses weakened the ability of New Orleans to raise revenue to fund basic government operations and provide public services. As a result, by the late 1970s, the city was experiencing a fiscal crisis, forced to slash funding for public services, while financially pressured to expend greater funds to leverage capital investment and develop new strategies for engineering urban redevelopment.

During the 1970s and early 1980s, state and local leaders viewed the Louisiana World Exposition as a straightforward matter of rational and objective urban planning to promote tourism-oriented growth and revitalization. Yet, early on, racial conflicts and struggles shaped and defined debates over the city's role in the exposition. In 1981, a major dispute erupted between Mayor Dutch Morial, the City Council, and the state government over whether the city could afford to back the fair. According to a letter sent by Mayor Morial to Floyd W. Lewis, chairman of the LWE board:

At present time, we are not sufficiently informed or involved in the major policy decisions that we feel we must be involved in. . . . [While the Exposition] is essentially a private undertaking, [it will] require a substantial amount of city involvement, particularly in relation to transportation problems and parking, streets, sewerage, and drainage, sanitation, and security.[18]

Mayor Morial feared the exposition site would privatize a vast area of urban space and deprive citizens of any permanent residual benefit in the form of new structures or land uses to enhance the public domain. Councilmen Mike Early, Joseph Giarusso, Sidney Barthelemy, and Jim Singleton, whose district included the exposition fairgrounds, became strong opponents of the LWE. Along with Morial, these City Council members castigated the LWE and fair organizers for refusing to hire racial minorities and low-income people to work at the fair. "We are fearful," Morial said, that the fair may pass up local workers "because of a perceived lack of qualifications. . . . This is especially true as it pertains to residents of the city's housing developments and other low-income neighborhoods. As a consequence, it appears that many of the jobs at the fair may end up being held by migrants and people outside the city of New Orleans."[19] More broadly, during the initial years of fair planning, Morial and city council members repeatedly accused the LWE for being interested only in what was happening on the fair site and ignoring the interests of New Orleans residents and neighborhoods as a whole. According to Morial,

> The world's fair representatives ought to stop coming before this council, saying that they're the private sector concerned only with what happens on their 80-acre site and that's all. I challenge Mr. Schmitz (chairman of the LWE board) and Mr. (Peter) Spurny (general manager of the world's fair), to get off that tack. The city would be remiss if it didn't try to get all it can as a residual of the world's fair. Now that's the way the cookie crumbles and I want to see New Orleans get a piece of the cookie.[20]

We can understand the disagreements between the city officials and exposition planners over the role of the private and public sectors as part of a larger struggle that reflected the volatile mix of class power and racial exclusion in New Orleans during the early 1980s. The *Times-Picayune* reported that controversy between Mayor Morial and the state government was a political dispute over how much public monies the state of Louisiana should contribute to New Orleans for street repairs, new sidewalks, and site preparation. Members of the LWE and other exposition supporters argued that the city might not receive direct, short-term benefits from the exposition but would receive the long-term benefits of increased tourism-oriented redevelopment. Such long-term financial benefits would, in turn, have trickle-down effects in the form of abundant tax revenue and public resources that would flow into poor neighborhoods, schools, and other public institutions, thereby benefiting the entire city. During years of planning for the fair, it became common practice for the LWE to assert the fair's status as a purely "private venture" that was risking capital and resources to help revitalize New Orleans. At the same time, city officials and state representatives from New Orleans complained they were being ignored by the LWE even though the city had spent millions on the fair. "When we approach the fair," according to councilman Sidney Barthelemy, "we're told it's a private venture."[21]

When challenged repeatedly by city leaders to help support the city, the LWE maintained that they did not have the political expertise or credibility to lobby for more state aid for the city of New Orleans. One skeptical editorial in the *Times-Picayune* noted that an atypical feature of the Louisiana World Exposition was that the fairgrounds "would be largely private property leased to the fair that would revert to its owners, with whatever value enhancement due to the fair and fair-induced development, when the fair is over."[22] The highly proclaimed residual effects left by fairs in other cities such as public auditoriums, museums, parks, and so on, would not remain or would be only small scale. LWE officials and state leaders, including Governor David C. Treen, threatened to withdraw support and abandon the exposition if it did not have the full support of the New Orleans mayor and city council.[23]

Claims that the Exposition was a private venture that was not accountable to the public sector failed to sway skeptical city officials and galvanized opposition, sparking calls by angry leaders to audit the LWE and force the organization to open its financial books for public scrutiny.[24] During these years, accusations of racism and racial discrimination permeated public debates over the exposition as African American officials and civil rights activists attempted to define New Orleans residents and neighborhoods as victims of an elite white power structure bent on locking blacks out of the decision-making process. In the aftermath of Morial's reelection in 1982, the mayor expressed that white elites were patronizing and refused to work with him and the city. As Morial remarked, "I don't know why people want me to deal politically different than any other mayor. Is it because I'm a nigger? Because I'm a nigger, I've got to be shat on by everyone else?"[25] Racial conflicts over the fair intensified in 1982 when Rev. Jesse Jackson joined Morial and the City Council in criticizing the world's fair as part of a larger process of white elite attempts to marginalize the black community. The world's fair "has a choice of dealing with the black community as trading partners or as civil warriors," proclaimed Jackson. New Orleans's African American population "ought not to have demean itself by begging for menial jobs or negotiating for a few enterpreneurial opportunities. We have the people and we have the capital."[26]

Jackson's protests were amplified by City Councilman Jim Singleton, who denounced the LWE for hiring only a few blacks for staff positions and none at the executive level:

> Now I'm ready to put [the LWE] and the community on public notice that unless they change their hiring policies, I intend to start putting their requests for building permits and zoning changes in deep freeze. . . . I'm not setting quotas or telling them whom to hire . . . but in city that is more than 50 percent black, they are certainly making it tough on black elected officials who have supported the fair when their staff organization is overwhelmingly white and includes no black executives.

As Singleton elaborated, the LWE "tells us the fact that white females make up 60 percent of their staff, and that demonstrates their good faith to equal opportunity for all minorities. I'm sorry but that isn't my idea of minority involvement. . . . It's my belief that the fair doesn't want to hire blacks right now. My message to the fair is that hiring blacks isn't as optional as they seem to think it is."[27] Other public officials, including Louisiana Representative Louis A. Charbonnet III, complained that the LWE "has not been fair to our citizens, to women or to blacks."[28] U.S Congresswoman Lindy Clairborne Boggs derided the fair for its lack of diversity, claiming that "there hasn't been enough interest in it [by blacks and women] to make certain there is proper inclusion of minorities."[29]

Racial protest and antagonism punctuated the planning and staging of the 1984 Louisiana World Exposition as different groups and interests struggled to project different interpretations of the exposition and its relationship to New Orleans. In February 1984, several African American artists threatened to launch a class-action suit against the LWE and other art and culture organizations in New Orleans "to address the reprehensible and blatant omission of Black artists in the proposed exhibition, 'Louisiana: Major Works 84.' " This protest against racial exclusion reflected a broad-based struggle to remedy "the inadequate local representation of the Blacks arts community." Black artists assailed exposition planners for selecting only one African American out of fifty-one artists to represent Louisiana art. "We don't think it is equitable," according to one artist, "to suggest to the 'world' that this one person is the total of Black artists in Louisiana of importance." According to a letter sent by several artists to Mayor Morial,

> To have given to this arts community unselfish time, expertise, and what little finances we have and to still be excluded will certainly no longer be tolerated. . . . Why is it every time there is a community, "mainstream" arts exhibition, Black artists have to remind those "in charge" of [our] existence? . . . This concern is not just for the short-term period of this exhibition, but for the long-term future of Black artists in this community and the self-esteem of the Black community at large.[30]

The preceding quotes communicate a powerful message of opposition and protest against racial exclusion and tokenism. These criticisms were not just aberrations or isolated complaints from a few disgruntled artists. Reflecting a broader civil rights struggle against racial segregation and inequality, black artists and cultural organizations agitated for social justice and broader recognition of the wide range of African American artistic contributions to New Orleans history and culture. On the one hand, African American artists argued that their exclusion from the 1984 Exposition revealed the exposition to be an "inauthentic" representation of New Orleans culture and heritage. On the other hand, like the Colored Exhibit at the 1884 Industrial and Cotton Centennial Exposition, the 1984 Louisiana World Exposition sufficed as a political vehicle for black protest, as well as a forum to contest social deprivation and further resistant agendas. Also similar to the 1884 Exposition a century earlier, the 1984 Exposition reflected a struggle among tourism boosters, local elites, and grassroots organizations over the meaning and content of local culture and authenticity. In 1984, as result of protest and mobilization, black leaders were successful in pressing state legislators to create the Louisiana Black Culture Commission and the Division of Black Culture. Six years later, in 1990, thirteen African American business owners established the Black Tourism Network (BTN) to increase opportunities for African Americans in the tourism industry. In

1996, the state of Louisiana created the multicultural branch of the Louisiana Office of Tourism to work with the BTN in identifying historical African American sites and hosting a major multicultural tourism summit. These developments represented the formation of new organizations to raise awareness of African American heritage and affirm tourism practices as an important source of authenticity invention.

Beyond Bread and Circuses: Localization and Cultural Hybridization

> The world will truly be focused on New Orleans. . . . An international exposition, a World's Fair, is a lot more than just a lot of exhibits from different countries. It's a happening. It's an experience. It's a celebration. It's an event. It's a once-in-lifetime experience. . . . And it's more than birds, balloons, bands, fireworks, and flags . . . it's a catalyst for development. It's a catalyst for tremendous economic impact.
>
> —Peter Spurney, executive vice president and general manager of the Louisiana World Exposition, September 20, 1980[31]

Scholars have long condemned world's fairs and other tourism-oriented spectacles as instruments of hegemonic power that shift attention away from everyday social problems in the city and pacify local people, a form of ideological manipulation referred to as "bread and circuses."[32] This metaphoric phrase suggests that if oppressed people receive food and entertainment, they will forget about their problems and believe in the beneficence of the system. Critical scholars argue that the intent of most tourist attractions, including world's fairs, is to further commodification and mollify people through the ideology of consumption and entertainment.

Yet residents and tourists are not simply passive recipients of accepted meanings produced by advertisers, tourism boosters, and place marketers. They are actively involved in the production of meaning and produce meanings, some which are unexpected and intensely resisted by tourism interests and other supporters. Indeed, urban spectacles like world's fairs are cultural battlefields, sites of struggle where powerful economic and political interests are often forced to defend what they would prefer to have taken for granted. In this conception, tourist attractions and other entertaining spectacles reflect the different meanings that residents have about tourism, evince conflicts over representations of authenticity, and express the different bases for people's acceptance or resistance to dominant tourism images. In short, tourist sites, attractions, and spectacles such as world's fairs have a Janus-faced quality. They have the potential for creative encounters and can offer opportunities for people to engage in new forms of authenticity construction and cultural invention.

Like the 1884 Exposition a century earlier, the 1984 Exposition spearheaded the growth of new aesthetic networks and heritage networks that played a major role in generating new meanings of local culture and heritage. Aesthetic networks comprised a collection of cultural organizations dedicated to bringing together artists, musicians, and collectors to celebrate local culture. Heritage networks included a spectrum of local and regional historical societies and historic preservation organizations. These networks organized a variety of exhibits on creole and Cajun ethnicity, Louisiana folklore, and the Mississippi River as symbols and displays of local culture. A Centennial Pavilion was created as a replica of the Main Building from the Industrial and Cotton Centennial Exposition, and the Christian Pavilion contained an exhibit last displayed at the 1884 Exposition.

On the grassroots level, tourism from below was evident in the development of new organizations and new cultural institutions for building local awareness of culture. During the initial years of exposition planning, the prospect of a world's fair attracted the interest of historic preservationists, artists, nonprofit organizations and community groups interested in showcasing New Orleans to the world. As a result, in 1981, the Arts Council of Greater New Orleans and the Mayor's Committee on Arts and Cultural Development merged to form the Arts Council of New Orleans to represent the arts community and promote local culture through a series of programs, projects and services.[33] Other groups that formed during the late 1970s such as the Community Arts Center (CAC), Save Our Cemeteries, and the Historic District Landmarks Commission (HDLC) reflected a growing awareness that neighborhoods and other cultural sites should be preserved as representations of local authenticity. While the creation of these organizations predate the 1984 Exposition, the planning and staging of the New Orleans World's Fair was a major catalyst for generating grassroots support to identify elements of New Orleans's past worthy of public display and commemoration.

In addition, the exposition played a major role in supporting and legitimating historic preservation as a significant cultural practice and expression of collective memory. Scholars have long known that collective memory is not historically fixed or static but emerges out of a context of social conflict and shifting networks of power and influence. Collective memory, according to Clifford Geertz, is a pattern of "inherited conceptions expressed in symbolic forms by means of which . . . [people] communicate, perpetuate, and develop their knowledge about and attitudes toward life."[34] Jeffrey Olick and contributors suggest that not only do particular meanings and forms of collective memory change over time, but also the processes of constructing memory varies historically.[35] Research by Diane Barthel on identity and preservation movements, Robin Wagner-Pacifici and Barry Schwartz on monument-making, and John Walton on the production of historical narratives in Monterey all represent scholarly efforts to link the politics of collective memory formation and transformation to current problems and struggles over community empowerment.[36]

These points resonate with happenings in New Orleans during the planning and staging of the 1984 Exposition. New Orleans's main historic preservation group, the Preservation Resource Center (PRC), sponsored an exhibit at the exposition that featured an 1830s creole cottage. Creators of this "Living in New Orleans" exhibit believed that "something should be done at the fair to promote the city's historic architecture and neighborhoods." Estimates suggest approximately 500,000 people went through the PRC's exhibit and, according to sponsors, "all learn[ed] about [the] livability and rich cultural heritage of the city's many historic neighborhoods."[37] Such a sentiment was reminiscent of local writer Grace Elizabeth King's interpretation of the 1884 Cotton Centennial Exposition as awakening local culture and "opening . . . the past history of the city, not only to strangers, but to the citizens themselves."[38] Later, the PRC established the African American Heritage Preservation Council to promote the preservation of local ethnic heritage, creole culture, and African American collective memory through workshops, education programs, and tours through neighborhoods. These developments reflect interest in expressing to the world the accomplishments of African Americans and legitimating an inclusive conception of urban culture that portrayed the black community as major participants in the creation of New Orleans's collective memory.

In short, the 1984 Louisiana World Exposition provides an example of the intersection of the tourism from above and below. On the one hand, the 1984 Exposition contained an unprecedented display of local cultural artifacts, regional foods, and customs that were presented before a global audience, thus raising the international profile of New Orleans. At the same time, a combination of global-local networks, public policies, corporate actors, and other organized interests worked to transform a vast area of the city into an entertaining space for people to gaze on exotic cultures, histories, and products from far away places. On the other hand, the 1984 Exposition illustrated the processes of localization and cultural hybridization in the constitution of touristic culture. Localization was expressed in the actions of local groups and cultural organizations to retain a "sense of place" in local products and creations, while hybridization showed in the production of cultural innovations and new inventions of authenticity. The PRC's creole cottage at the exposition represented local efforts to display markers of creole ethnicity as reflective of New Orleans's distinctive authenticity.

Through protest against marginalization, African American leaders and activists used the exposition as an outlet for political contestation and cultural expression. A major effect of this increased attention was the elaboration of new cultural knowledge that positioned African Americans as stewards of New Orleans and creole culture. By this time, diverse groups of people, including African American activists and cultural authorities, were reappropriating "creole" as an inclusive term symbolizing the language and folk culture native to southern Louisiana where African, French, Spanish, and Caribbean influence took root historically and culturally. As a result, by the 1990s, creole festivals dotted the Louisiana and southeast landscape, while historical societies, cultural centers, and international publications promoted creole culture.

It would be wrong to view localization and hybridization as simple reactions to extralocal trends or residual products of global level changes. Instead, they are in large part immanent to tourism from above, and they reflect local efforts to resist, absorb, and transform the global processes of commodification and standardization to produce new and locally distinctive cultural traditions. In the literal sense, no one can produce tourism globally because tourism depends on local connections and local networks of activity. As an uneven and contested process, tourism involves a set of global forces imposed from above in conjunction with localized actions and organizations attempting to preserve place difference, local traditions, and indigenous cultures. These points resonate with the work of Arjun Appadurai, Ulrich Beck, Mike Featherstone, Scott Lash, Roland Robertson, John Urry, and others, who argue that globalization and other macro-level trends do not mean the world is becoming more homogeneous.[39] Rather, the trends associated with tourism from above are highly contradictory, both in content and in their multiple consequences.

Urban Branding and the Holy Trinity of New Orleans Tourism

A brand is more than a name, logo, or slogan and it is not built only through advertising. Genuine brands are the result of a comprehensive strategy that encompasses the entire destination *experience* from the visitor and prospective visitor point of view. . . . Brand names are well known but similar, like supermarkets, car dealerships, and fast-food restaurants. The distinguishing factor that sets a "real" brand apart from others is its set of distinctive characteristics and its experience. . . . You get to be a real brand *only* when your customers (visitors) say you are distinctive.　　　　　　　　　　—Brand Strategy, Inc., 2004[40]

While the 1984 Louisiana World Exposition helped foster new appreciations of local culture and heritage, it did little to remedy the economic problems of New Orleans, and by the late 1980s the city was experiencing an unrelenting fiscal crisis and intensifying poverty.[41] During this time, local business interests and tourism boosters joined with state and local governments to establish new tourism organizations and place marketing strategies to bolster the economic fortunes of the city. In 1990, the State of Louisiana and the City of New Orleans established the New Orleans Tourism Marketing Corporation (NOTMC) as a private, nonprofit, economic development corporation to market New Orleans as a leisure destination. During the 1990s, the City of New Orleans created the Mayor's Office of Tourism and Arts to serve as a liaison to the tourism industry and arts organizations. In 1995, the state of Louisiana and the City of New Orleans passed statutes earmarking a portion of the local hotel-motel tax to the New Orleans Sports Foundation to attract professional sports events to the city. This tax was also set aside for the Greater New Orleans Tourist and Convention Commission (GNOTCC) to attract foreign travelers to the city. The GNOTCC

Fig. 6.4. Over the last decade, tourism organizations have launched promotional campaigns to elide the distinction between residents and tourists, to urge residents to embrace the consumption practices characteristic
of tourists. In this advertisement from the late 1990s, the NOMCVB
encourages New Orleans residents to be tourists in their own hometown.
Yet, unlike tourists, residents are locked into everyday local struggles and
conflicts, shared experiences of the mundane and commonplace, and
collective practices to create stable rules and traditions to give meaning to
their lives as members of a community. Such actions are the antithesis of
touristic experiences, which are explicitly designed to be worry-free, spectacular, extraordinary, and short term. Today, past distinctions between
tourism and other aspects of culture are eroding as tourist modes of
staging, visualization, and experience increasingly implode into everyday
life. (Reproduced by permission of Tulane University, Howard-Tilton
Memorial Library, Special Collections)

was renamed the New Orleans Metropolitan and Convention and Visitors Bureau (NOMCVB) in 1995. By the end of the 1990s, the NOM-
CVB had established offices in several foreign countries to promote the
city's culture and attractions on a global scale. The legalization of gambling in Louisiana in the 1990s and the opening of a Harrah's casino in
New Orleans also expanded the base of monies to fund local tourism
marketing agencies such the NOTMC.[42] As a result of these institu-

tional transformations, by the late 1990s, metropolitan residents were now viewed by tourism organizations "as if tourists" and were subject to strategic and methodical promotional campaigns urging them to acquire the knowledge and visual orientation characteristic of tourists (fig. 6.4).[43]

Since the nineteenth century, New Orleans has engaged in various forms of place promotion and marketing to enhance local distinctiveness and project a favorable image to a global audience. What is new in recent years, however, is the concerted and highly organized effort by major tourism organizations in the metropolitan area to *brand* New Orleans as a historic city and entertainment destination. Urban branding is a process of creating a set of metonymical connections between a city's iconic representations in which one representation refers to another through entertaining experiences and pleasurable associations across time and space.[44] In this sense, the brand image is a visual cue that acts as both an attraction for potential tourists and as a cultural framework for authenticating the tourist's experience once they arrive in the city.

New Orleans has long been called "The City That Care Forgot" and "The Big Easy," a destination where visitors can "Laissez Les Bon Temps Roule" or "Let the Good Times Roll." Since the 1990s, tourism organizations such as the New Orleans Tourism Marketing Corporation (NOTMC), the Louisiana Office of Tourism, the New Orleans Metropolitan Conventional and Visitor Bureau (NOMCVB), and the New Orleans Multicultural Tourism Network (NOMTN) have established partnerships to elaborate and extend these and other slogans through a series of strategic branding campaigns that aim to define New Orleans as America's "most authentic city." Such campaigns are employed synergistically to maximize exposure of New Orleans to a global audience. As the NOTMC Corporation's 2002 Annual Report notes:

> The new comprehensive branding campaign focused on the food, music, ambience, and good times New Orleans offers any time of the year. It marks a shift from the purely direct-response approach of prior years by adding a strong image component. In our creative testing in 2001, the concept of "authentic fun" and the message "happenin' every day" got very positive responses. In 2002, it delivered as tested. Our Summer Campaign pushed traditional inquiries 10% beyond the previous year's campaign.[45]

The 2003 Annual Report of the NOTMC notes that their "creative strategy" is to expand on the "New Orleans: Happen' Every Day" theme to "highlight food, music, and history"; "show the day with the night"; "reflect authentic, fun positioning"; "utilize photography"; and have "images of family/children (conveys safety)."[46]

This branding campaign connects with the marketing efforts of the New Orleans Metropolitan Convention and Visitors Bureau (NOMCVB). In 2003, the NOMCVB began "disseminating a strategically crafted set of core messages that 'brand' the city as a premier destination." As the 2003 Annual Report of the NOMCVB tells it, "The NOMCVB is branding New Orleans as . . . an energetic and vibrant city not only to visit but also in which to live, work, and do business. The CVB's communication emphasizes New Orleans' unique blend of European, African, and Caribbean culture and its preeminence as a center for art, music, and food." At the same time, the NOMCVB is "branding itself as the national leader in best practices and customer service." In short, branding campaigns launched in recent years by the NOMCVB and the NOTMC embrace strategies of place differentiation and image specialization to create commercial value, draw visitors to the city, and cement their status as definers of local authenticity.[47]

Urban branding is illustrative of a wider tourism promotion strategy to expand New Orleans's urban iconography through the use of sophisticated niche marketing techniques. As reflected in the work of Paul Chatteron and Robert Hollands, John Hannigan, Allen J. Scott, and other scholars, niche marketing refers to the development of new forms of cultural fragmentation, differentiation, and specialization that split consumers and markets into ever-smaller segments or niches, resulting in heterogeneity rather than homogeneity.[48] Niche marketing is simultaneously about diversity and homogeneity, or "homogenized diversity." Place marketers and tourism officials seek to create and exploit niche markets by erasing the diversity of social groups and defining and thus homogenizing families, baby boomers, senior citizens, African and Hispanic Americans, and Gays and Lesbians as consumers.

In tourism marketing, all groups and subcultures—except nonconsumers—are potential niche markets. Tourism organizations like the NOTMC project only those images that appeal to high-income groups that have the greatest consumption power or consumption-creating potential. Indeed, profit making and organizational survival dictate that tourism agencies create more and more niches because each new niche group amounts to a new market to tap into to create consumer demand to travel and spend money, a process discussed by scholars such George Ritzer, Scott Lash, and John Urry, among others.[49] As one leader within the tourism industry told me,

> Prior the mid-1990s, we were not able to capture that multicultural tourism market because of the way we sold ourselves. We never promoted the history, the culture, the Islenos, the Germans, all the folks that made New Orleans what it is. These groups are an untapped resource that no one has really stumbled upon it yet. There are pockets of groups that should be promoting themselves but they just have not realized the profit potential yet. The Islenos and the German influence, you have little bits of pieces here and there, and some people know about this, but it is still an untold story. So, I think there are a lot of ethnic groups like that who need to be examined.[50]

Broadly, urban branding and niche marketing involve a mix of claims to distinction and assurances of predictability and comfort based on homogeneity and standardization. In New Orleans, this narrative of distinction is constructed around three themes—history, music, and food—that constitute the "holy trinity" of New Orleans tourism. The following quote from one official of a local tourism organization describes this holy trinity of history, music, and food that connect and unite the disparate elements of the city and region:

> The images [New Orleans tourism organizations] use to promote tourism are evocative and emphasize the holy trinity of New Orleans tourism: food, music, and history. All the cultures of New Orleans emphasize these elements and we use them to promote the city and its peoples. We advertise in regional markets, consumer magazines, and on cable television. Our emphasis is on the authenticity and heritage of New Orleans.[51]

Collapsing urban complexity into a series of formulaic images—food, music, and history—is a major element of the homogenization and rationalization process associated with tourism from above. Reflecting the shift to a touristic culture in New Orleans, the tourism officials I interviewed embrace a consumer demand–driven view of local culture and place, a view underpinned by a logic of what is most likely to appeal to tourists. Importantly, place marketers and tourism professionals now espouse views of New Orleans culture and authenticity that reflect travel trends and tourists' ways of viewing the world. That is, the different representations of local culture—including what is distinctive and unique about New Orleans—are chosen from a variety of vocabularies, symbols, and codes to appeal to the traveling consumer.

Going further, according to my interviews and the quotes from the NOTMC and Brand Strategy, tourism boosters and officials believe that tourist's tastes, habits, and tourism market prerogatives should be the definers and structuring characteristics of local authenticity. Thus, advertising New Orleans as a site of delicious food, quality music, and rich history fulfills several goals, including showcasing the different local cultures, enticing diverse kinds of tourists to visit the city, and generating business opportunities within the local tourism industry. The narrative's lack of specificity leaves it open to many interpretations and creates a discursive space for the inclusion of different peoples and ethnic backgrounds. In 2003, for example, the website of the New Orleans Multicultural Tourism Network (NOMTN) told people that "New Orleans is a gumbo of cultures that blend together, yet maintain their own unique flavor." As a quote from the NOMTN website tells it:

> With a history older than that of the United States, New Orleans is a contemporary city steeped heavily in the past. Its people still reflect the diversity of its ancestors, an eclectic mix of Native American, European, African, Caribbean, Acadian, and Hispanic Cultures, out of which was born the most unique bloodlines in the world. When you visit New Orleans you will definitely see the world.[52]

As far as possible, tourism boosters attempt to construct New Orleans as an "experiential brand" in which the city itself signifies a treasure trove of sensory, affective, and cognitive associations that result in a variety of memorable brand experiences. Central to this process of developing an experiential brand is the creation of an evocative narrative with food, music, and history serving as unifying elements of New Orleans culture and collective memory. Interestingly, tourism boosters have explicitly focused their branding efforts and niche marketing strategies on music because they view it as a major element of cultural life with a built-in sense of nostalgia. Musical lyrics imagine and memorial-ize past times, offer an alternative to the rhythms of everyday life, and suggest different ways of viewing the present. Music does not just invoke an imagined past and future; different genres connect with different places. In recent years, for example, city elites and tourism boosters have attempted to brand jazz music as authentically New Orleans in an effort to generate inward investment and stimulate the growth of a local music industry. In 2002, local leaders established the New Orleans Jazz Orchestra as a nonprofit jazz education and performance organization that had as its purpose "the celebration, proliferation, and structured branding of New Orleans jazz" and the development of a "New Orleans based jazz tourism programming." Central to this initiative has been the emphasis on "building national awareness about the role New Orleans has played and continues to play in American culture." Advertisements proclaim, "New Orleans jazz is a way of life for New Orleanians" and New Orleans's "spirit created America's only indigenous music."[53] These strategic efforts supplement a major branding campaign launched by the Mayor's Office of Economic Development in August 2004 to "facilitate future collaboration among the businesses and entities that promote Jazz." As New Orleans Mayor C. Ray Nagin puts it, "New Orleans is the birthplace of Jazz and Jazz is the foundation for all music in America. We need to capitalize on this and begin branding the world-wide appeal of Jazz as a uniquely New Orleans experience."[54]

In the aftermath of the Katrina disaster, New Orleans's major tourism organizations are elaborating on their past branding campaigns and creating new campaigns to alter people's perceptions and images of New Orleans using brand elements such as new slogans and logos (table 6.2). In April 2006, the Louisiana Recovery Authority earmarked $30 million for tourism and convention marketing. The NOMCVB is using a portion of this money to "re-image and re-brand" the Ernest N. Morial Convention Center, the site of an internationally televised humanitarian crisis in the days after Hurricane Katrina.[55] The NOTMC, whose hotel tax-dependent budget was negatively affected by the Katrina disaster, has joined forces with the Louisiana Office of Tourism to launch a "Fall in Love with Louisiana All Over Again" advertising campaign. Through urban branding, tourism organizations seek to counter negative publicity by projecting images of rebirth, renaissance, and reauthentication. Indeed, the city government's effort to brand New Orleans as

TABLE 6.2

Major New Orleans Tourism Organizations Engaged in Post-Katrina Branding Campaigns

Tourism Organization	Mission and Objective	Image-Building Themes and Slogans
New Orleans Metropolitan Convention and Visitors Bureau (NOMCVB)	Offer convention services; provide information to visitors	"Fall in Love with New Orleans All Over Again" "Still America's Most Romantic, Walkable, Historic City—New Orleans" "Authentic and Real: Like No Other Place" "The Rebirth of New Orleans: Ahead of Schedule" "You'll Love the New New Orleans"
New Orleans Tourism and Marketing Corporation (NOTMC)	Foster jobs and economic growth by developing the New Orleans tourism industry Promote New Orleans as a leisure tourism destination, especially during the winter and summer months	"New Orleans: Happenin' Every Day" "Fall in Love with Louisiana All Over Again" (in collaboration with the Louisiana Office of Tourism)
New Orleans Multicultural Tourism Network (NOMTN)	Promote New Orleans as a multicultural destination; increase meaningful participation for people of color in the tourism industry	"Do You Know What It Means to Miss New Orleans?"
New Orleans Jazz Orchestra (NOJO)	Provide information, education, and performances to advance jazz's role in American culture and New Orleans's role in jazz	"Jazz at the Center of Rebirth" "We Lift Our Instruments to Lift Our City"

the birthplace of jazz has accelerated in the aftermath of Katrina as city and state leaders announced in May 2006 their desire to create a twenty-acre performance arts park to be anchored by a new National Jazz Center in downtown New Orleans.[56]

The need for an unequivocal focus in marketing New Orleans is a primary motivator for re-branding the city as a premier tourist destination. For New Orleans elites, post-Katrina urban redevelopment is as much about accumulating brand value as it is about zoning, tax subsidies, and other conventional aspects of planning and policy. As a set of advertising slogans, branding assists in reducing the uncertainty of the urban experience by making the image of New Orleans and its cultural products transparent and understandable. Producing and circulating brand values is tantamount to rearranging commodity images into chains of meaning and cultural signification to make New Orleans attractive and accessible to the imagination. Thus, what defines contemporary tourism planning and marketing campaigns today is the attempt to build brand loyalty and insinuate branding practices more deeply into the lives of visitors and residents.

As I show in the next two chapters, struggles over meanings and definitions of local authenticity are omnipresent in New Orleans and are embedded within a larger tourism discourse that structures how people think about the city and its identity. Tourism marketing campaigns that appropriate cultural imagery, symbols, and themes are not neutral and objective. They are strategic and methodical, and they reflect concerted attempts by tourism organizations to legitimate themselves as community "experts." As I point out, antagonism and struggle over tourism has become particularly acute in recent years as local residents have opposed government and corporate efforts to commercialize Mardi Gras and to transform the French Quarter into an upscale entertainment destination that is antithetical to residential life. These conflicts are rooted in opposition to the homogenizing effects of tourism from above and feed local struggles to advance new grassroots conceptions of authenticity and tourism from below.

7

A Repertoire of Authenticity

Contested Space and the Transformation of the French Quarter

Are tourists ruining the Vieux Carre? A lot of people say they are, a lot of people say they already have, and a lot of other people say more tourists should be attracted, made to stay longer, and convinced to spend more. . . . Numerous long-time Quarter business people, residents, and tourists who have visited the city over the years gone by say that the caliber of tourism in the Vieux Carre is changing. . . . They say the French Quarter is becoming an amusement park type tourist trap.

— J. E. Bourgoyne, *Times-Picayune*, December 23, 1973[1]

We can all see it coming already. In a few short years, the French Quarter will be a ghost town of vacation condos, time-shares and bed-and-breakfasts, burned out as a tourist destination. Ads will try to lure locals to "rediscover Quarter living." Bankrupt T-shirt shops will be artfully restored into corner groceries with Sicilian names. Cheap sunglasses booths will be turned back into fruit stalls at the French Market, artists will be paid to paint on Jackson Square—anything to revive a lost authenticity. But it will be too late. Because that fascinating web of lives that has formed Quarter culture for generations—Creoles, Italians, artists, musicians, entertainers, bon vivants, and bohemians—will have vanished. . . . Soon the transformation will be complete . . . and the vital heartbeat residents gave to the neighborhood will be gone.

— James Nolan, local writer, *Times-Picayune*,
May 20, 2001[2]

If it weren't for the French Quarter, we would not get any tourism or convention business. This is where it all starts. This is the nucleus not only for New Orleans tourism but Louisiana tourism. Statewide we are it. We drive the state economy, and the state could not survive if it were not for the French Quarter. Bourbon

Street, the architecture of the French Quarter, and Jackson Square
—these are the things that people take pictures of when they come
to Louisiana.

—French Quarter business owner[3]

The preceding quotes communicate three very different interpretations of New Orleans's most famous neighborhood and how it has
changed over the decades. The first quote, from the 1970s, expresses
fears about the French Quarter becoming an amusement park for tourists; the second quote laments the loss of neighborhood authenticity; and
the third quote describes the French Quarter as the economic engine of
New Orleans and the state of Louisiana. These quotes reveal the multifaceted nature of the French Quarter, including its status as a specialty
shopping area, an entertainment complex, a residential area, and a focus
of culture and historic preservation of regional and national importance.

These quotes also convey different conceptions about the meaning of
tourism and the role it plays in neighborhood life. Complaints about
tourism's effect on the French Quarter and calls for expanding tourism
to revitalize the neighborhood span many decades, and there have always been a variety of opinions on how to "improve" the neighborhood. In recent decades, the French Quarter has become a battleground
of intense conflicts over commercial revitalization, historic preservation,
and neighborhood integrity. During the 1970s, neighborhood groups
mobilized to fight the privatization of the historic French Market, the
expansion of large-scale hotels, and the building of the retail center,
Canal Place. Since this time, residents and businesses have teamed with
historic preservationists and other activists to protest the growth of fast-
food restaurants, mall-like shops, and chain-like clothing stores that
cater almost exclusively to tourists.[4] In 1988 and 1989, the National
Trust for Historic Preservation identified the French Quarter as one of
the eleven most endangered places in the country due to the threat that
commercial business growth posed to the residential character of the
neighborhood.[5] In recent years, residents and neighborhood organizations have lamented the increase of hotels, bed and breakfasts, time-
shares, condominiums, and large entertainment clubs.[6] For most of its
history, the French Quarter functioned as a residential neighborhood
composed of diverse groups of people. Since the 1960s, however, the

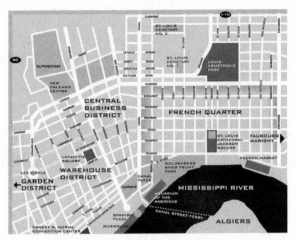

Fig. 7.1. Map of the Central Business District and the French
Quarter. (Reproduced by permission of Tulane University,
Howard-Tilton Memorial Library, Special Collections)

area has been transformed into an entertainment destination, marketed
vigorously by tourism promoters, and redesigned to bring visitors into
the city (fig. 7.1).

The expansion of tourism and entertainment in the French Quarter
over the decades has paralleled the racial and class transformation
of the neighborhood. Between 1940 and 2000, the population of the
French Quarter plummeted from 11,053 to 4,176, a loss of more than
50 percent of its population. Interestingly, after the 1960s, as New Orleans shifted to a city with a majority of African Americans, the French
Quarter neighborhood became more white. From 1940 to 2000, the
number of whites living in the French Quarter increased from 79 percent to 91.9 percent, while the number of blacks dropped from 19.7
percent to 4.3 percent. Only 116 children younger than 18 years lived
in the Vieux Carre in the year 2000. This number represents only 2.7
percent of the total population of the neighborhood. Of the almost
3,000 households in the Vieux Carre, more than 97 percent do not have
children younger than 18 years.[7] In the three census tracts that make up
the French Quarter, both median incomes and property values have increased, especially during the 1990s, and escalating rents and conversion of affordable single-family residences to expensive condominiums
have pushed out lower-income people and African Americans.[8] Overall,
in the past sixty years, the French Quarter has witnessed a loss of pop-

ulation, a decrease in percentage of minority residents, and huge increases in median household value and cost of rent.

Hotels, Entertainment Chains, and Tourism Growth in the French Quarter

> There's no way you can have a perfect night in New Orleans if you don't
> go to Bourbon Street. . . . The fun, the color, the noise. I love it. No city
> in America has anything like Bourbon Street.   —Larry Flynt, 2004[9]

One of the most striking transformations in the French Quarter and surrounding areas over the past few decades is the growth of transnational hotel firms, transient lodges, and other hotel accommodations. Despite passage of the 1969 moratorium barring new hotel building in the French Quarter, hotel development continued unabated during the 1970s and later. Between 1969 and 1978, six hotels with 695 rooms opened in the neighborhood. During this time, hotel developers attempted to circumvent the hotel moratorium by converting small homes and residential spaces into "guest houses" and other accommodations. In response, in 1978, the New Orleans City Council passed a law banning the opening of new guest houses and the expansion of existing ones. Despite this ban, between 1979 and 1982, four more transient or rental homes opened, adding 79 more hotel rooms to the French Quarter. In the 1980s and later, the City Council enacted laws to relax the restrictions of the 1969 moratorium and invalidate prior legal constraints on expanding hotel development. In 1982, for example, the City Council passed an ordinance to allow new hotels on Canal Street and in the French Quarter but in existing buildings only. Overall, from 1960 to 1982, the French Quarter experienced a growth of 3,554 hotel rooms.[10]

Over the past decade, the City Council has issued permits to allow hotel firms to exceed the height restriction of seventy feet and to purchase residential buildings next to hotels and convert them into lodging. In August 2000, historic preservation and resident groups launched a lawsuit to halt the planning and construction of a sixteen-story Marriott hotel in the French Quarter, arguing that the city violated its own laws by approving a new structure more than twice the height allowed by neighborhood zoning ordinances.[11] Despite vehement opposition from business owners and residents, in August 2004, the New Orleans City

Planning Commission voted 6 to 1 to grant a single exception to the thirty-five-year-old prohibition against new or expanded hotels in the French Quarter.[12] Local residents and lawyers representing the French Quarter Citizens and the Vieux Carre Property Owners, Residents, and Associates (VCPORA) argue that these recent developments essentially nullify the original moratorium, encourage unrestricted development that is not open to public comment, and give hotel developers unbridled freedom to build hotels and ignore the historic integrity of the neighborhood.

The growth of hotels and other transient accommodations in the French Quarter reflects a larger entertainment-oriented urban revitalization strategy adopted by the city government to increase tax revenue and aid civic image building, a trend also observed by Mark Gottdiener in his analysis of theming and Paul Chatterton and Robert Hollands in their examination of nighttime urban playscapes in the United Kingdom.[13] For New Orleans leaders, civic image building is akin to image reconstruction and the presentation of a safe and secure French Quarter that is open to all kinds of capital investment, even commercial development that portends a transformation in the residential base of the neighborhood. Yet these trends have not gone unopposed. During the 1980s, historic preservationists and neighborhood residents banded to protest the planning and construction of the Audubon Institute's Aquarium of the Americas, a tourist attraction that opponents interpreted as a major treat to neighborhood authenticity. For opponents, the Aquarium represented the latest manifestation of the increasing power of large corporations in undermining the residential character of the French Quarter and sanitizing space for commercial profit. Proponents considered the aquarium to be an important complement to the city's expanding tourism infrastructure that portended a new era of economic revitalization and growth. According to Ron Forman, president of the Audubon Institute,

> How can we afford not to build the aquarium? We have a choice. We can all die, sit here and be unemployed, or move to another city. Or we can find ways to invest in a project that will bring jobs, help our tourist industry and bring culture and education to our city. To me, the choice is clear.[14]

For Forman and other supporters of the aquarium, the intractability and contrariness of neighborhood resident groups imperiled urban redevelopment and suggested that preservationist causes were culturally backward. Neighborhood groups such as the VCPORA argued that the aquarium was "incompatible with the historic character of Vieux Carre" and "totally out of scale with the Vieux Carre."[15] For Forman, the aquarium battle was part of a larger struggle to legitimate corporate-driven tourism development against the grassroots opposition of neighborhood residents and historic preservationists. According to Forman, "I'm very often like a bulldozer with blinders. I keep going straight ahead until the goal's accomplished. We don't have time for people who say no. We just ask them to get out of the way."[16] In the end, voters approved a $40 million financing package, and the aquarium opened in September 1990.

The defeat of historic preservationists and resident groups in the aquarium conflict emboldened corporate interests to launch even more ambitious proposals to expand tourism and commercial development in the French Quarter. In 1992, city planners rezoned the first two blocks of Decatur Street as a French Quarter Entertainment District, a move meant to spur redevelopment of several vacant commercial properties and create an anchor of commercial revitalization that could have spillover effects into surrounding areas. Large firms such as the House of Blues, Coyote Ugly Bar, Planet Hollywood, Jimmy Buffet's Margaritaville Cafe, and Harrah's Casino have all opened since the early 1990s. Bourbon Street began to experience a new wave of corporate investment with the opening of the Chateau Sonesta Hotel in 1995, Larry Flynt's Hustler Club in 1996, Redfish Grill in 1997, and the Storyville District Jazz Club in 1999. In 1998, Don Kleinhans, a national adult entertainment investor, opened Utopia, a music and dance club at 227 Bourbon Street and Opulence, a nightclub, a few doors away. Bourbon Street has long been one of New Orleans's most valuable commercial real estate strips.[17] Nevertheless, space on the street has become more desirable as the tourism industry has expanded since the 1980s. The construction of upscale hotels along Canal Street and in the Central Business District has increased foot traffic within the French Quarter and encouraged investors to renovate properties in the first few blocks of Canal Street and turn old bars on Bourbon Street into upscale themed music clubs. These tourism-driven commercial developments suggest a new era of the increasing dominance of chainlike entertainment venues, with big brands taking over large parts of urban space.

A further manifestation of the growth of tourism is the proliferation of visitor-oriented shops and retail stores that cater almost exclusively to tourists, a trend closely associated with the restructuring of the commercial base of the neighborhood. In an analysis of commercial change in the French Quarter, Catherine Vesey found that from 1950 to 1999, the number of souvenir and T-shirt shops increased from twenty-six to 110, retail apparel stores increased from fourteen to forty-two, music clubs increased from seven to twenty-seven, and art galleries increased from ten to forty. In addition, from 1950 to 1999, the number of groceries decreased from forty-four to four, miscellaneous food stores declined from forty-four to nineteen, hardware stores from thirty-one to one, and laundry services from twenty-four to two. During this time, several mom-and-pop operations that had been stable fixtures in the neighborhood for decades closed, including LaNasa Hardware, Reuter's Feed and Seed, Morning Call coffee shop, Puglia's grocery store, and Weirlein's music store. Interestingly, the number of warehouses, industrial services, freight distribution, and manufacturing services plummeted from 131 to two. Today, souvenir shops are the most prevalent retail business in the area. Overall, from 1950 to 1999, residential-oriented businesses, such as barbers, department stores, shoe shops, small-scale groceries, and laundry services decreased more than 15 percent, while tourist-oriented businesses, such as T-shirt shops, poster shops, daiquiri shops, and commercial tourism information centers expanded by 32 percent.[18]

In sum, over the past few decades, the French Quarter has undergone a dramatic sociospatial transformation. High-class fashion outlets and expensive retail stores have taken over the old Jackson Brewery, transforming an old factory into a suburban-style shopping mall (fig. 7.2). Designer bars, chain restaurants, and souvenir shops have gradually replaced former working-class corner cafes and food shops. Many small antique dealers and art galleries have left the French Quarter and moved to Magazine Street, where they can afford the rents. On Royal and Chartres Streets, a proliferation of private art galleries and antique dealers have opened, often displaying works at expensive prices. New dance bars that never close have replaced the old jazz clubs on Bourbon Street. Streets and buildings valued and protected for the architectural and scenic effects are juxtaposed with areas of corporate tourist development and privatized areas of retail shopping and entertainment. Indeed, the last of the corner cafes and local coffee shops are today competing for space with some of the largest corporations in the world.

Fig. 7.2. Aerial view of the French Quarter, showing Jackson Square and the Jackson Brewery in 1984. This photograph was taken before the redevelopment of Woldenberg Park and the building of the Aquarium of the Americas. For most of its history, the French Quarter functioned as a residential neighborhood composed of diverse groups of people, land uses, and stores serving both residents and tourists. Since the 1960s, however, the French Quarter has become a relatively affluent and exclusive enclave, marked by a proliferation of corporate entertainment and tourism venues. (Reproduced by permission of the New Orleans Public Library, Louisiana Division and the City Archives)

Contested Space and a Repertoire of Authenticity

Both the city and the residents want to preserve the buildings, but for two conflicting reasons—one to attract tourists, the other as a place to live. Who will win? I don't know.

—Mary Morrison, French Quarter preservationist,
on the threat tourism poses to the French
Quarter's residential ambiance, 1998[19]

City leaders, residents, and tourism officials all recognize that the French Quarter has experienced a massive increase in visitors and a proliferation of entertainment venues and tourism-oriented stores in recent decades. Resident groups, neighborhood organizations, and city agencies have organized symposia and public meetings and initiated studies to gauge the impact levels of tourism.[20] There is no consensus on the meaning of tourism, whether tourism has positive or negative effects, or what should be done about tourism in the French Quarter. Perceptions of tourism impact problems and their remedies vary widely among residents and city leaders. The lack of consensus does not break down to a clear demarcation between those in favor of tourism and those against it. Residents have a variety of different, complex, and ambivalent positions about tourism. Indeed, the residents I interviewed were unanimous that tourism is a major sector of the metropolitan economy and that New Orleans and the French Quarter are dependent on tourism. Yet many residents assert that tourism in recent decades has changed to a point where it is destroying the cultural fabric of the French Quarter. Others argue that tourism has brought many benefits to the French Quarter, including more affluent residents and lucrative capital investments to preserve historic buildings and revitalize space. Still others hold contrasting positions and maintain that tourism has undermined the ambiance and uniqueness of the French Quarter while at the same time providing an opportunity to showcase the rich culture and heritage of the neighborhood and city. In these and other cases, residents have invented new understandings of the neighborhood that seek to contest and limit tourism, and to control and expand tourism.

Over the decades, the dramatic expansion of tourism has encouraged French Quarter resident groups to cultivate a repertoire of authenticity that they use to legitimate both the processes of and their role in neighborhood redevelopment. French Quarter residents invoke claims of authenticity by producing several narratives that emphasize themes of nostalgia, exploitation, victimization, and neighborhood empowerment. One theme locates authenticity not in the present but in the past, in a narrative of past grandeur where genuine social relations and close neighborhood ties defined the French Quarter. Many long-term residents argue that in olden times the French Quarter was a small community of diverse people who lived in relative harmony. One resident and neighborhood activist, Mary Morrison, who moved to the French Quarter in the 1930s, noted in 1972:

> 33 years ago [the French Quarter] was a heterogeneous citizenry of Negroes, Italians, still some old and illustrious Creole families. . . . We also

had Chinese, Filipinos, Puerto Ricans, as well as Anglo-Saxon or Scotch Irish. . . . Here people were born, lived, were married and died in the same house. This gave tremendous color, stability, and vitality to the Quarter."[21]

According to one resident who has lived in the neighborhood since the 1940s, "I liked the small-town character of the French Quarter. . . . I liked that people knew each other and cared for each other. I could walk many places and have coffee with friends. It was a great neighborhood to live in."[22] In the interview quote below, one resident reminisces about how the old French Quarter was a place of families and close associations. As this person told me,

> When I think about the 1960s, [the French Quarter] was a much quieter neighborhood. There were many more full-time residents. There were many more businesses that were attuned to the residents who lived here as opposed to the tourists who come here. There were wonderful little restaurants that had "typical" New Orleans food for New Orleans people and not something for the tourists. We had wonderful vegetable/fruit stands over in the French Market. And these were for local people. Both of our children were born while we were in the French Quarter, 1962 and 1964. And it was a great place to have children and there were lots of other families with children. We had a parent/children social group, and we got together and had Easter egg hunts, Halloween, and so on. And my husband worked in the French Quarter, he walked to work. I would meet him with the stroller when he was finishing work, and we would take a walk with the children on the way home. It was really a very, very pleasant place to live.[23]

Closely related to the narrative of past grandeur are tales of deep sadness, regret, and loss over what residents see as the decline of neighborhood institutions, shared culture, and community identity. Indeed, the theme of nostalgia is pervasive throughout my interviews with residents, especially older ones who have lived in the French Quarter for decades. In interviews, residents recollect about a time when the French Quarter was a place of hominess and authentic relations. While the neighborhood had its share of problems, residents maintain that crime was relatively nonexistent and the neighborhood was much more family friendly and accommodating toward children than today.

Many residents mention the names of locally owned grocery stores, coffee shops, and other businesses where everyone supposedly knew everyone else. In this interpretation, residents were close friends, and relationships with neighbors were warm and cordial rather than distant and reserved. "One thing was the camaraderie of everybody," as one person told me. "You knew everybody on the block, you knew half the people in the Quarter. It was like living in a small town." For this person, "there were any number of mom-and-pop so-called stores, where mom and pop ran the store downstairs and lived upstairs. It seemed like they were on every corner. They are all gone now, and I regret it. You knew your neighbors, and the neighbors knew you. It was a wonderful lifestyle that no longer exists."[24] In the old days, according to some residents, people took pride in forging a self-sufficient neighborhood, with hard work and determination being the basis for the French Quarter's authenticity. "The French Quarter was a self-sufficient community," as one person told me: "There were lots of corner stores that supported the residents. They all employed people who lived in the neighborhood. In fact, all you needed to live and survive was here: food, entertainment, recreation, we had parks and schools for children. There were five drug stores, lots of cleaners, hardware stores, grocery stores, movie theaters. All that has gradually disappeared."[25]

In the quote below, one long-time resident reminisces about a time, not so long ago, when a close friend operated an antique store in the neighborhood. For this person, the memory of an old antique store signifies a bygone time when social relations in the French Quarter were rich in meaning and significance. Here local ties among French Quarter friends internalized the bounteous charm and unique character of the neighborhood, creating and projecting a magical and enchanted world. For this person, the growth of tourism is tantamount to the disenchantment of French Quarter and the growth of generic landscape. As this person told me:

> Thirty years ago, a friend of mine, she passed a way a long time ago, owned a beautiful antique shop on St. Peters Street. It was an old building, wooden floors, and lots of antiques. I had never really been into an antique store until I moved to the French Quarter and began visiting them. And that got me interested in collecting antiques, which I have been doing now for over thirty years. She knew lots and lots of people.

And I loved visiting her shop, which was the most beautiful place you could ever see or enter. You could walk in broke and just want to have everything in the store, and somehow you could find the money to buy something. And these were the days when it would not break your pocketbook to buy antiques. But the year before the 1984 World's Fair, she came to me and said, "I have some bad news, I am closing up. The World's Fair is coming and the owner of the building is raising the rent." She told me that there was no way she could stay in business in the French Quarter. It was a very sad experience, and there is not a time that I don't walk by there and think about her wonderful place. But, at any rate, that example is part of the larger change that has taken place in New Orleans, of how tourism has affected the city in a negative way. Now her old antique shop is a place where you can buy all the tourist T-shirts that your heart desires.[26]

It is important to point out that the nostalgic story told by residents constructs an image of the French Quarter as a place where diverse people—including artists, poor people, blacks, and whites—lived together in peace and tranquility. Many of the white residents I interviewed denied that racism played any role in history of the French Quarter. While they acknowledged the centrality of racial segregation in New Orleans, they asserted that the heterogeneity of the French Quarter voided racial animosity and made racial discrimination nonexistent. "Race and ethnic relations have always been good in the French Quarter," according to one resident; "I have always felt a great deal of goodwill from people of other races. This is one of the reasons I tell people why I have always loved living here."[27] According to a resident who grew up in the French Quarter in the 1940s:

I came up in the French Quarter, and in those days the French Quarter was *real*. It was a blue collar Italian ghetto—that's the best way to describe it—filled, literally, with 15,000 people. . . . Back then it was families, all working people, and it was integrated. We didn't know it; it was just a matter of fact that we lived together; blacks and whites side by side. There was no big issue over it; the only time there was an issue was when you involved the government thing: black kids went to one school, white kids went to another. But as neighbors, we lived as neighbors: you'd pass food over the fence and things like that.[28]

In my interviews, white residents interpret the French Quarter as a place where racial tolerance and acceptance were and continue to be the foundation of neighborhood authenticity. Unlike the white working-class residents that Maria Kefalas studied in the Beltway neighborhood of Chicago, the white French Quarter residents I interviewed do not express overtly racist sentiments or belief systems.[29] Residents frame race and racial differences in a vocabulary of class and culture that creates and affirms symbolic and social distances between the French Quarter and surrounding black neighborhoods. French Quarter residents' views of the city and their neighborhood accepts the reality of racial inequality, while explicitly denying that racial discrimination or segregation has any meaningful role in neighborhood life. Racism, poverty, and other social problems are the problems of "other" neighborhoods, not the French Quarter, according to residents. Assertions that race relations have always been inclusive, peaceful, and harmonious are a strategic means of asserting cultural distinctiveness and creating a sense of moral worth and social status. For residents, racial diversity is the social glue that holds the French Quarter together and elides class and racial conflicts. This conflict-free understanding of the French Quarter is widespread and uncontested in my interviews. Neighborhood residents suggest that, in the past, living in a close-knit community with shared schools and businesses helped foster a deep community identity that transcended race and class divisions. Even today, residents use the language of "multiculturalism" to claim that racial unity and openness define the French Quarter.

These views should not be taken at face value but interpreted with a skeptical eye. Many of the sentimental comments that come through in my interviews express a discourse of cultural "loss" and neighborhood "decline." At the same time, the resulting portrait of the French Quarter as a place of racial "diversity" reflects the nuanced complexities of residents struggling to understand and navigate a constantly shifting neighborhood terrain. On the one hand, the somber accounts suggest that the social and cultural connections that interwove French Quarter families and neighborhood associations have disintegrated, contributing to widespread anxieties about rootlessness, anomie, and impersonalization. On the other hand, like all nostalgic narratives, tales about the past are told in the present by people who selectively incorporate some aspects of history while excluding other parts. Nostalgia is an important ingredient in the process of meaning-making that draws on New Orleans's urban iconography to give a selective and partial interpretation of the present in light of a believable past.

Sociologists and other scholars have long known that the discourse of urban decline is constructed in nostalgic terms that draw on and invoke a variety of myths and interpretations about the past.[30] Indeed, the cynical reading of the past by French Quarter residents resonates with Georg Simmel's famous observation that nostalgic sentiments "are nothing other than the rosy illumination of a past that has been spared the shadows of the present." The "pessimism concerning the present day," according to Simmel, becomes a "glorification of the past."[31] Robert Beauregard's interrogation of the "discourse of decline" suggests that people's evocations of urban decline are "not an emotionally flat rendition of objectively specified conditions but highly charged stories built up of layers of personal and collective meanings."[32] As a major component of the repertoire of authenticity, nostalgia is a framing device that closely approximates what sociologist Erving Goffman called a "schemata of interpretation" that enables individuals "to locate, perceive, identify, and label events in the world at large."[33] Nostalgia involves simplifying the world by selectively punctuating and encoding situations and neighborhood experiences to identify a problem and challenge competing explanations of reality. Importantly, what specific nostalgic themes and symbols people choose to accentuate (and exclude) are connected with target audience of the tale. Quoting Philip Kasinitz and David Hillyard, "arguments about neighborhood identity are always made in part for audiences beyond the neighborhood's boundaries."[34] In this sense, the idealization of the past allows local residents to construct a story of the French Quarter "community" within a framework that is recognizable, understandable, and credible to others. Inevitably, this process involves emphasizing some aspects of the past while downplaying other interpretations.

Another major element of the repertoire of authenticity is the sense of exploitation and victimization. Residents strategically deploy various symbols and persuasive devices to claim that they and their neighborhood have been overburdened with and exploited by tourism venues. In the quote below, one neighborhood coalition leader excoriates tourism boosters and the city government for having little concern with the French Quarter's authenticity and distinctive sense of place. Reflecting a long history of conflict and struggle over tourism in the French Quarter, the following quote conveys a sense of urgency, imminent threat, and community destabilization. At the same time, this person maintains that historic preservation and residential life are what give the French Quarter its tourist appeal:

> A couple months of ago [in 2003], in the 300 block of Decatur Street, there was a proposal before the city government for a bar to open in a beautiful building. It had just been rehabilitated and reconditioned, and the name of the bar was going to be "Freaks and Hos." They were going to have 300-pound strippers, dwarf-tossing, and midgets as the waiter staff and bar staff. I mean does something like that add anything to the historic charm and character and the tout ensemble of the French Quarter? I think not! The tourism industry tries to cram as much as possible here in the French Quarter. The prevalent thought is that preservation is anti-economic development, but I think that the best economic development you can do is to save the French Quarter from tourism. So, all these things, like bars like "Freaks and Hos," allowing the building and expansion of hotels, allowing them to proliferate, strike at the core of what originally drew people to the French Quarter. And if we just want this to be an overgrown theme park or a Disney World, well, fine, but move out all the residents, shut up the front with a big gate, hose it down once a week, and run the tourists through.[35]

The preceding quote reflects a long tradition of neighborhood opposition to entertainment and commercial venues that residents identify as a threat to the quality of life and stability of the French Quarter. Residents validate, amplify, and transmit these and related sentiments of victimization and exploitation through resident networks, heritage networks, and other connections with grassroots cultural groups in New Orleans. Residents blame city leaders and elected officials for allowing hotels, condominiums, and bed and breakfasts into the French Quarter while refusing to enforce zoning ordinances to protect the residential fabric of the neighborhood. Others note that the effort to keep hotels out of the French Quarter has been a multidecade battle that has intensified in the 1990s and later, as city leaders have turned to tourism to remedy the long-term economic decline of the metropolitan economy.

Still other long-time residents single out the proliferation of T-shirt shops and guided tours as symptomatic of the ongoing destruction of the distinctive charm and culture of the French Quarter. According to residents, T-shirt shops cater only to tourists, project false representations and stereotypes of the city and its population, and do nothing to enhance residential use-values. Residents assail haunted tours, voodoo tours, and other guided walking tours as neighborhood exploiters who manufacture falsehoods, promote totalizing and stereotypical views of New Orleanians, and transmit asinine stories about the French Quarter. Complaints against rowdy drunks, crowded sidewalks, loud bar music, and pervasive loss of privacy dominate my interviews.

Finally, in recent years, residents have protested the building of a Harrah's hotel and casino on Canal Street. Neighborhood organizations such as the Vieux Carre Property Owners, Residents and Associates (VCPORA) and the French Quarter Citizens view the growth of corporate gaming and casinos as more evidence that city leaders have no genuine concern for the residential nature of the community and are more interested in transforming New Orleans into a contrived Las Vegas–style casino mecca and theme park. Rather than nurture local culture, residents argue, global entertainment corporations like Harrah's tap into and exploit the uniqueness and distinctiveness of the city for their own profiteering interests. In this interpretation, tourism is a corrupting force that plunders local culture and leaves behind a prosaic landscape that is empty of authentic content and communal value.

"Of Space" versus "In Space": Authenticity Struggles as Liminal Practice

It is important to understand, when thinking about tourism and New Orleans, to distinguish between being in the French Quarter and being of the French Quarter. When you think about the House of Blues and the Hard Rock Cafe, you have to remember that these big chains and other large hotels and other firms are in New Orleans but not of New Orleans. That is the big difference, being in some place and being of it. Much the same way that New Orleans is in the USA but not really of the USA, although it is becoming more homogenized like other American cities over time. I have used this phrase many times in the past. New Orleans was once the largest city in the South but not of the South. In the very beginning, New Orleans was anti-American. New Orleans was Catholic and Latin. And that is exactly its charm. That is why people hate us, and love us at the same time.

—French Quarter resident and Mardi Gras float builder[36]

We can interpret the discourse of decline, loss, nostalgia, and exploitation as illustrative of a repertoire of authenticity that residents draw on to claim ownership and thus the power to define the French Quarter culturally. Residents invoke themes of sentimentality and victimization to claim that they, not city leaders or tourism officials, are the "authentic" voice and genuine owners of the community. This discourse accepts the growth of tourism while seeking to contest, negotiate, and control the process of tourism development. Several residents make distinctions between those individuals and business that are "in" the French Quarter but not "of" the French Quarter. Residents invoke this dichotomy to distinguish between those groups and individuals who they view as contributing to the charm and character of the neighborhood versus those who exploit and take advantage of the neighborhood. The dichotomy also operates as framing strategy to affirm collective identity and claim membership in a neighborhood with locally distinctive networks and close friendship ties. Assertions over who is "of" versus "in" the French Quarter reflect conflicts over neighborhood identity and intimate authenticity struggles as liminal practice.

Scholars in diverse fields have used the concept of liminality to refer to ambiguous and ambivalent meanings people assign to geographical sites and social practices that are in influx and upheaval.[37] A liminal space can be a geographical site such as a porch that sits between the private home and public neighborhood; a table at a sidewalk café that occupies a space between a commercial business and a larger public world of the street; and an airport or subway station where everyone is always arriving and departing. Liminality expresses a vocabulary of rupture, discontinuity, and transition. We can view the French Quarter as a liminal space where the commercial space of tourism and corporate entertainment intersects with the residential space of home and neighborhood life. The sentiments of nostalgia, victimization, and exploitation in residents' voices express the volatile currents of tourism expansion and transformation in a fragile neighborhood where the boundaries between home and entertainment are imploding.

Constructing a repertoire of authenticity is neither a process of adaptation to changing social conditions nor a mode of resistance against tourism expansion. To assert that residents are adapting to their changing conditions dismisses the symbolic forces that motivate their decision making and the role of tourism and neighborhood space in anchoring meaning and action. Alternatively, the resistance trope simplifies the agency exercised by residents because it cannot explain why some residents oppose the tourism redevelopment while others are enthusiastic and welcome it. Indeed, a major ingredient in the repertoire of authenticity is the effort by residents to construct and project an image of the French Quarter as an important source of cultural innovation. In interviews, many residents see the French Quarter as the birthplace of many of New Orleans's famous cultural forms, including jazz music and creole architecture. Residents view their neighborhood organizations—for example, the Vieux Carre Property Owners, Residents, and Associates (VCPORA) and the French Quarter Citizens—as carriers of local heritage and culture, a vanguard of authenticity. Neighborhood promotional materials often mention a long list of artists, musicians, and famous writers who were drawn to the area, including William Faulkner, Tennessee Williams, Ernest Hemingway, and F. Scott Fitzgerald, among others. Residents maintain that these famous people contributed to the ambiance and prestige of the neighborhood's culture and heritage.

In addition, some long-time residents see themselves as providing cultural leadership and education to new generations of residents who are moving into the French Quarter. The theme of cultural preservation and empowerment counters marginalization and acts as a galvanizing force to unite residents around a shared identity as custodians of French Quarter culture. Residents view themselves as important agents in telling the story of the history and development of the distinctive neighborhood. They are vividly aware and understand the importance of defining the neighborhood in a way that includes them. By asserting leadership and control over "their" neighborhood, residents seek to define the French Quarter's public image and shape how other people view the area. In this way, residents portray themselves as the authentic voice of the neighborhood and therefore essential to the process of tourism development. As one leader of a French Quarter resident group told me,

> I believe that the residents are the cultural core of what makes the French Quarter charming. We are the people who are keeping the places up which inspires people to have conversations about them. We wash the sidewalks, trim the trees, keep the sidewalks clean, plant the flowers. We are the ones that maintain and preserve the French Quarter.

We are the custodians of the French Quarter that make it a place worth visiting. The tourism industry doesn't do anything but help encourage people to visit. We are the ones that make it possible to have a tourism industry, and tourism would be nothing without us.[38]

To be sure, both tourism and authenticity have different meanings and uses for French Quarter residents. Some residents, especially those who embrace vehement anti-tourism sentiments, are deeply cynical about the residential future of the neighborhood. In this fatalistic view, tourism is akin to a juggernaut of cultural homogenization that is wiping out the charm, character, and distinctiveness that has historically made the French Quarter appealing. Yet it is important to note that cynical sentiments are not monolithic but are varied and contested. They may not represent the French Quarter population as a whole, and they may represent more of a vocal subgroup than a norm. Indeed, many residents I interviewed disagree with the view that tourism breeds negative consequences *in toto*. For some residents, tourism can help foster a sense of uniqueness and encourage a feeling of community pride. In this interpretation, tourism can be a mechanism for promoting and reinforcing local authenticity and identity. Still other residents I interviewed feel that tourism can be an institutional vehicle for showcasing the rich tradition and heritage of the city to other people who live in far away places. "Tourism has forced us to realize that we have something that needs to be saved," according to one resident; "other people have made us realize that we have something valuable, and there's a need to preserve buildings, cemeteries, and culture."[39]

Other residents see tourism as a double-edge sword that can have corrupting effects, while at the same time creating the social conditions to grow and nurture new authenticities. In the following three quotes, local residents reflect on how tourism has affected meanings and conceptions of local authenticity. These people reject totalizing views of tourism as a force of cultural erosion and emphasize the possibilities and positive aspects of tourism. Yet their views are not singular, fixed, or uniform. According to one resident:

I think tourism can help preserve local culture, but it can also destroy local culture. It depends on how it is managed and regulated. Our neighborhoods are a cultural treasure. When you have a historic commercial corridor coming back, then that helps the culture. But it can also be a problem. We can lose our history and culture if we are not careful, they are delicate things and worthy of preserving and cherishing. Not just for us but for our future generations. In a way, tourism is helping us to create more awareness among our residents of their heritage that they may have forgotten. We are building neighborhood pride.[40]

As one leader of a French Quarter resident's group put it:

I think that authenticity matters on its own. Maybe your average visitor does not know it or care, but I think it still matters. Authenticity and interestingness are related. A socially diverse place adds to the texture of the interaction that people have in the neighborhood. Take my block, for example. I like that the people across the street are working people and not day traders. We have different things to talk about because we come from different occupational backgrounds. This is the culture that continues to animate the French Quarter. It is a culture of residential life and community. It is not some place without residents like Disneyland. People who come to New Orleans are interested in authentic experiences. They want to see and experience the city and its cultures and history. We therefore have a financial incentive to make the city more authentic. We have to maintain our authenticity and create new authentic experiences.[41]

Finally, one person who heads a grassroots neighborhood conservation organization told me how he believes local people can appropriate tourism for their own purposes, using tourism for not only preserving local culture but also creating new cultural forms:

There is an element of tourism that corrupts culture and commercializes it. It does all those things, it packages it for tourist consumption. But then if the locals are smart enough, then they can take that product and repackage it and make it authentic. We have plenty of artists who are constantly representing the city in different ways and redefining it through their paintings and art. All the stuff of the city—its art, culture, history, and heritage—becomes recycled again and again to create new things for locals and tourists to see, appreciate, and think about new things. That is what is important. By representing culture and history in new ways, building on the old to create the new, we can create new culture and heritage, and we don't freeze the past in time, as if it is some unchanging and static thing. So, I don't think that we will ever run out of creative ideas.[42]

These voices reveal a nuanced and multifaceted understanding of tourism and provide insight into the tourism from below processes of localization and hybridization. Localization implies efforts by local residents and groups to absorb and transform the generic and standardized products of tourism from above to promote and enhance local authenticity and distinctiveness. Hybridization is a process by which local people use tourism institutions and practices to produce new authenticities and cultural innovations. Localization is evident not only in resident voices but also in the actions of neighborhood coalitions, festival organizers, and other grassroots organizations. For decades, for example, the Spring Fiesta Association has used tours of French Quarter homes, gardens, and a parade to "preserve and share the cultural heritage of New Orleans."[43]

In addition, French Quarter resident groups such as the VCPORA and the French Quarter Citizens have long contested the growth of chain entertainment stores and worked to preserve the historic character and architecture of the neighborhood through overt demonstrations and litigation. Over the years, these neighborhood coalitions have teamed to produce video documentaries and informational programs and to sponsor tours and fund raisers to build solidarity and educate others about the positive benefits and negative consequences of tourism. Moreover, the growth of festival volunteer organizations, such as the French Quarter Festivals, provides insight into how local people harness tourism practices to promote both localization and hybridization, especially in the realm of music. As one leader of the organization told me:

The first French Quarter Festival effort was designed in 1984 to focus on our local culture in New Orleans. That festival was the springboard for what we created next, which was called Creole Christmas, and it evolved into Christmas, New Orleans Style. While the French Quarter Festival was a local event that grew to attract tourists, Christmas, New Orleans Style always started as a tourism event with the hope that locals would appreciate it. Satchmo Summer Fest is the same kind of event. We have all this history, nostalgia, and tradition, and we decided to capitalize on that. We always talked about the need for some sort of event that focused on jazz. Satchmo Summer Fest was an event that not only was about perpetuating the idea that New Orleans is the birthplace of jazz but also [provided] an economic development tool by stimulating tourism. So, all our events have different threads that go through them, but the one continuous thread is that they all focus on New Orleans and our music and food and our people and culture, because we really don't want to be Anywhere, USA.[44]

Held annually in conjunction with the French Quarter Festival, the grassroots New Orleans International Music Colloquium (NOIMC) offers informal presentations, panels, and interviews to "promote and disseminate to the general public, research on New Orleans music and culture." The colloquium includes a variety of music styles and genres, including opera, traditional jazz, gospel, rhythm and blues, brass bands, "and all of the music performed or recorded in New Orleans." More important, the goal of each colloquium is to provide opportunities for local researchers "to describe the origins and development of music" in New Orleans "through their unique local perspective." Here musicians and researchers are instructed to "experience the colloquium and create your own definition of New Orleans music."[45]

Lessons of the French Quarter

Entertainment firms locating on Bourbon Street work to undermine the small-town character of the French Quarter. First, I have problems with large corporations to begin with. I think they are an alternative government with the power they have. Second, I have problems with the homogenization of culture, of cultural life, whether it's strip clubs or whatever. So, we have maybe 200 Larry Flynt Hustler clubs around the country and they are no different from the other. You can get one in Los Angeles, Chicago, Miami, wherever. I find that upsetting and absurd. They spend big bucks on buildings and wipe out the charm and character of old neighborhoods.

—French Quarter resident and property owner since 1976[46]

I am a businessman and I believe in the free market concept. I believe that anybody has a right to be in the French Quarter and do business if they are doing things legally, if they obtain the proper permit; everyone has the same legal access to the same piece of real estate in the same spot. I don't see any reason to keep say the House of Blues out versus Larry Flynt's Hustler Club. I think it is a question of doing your business smarter and being on top of your industry, and being competitive. So, I am not necessarily against large, out-of-state corporations coming into the French Quarter. Again, we are dealing with a free market here.

—French Quarter restaurant owner and resident
since the 1960s[47]

The comments in the preceding section draw attention to the importance of understanding authenticity as plural, conflictual, and contested. Rather than making the case that tourism undermines authenticity, the data and interviews suggest that tourism redefines the discourse of authenticity and helps promote the invention of authenticity. In the case of the French Quarter, past elements of neighborhood authenticity have acquired new meanings and salience in relation to expansion of tourism in New Orleans. Today, the French Quarter is simultaneously real and imagined, organized and authenticated as a distinctive place by tourism practices and cultural representations. While individuals and groups construct their own realities and identities, they are not free to unilaterally pick and chose what significations to include in their definitions of authenticity. "No doubt agents do construct their vision of the world," according to Pierre Bourdieu, "but this construction is carried out under structural constraints."[48] Past conditions, rules, and structures feed forward to constrain present social action, while presenting opportunities to forge new authenticities. Narratives of the past and assertions of authenticity are less about the "history" of the French Quarter itself and more about the construction of present-day neighborhood identities.

Despite their diverse work, early critical descriptions of tourism by Daniel Boorstin, Dean MacCannell, and others conceptualized tourism as a process of cultural erosion and degradation that transforms indigenous and authentic places into saleable items (commodities) devoid of emotional and communal life.[49] Missing from such accounts is an examination of the ways in which assertions of authenticity draw on partial and incomplete conceptions of the past to deal with current problems, conflicts, and struggles. As a fluid and hybrid category, authenticity is fashioned in power struggles of factions and groups to create and control material resources and the contents of collective representation. In this sense, the social construction of authenticity is always marked by dispute and contestation, as different actors engage in narrative manipulation and deploy ideological arguments that draw on the French Quarter's most idealized characterizations. In the case of the French Quarter, authenticity operates as a collective representation which contains vocabularies and symbols that structure residents' abilities to think and act. Thus, the powerful forces of commodification and rationalization that characterize tourism from above do not annihilate local authenticity but cultivate and call forth new conceptions of authenticity that, in turn, mobilize people to reaffirm the uniqueness of place.

One lesson we can learn from the French Quarter is that tourism is not about balancing its "positive" impacts against its "negative" consequences. Much of the tourism policy literature assumes that local communities are "authentic" communities that "suffer" or "benefit" from the development of a tourist infrastructure. In these either/or accounts, tourism becomes an "external" force that "impacts" a community. Lily Hoffman, Susan Fainstein, and Dennis R. Judd, among other urban scholars, have noted that this either/or perspective on tourism ignores the complex matrix of economic, political, cultural, and spatial interactions that constitute the tourism industry.[50] Another problem with the bi-polar "impacts" thesis is that it too often loses sight of everyday social life and the spatial practices that link the lived activity of urban residents with tourism. A lack of critical depth and reflexivity fails to illuminate the contingencies, conflicts, and struggles tied up in notions of tourism influences and local constructions of authenticity. The tourism from above and below heuristic helps us see large-scale social processes and local actions as a dyad acting as an interactive and reciprocal process. To paraphrase Pierre Bourdieu, who focused on the dialectical relationship between objective structures and subjective phenomena, tourism from above constitutes the structural constraints and extralocal processes that constrain local action while providing opportunities for cultural invention and authenticity creation that feed into and define tourism from below.[51]

In this perspective, multiple conflicts and struggles shape the historical development of urban tourism in a variety of unforeseen ways. Processes of tourism from above can encourage the creation of new subcultures, modes of authenticity, and artistic productions that, in turn, serve as cultural fodder to satisfy the voracious appetite of tourism publicity, marketing, and advertising. Indeed, many of the nostalgic tales that French Quarter residents told me have been coopted and commodified into tourist guidebooks and coffee table books. Old stories and nostalgic images of the French Quarter are recycled through the medium of tourism advertising and discourse and are then appropriated by local residents to construct a repertoire of authenticity to challenge marginalization and to contest the power of large corporations over urban space. Tourism images and discourses provide the cultural resources that local people can reappropriate and rework to construct a distinctive repertoire authenticity that they draw on to influence the process of neighborhood redevelopment.

In addition, the active role of French Quarter residents in the construction of authenticity complicates urban theories that describe tourism as tantamount to a process of Disneyization that transforms neighborhoods into ageographical theme parks bereft of real authenticity.[52] During the 1980s and 1990s, many scholars expressed alarm that cities were adopting the features of a Disney theme park—for example, the production of entertainment and spectacle in a controlled and surveilled space–to revitalize urban neighborhoods and commercial spaces. Even in New Orleans, local journalists have waxed nostalgically about the good-old days of the French Quarter before its transformation into a "creole Disneyland" dominated by the production of a fake or phony authenticity.[53] On the one hand, we can view Bourbon Street in the French Quarter as a "tourist bubble," a Disneyesque space where tourists can indulge the city's vice reputation to provide them with exotic experiences.[54] On the other hand, the intensity of debate over tourism and authenticity in the French Quarter reveals a more complex and nuanced picture than that provided by the Disney perspective of cities-as-theme park.

One limitation of the Disneyization perspective is that it uncritically assumes an "authentic" lost past that has been superseded by an inauthentic Disney present dominated by hype, spectacle, and simulation. A second problem with the Disneyization thesis is that it lacks specificity in analyzing how and under what conditions people use tourism institutions and practices to resist homogenizing trends and promote cultural invention, innovation, and authenticity creation. Third, and more broadly, the Disneyization thesis effaces human agency, posits a disconnect between urban spaces and residential practices, and suggests that contemporary urban neighborhoods could not possibly be authentic. Cobbling together different themes, symbols, and motifs to build a repertoire of authenticity is a complex process that reflects local efforts to counter exoticized and stereotypical views of local cultures, reconstruct notions of local heritage, and empower neighborhoods to gain control over redevelopment. In this interpretation, authenticity is contested terrain—a field of competing claims and discourses, where different actors engage in a process of constructing culture within a sociopolitical arena constituted by local power relations and global forces.

Finally, the devastation unleashed by Hurricane Katrina on New Orleans highlights how local constructions of neighborhood authenticity are linked to the production of class and racial segregation. Katrina revealed a profound disconnect between the branded and commodified image of New Orleans as a place of fun and entertainment and the disparaging image of New Orleans as a place of intense poverty and racial segregation. As pointed out, authenticity struggles express conflicts over ownership and control of urban space and illustrate the constructed nature of neighborhood boundaries and identities. Residents' definitions of themselves as custodians of French Quarter authenticity are deeply connected with both tourism development and neighborhood gentrification, the later process being bound up with the growth of class and racial segregation.

The French Quarter and adjacent commercial and residential areas upriver survived major flooding and damage from Hurricane Katrina. The idea of developing areas near the French Quarter as places of profitable commercial and tourist opportunities is moving forward and overshadowing the idea of rebuilding flooded residential spaces, especially high poverty neighborhoods. Since the disaster, major developers such as Donald Trump and others have planned major condominium developments, while Harrah's casino has launched a major expansion of its hotel. In particular, Harrah's has joined with the NOMCVB and city leaders to redevelop the area from the French Quarter to the convention center into an urban entertainment destination anchored by new restaurants, a themed jazz club, upscale bars, and global retail firms. These developments promise to further segment the residential space of the French Quarter from nearby commercial spaces and from surrounding residential neighborhoods with their shadow of segregated poverty. In addition, the use of tourism to attract capital to rebuild New Orleans portends a future of intense conflict between corporate elites and firms versus historic preservationists and neighborhood residents over what constitutes "authentic" New Orleans.

8

"The Greatest Free Show on Earth"

Intimations and Antinomies of Commodification and Carnival

People now go to the parades not to see beautiful floats or interact with others but to see how much they can catch. It has moved from a spectacle to a mall operation. It is a consumer thing. It's like Carnival has become a shopping binge. These longer and longer beads, all these novelties. The krewes are going to enormous lengths to outdo one another in the quantity and now the ingenuity of what is thrown. It used to be a great deal of effort that was put into art and skill to design the floats, now it is neither. All the beauty and uniqueness is gone. And the tourists just don't get it, they don't understand how Carnival has changed for the worse. All they care about is catching beads.

—Carnival historian and float builder[1]

I think visitors help us realize what we have. It is like when someone comes into your house and says, "that is a beautiful picture you have on the wall," and you say, "well, yea, I guess I am so accustomed to it that I had forgotten how beautiful, pretty, and valuable it is." I think, perhaps, that is how residents of New Orleans view Mardi Gras. Not all of them participate in it, and not all of them realize how important it is all the time. But they do when visitors come to town. But we cannot depend on visitors to preserve Mardi Gras, that is our job, not the visitors' job. They may make us realize that what we have is worth preserving, but it is not their job to preserve it.

—Carnival historian[2]

Unfortunately, and in part due to the way the news media has focused on the activities of those who "visit" and go to the French Quarter "after" the parades, it now appears that what many think about when they hear the words "Mardi Gras" are activities occurring in the French Quarter; i.e., flashing women (tourists who are drunk or need attention) and crowd surges (a spring break crowd trying to catch a glimpse)! This is not Mardi Gras. It has absolutely nothing to do with the "real" Mardi Gras celebration. Unfortunately, sex makes more news . . . so every news camera visiting our beautiful city for Mardi Gras heads for the spring break crowd on Bourbon Street . . . and does not give adequate coverage to those who spend thousands of dollars and months of time planning "The Greatest Free Show on Earth!"

—A local resident[3]

This book ends where it began, with Carnival and the Mardi Gras celebration. As reflected in literary, film, and music sources, New Orleans is probably most often identified with Mardi Gras, a celebration that symbolizes the city's joie de vivre while displaying submerged conflicts over race and class. In spite of the devastation caused by Hurricane Katrina, more than fifty parades, walking groups, and other informal processions took to the streets of New Orleans during 2006 to celebrate Carnival. For local leaders, Mardi Gras 2006 was an important statement of the city's strength and fast-paced rebuilding efforts. "Mardi Gras was a smoke signal to the rest of the world that New Orleans is on its way back," proclaimed New Orleans Mayor Ray Nagin.[4] For tribes of Mardi Gras Indians, black men who parade in neighborhoods dressed as Native American warriors, Mardi Gras 2006 revealed to the world that the back of the city's black community was weary but not broken. "After all Katrina destroyed, she couldn't destroy our spirit," mentioned one member of the Red Hawk Hunters tribe. "Though so many of us lost so much, it means a lot to be able to continue this legacy. The black culture is a creative culture, and it's here to stay," according to creole Osceolas Big Chief Clarence Dalcour. "Everybody here needs us to be here, it's what you call tradition."[5] While Hurricane Katrina dealt the city a major blow, local officials proclaimed Mardi Gras 2006 as a symbolic indicator of New Orleans's rebirth. More than 300 news outlets from around the world—including every European country, Russia, Taiwan, Australia, and China—visited New Orleans to report and showcase the Carnival festivities to a global audience.[6]

As New Orleans has changed economically, culturally, and socially over the decades, so has Mardi Gras changed with the times. The past three decades have witnessed a huge expansion in the annual number of parades and Carnival organizations (krewes), the number of visitors that attend Mardi Gras in New Orleans, and the money generated through the celebration. From 1857 to the late 1930s, there were approximately four to six parades per Carnival season in New Orleans. The number of parades grew to ten in 1940, to twenty-one by 1960, and to twenty-five by 1970. In 1973, the pressures of increased float size and swarms of tourists led the city government to pass an ordinance banning parades through the French Quarter, thus ending a 117-year tradition of parades rolling through the historic neighborhood. During the 1970s and 1980s, the number of parades increased dramatically, reaching a peak of fifty-five in 1986 and remaining between forty-five and fifty-three ever since. Local leaders have tracked the estimated economic effect of the celebration since the mid-1980s, and in 2000 overall spending from Mardi Gras hit the $1 billion mark for the first time, according to one economist.[7] "Economically, it is by far the single largest special event," according to Marc Morial, mayor of New Orleans from 1994 to 2002. "It's bigger than Jazzfest, it's bigger than the Sugar Bowl, it's bigger than the Super Bowl."[8] "It's the major annual event for this city," according to Michele Moore, spokesperson for the mayor's office; "we build many of our tourism and marketing strategies around Mardi Gras."[9]

Since 2005, the devastation of Hurricane Katrina has generated new calls to commercialize Mardi Gras and sell the celebration to corporate sponsors as expedients to rebuilding New Orleans. On the one hand, as I have pointed out in other chapters, commercialization has a long history in New Orleans's Mardi Gras. Major corporations have long used Mardi Gras themes in their advertisements to sell their products, and tourism organizations and other boosters have attempted over the years to establish Carnival balls and parades for tourists. On the other hand, residents and leaders have struggled to discourage overt advertising and corporate sponsorship in Mardi Gras in an effort to preserve the uniqueness of the celebration as an indigenous and authentic festival. Over the decades, the noncommercial nature of New Orleans's Mardi Gras has inspired the slogan "the world's greatest free show" to distinguish Carnival from other explicit money-making spectacles in the United States and emphasize the inclusive and localized nature of the festivities. In recent years, however, residents and Carnival leaders have lamented that commercialization has reached a point where it is hollowing out the rich authenticity and distinctiveness of Mardi Gras and transforming the celebration into a contrived tourist attraction that is antagonistic to communal interests and value (fig. 8.1).

The quotes at the beginning of this chapter communicate three different interpretations of Carnival: how it has changed over the years, and what it means to New Orleans residents. All three views express strong feelings and intimate Mardi Gras as a multifacted and contested celebration. Broadly, debates over commercialization and Mardi Gras express disagreements over meanings of authenticity in the city's signature celebration, who owns Carnival, and how should people use and celebrate Carnival to invigorate local culture.

Fig. 8.1, A–F (*opposite*). Since the 1960s, New Orleans's economic and political leaders have looked to Mardi Gras as a strategic marketing device and mega-event to attract tourists, consumption-oriented investment, and international media recognition for the city. Unlike most mega-events, Mardi Gras is not trademarked and is not sponsored by a body outside the city. While the city government does not earn revenue from licensing Mardi Gras, the celebration offers free exposure and publicity for the city through corporate advertising and global media coverage. In spite of its increasing extra-local and globalized character, Mardi Gras continues to exhibit features of an indigenous and localized festival marked by rich emotional ties, longstanding and venerable traditions, and a well-defined culture and historical authenticity. (A) Mardi Gras float den showing artists at work building the floats. It takes artists up to one year to design and construct some Mardi Gras floats that parade in New Orleans. The floats are decorated to depict different themes and almost all parades have at least 15 floats. (Reproduced by permission of the New Orleans Public Library, Louisiana Division and the City Archives). (B) The practice of wearing a mask, known as masking, during the Carnival season is one that dates back to the early Carnival celebrations in Europe. During the early nineteenth century masking was illegal in New Orleans. Today, many krewes follow a code of secrecy and wear masks and costumes to hide the identity of krewe members. Removing your mask during a parade is considered taboo and a cause for membership termination in some older krewes. (Reproduced by permission of Marc Pagani Photography). (C) Costuming and parading are widely practiced and enjoyed in New Orleans during the Carnival season from the Feast of the Epiphany to Fat Tuesday (Mardi Gras). While mass-media coverge of Mardi Gras centers on activities in the French Quarter and on Bourbon Street, Mardi Gras is a widespread festival that takes place on streets and neighborhoods throughout the metropolitan area. This female reveler waves to the crowds on Fat Tuesday, the last day of the Carnival season. (Reproduced by permission of Marc Pagani Photography). (D) Front view of an approaching float from the Krewe of Zulu on Fat Tuesday. Until the mid-1950s, local segregationist laws prohibited the Zulu parade and other African American organizations from traveling on St. Charles and Canal Streets, where the other major krewes paraded. Today, the Krewe of Zulu plays a major role in the annual Mardi Gras celebration. The Zulu King meets the King of Rex on Lundi Gras, and on Fat Tuesday Zulu is the first parade to roll with 30 floats and numerous bands. (Reproduced by permission of Marc Pagani Photography). (E) Zulu Warrior decked out in his elaborate costume. (Reproduced by permission of Marc Pagani Photography). (F) Mardi Gras Indians are groups of mostly African American Carnival revelers who hand-make their own costumes using beads and feathers. They have been parading on the backstreets of New Orleans outside the gaze of most visitors and media publicity for over a century. (Reproduced by permission of Marc Pagani Photography).

A

D

B

E

C

F

Rise of the Super Krewes and the Transformation of Carnival

> People came to Endymion's parade to do more than look. As the most
> generous club in Carnival, krewe members lived up to their motto,
> "Throw until it hurts." Literally, millions of beads, cups, doubloons
> and trinkets [are] tossed . . . no one goes home from an Endymion pa-
> rade empty-handed. Thanks to Bacchus and Endymion, four day hotel
> packages on Carnival weekend became an easy sell, much to the delight
> of tour operators. But Endymion did more than attract tourists and
> provide jobs; it played a major role in the democratization of Mardi
> Gras, opening its doors to some who had been barred from the old-line
> clubs. Endymion's membership represented, then as it does now, a cross
> section, a virtual microcosm of New Orleans, from cab drivers to attor-
> neys, from janitors to U.S. Senators. Without fanfare or fuss, Endymion
> opened its membership to the entire community.
>
> —Endymion Krewe history[10]

The past few decades have seen sweeping changes in the organization of
Carnival and the formation of new global-local connections that link
Mardi Gras with the processes of commodification and rationalization
that define tourism from above. The rise of "super krewes"—huge parades with gigantic and spectacular floats—in the 1960s and later represents a turning point in the history of Carnival. In 1969, the newly
formed Krewe of Bacchus debuted with the largest floats in Carnival
history and introduced several new Carnival traditions, including having a celebrity rider as its king (Danny Kaye) and an elaborate supper
dance with marching jazz bands. Bacchus was founded by local business
owners Owen "Pip" Brennan Jr., other members of the Brennan family
restaurants, and float builder Blaine Kern. Establishment of the super
krewes of Endymion in 1974 and Orpheus in 1998 copied the innovations of Bacchus, and all three krewes launched a new formula for enhancing the tourist appeal of Carnival.

Before the 1960s, Carnival krewes were limited to native-born residents of New Orleans, and membership was considered a rare privilege
and expression of upper-class status. The Krewe of Bacchus broke this
longstanding tradition and opened its membership to nonresidents, inviting business leaders from Houston, Dallas, and Los Angeles to be
members.[11] Unlike the parades of the old-line krewes of Comus, Mo-

mus, Rex, and Proteus, the parades of the super krewes contained hundreds of members, double-decker and tandem floats, and dozens of marching bands. In the nineteenth century, the old-line krewes represented a new form of elite cultural production to attract capital and investment to the city of New Orleans. The super krewes of Bacchus, Endymion, and Orpheus extended this basic impulse to harness Carnival for tourism and heralded the beginning of a new era in which krewes overtly and explicitly attempted to recruit nonlocals and celebrities to make Carnival more spectacular and entertaining.

In the quotes below, two Mardi Gras enthusiasts reflect on the development of the super krewes and note their significance to the dramatic expansion of tourism that takes place in the 1960s and later. According to an editor of popular local magazine,

> Mardi Gras's extension of tourism comes in the late 1960s when a few people within the hospitality industry want to create a spectacular parade that is really different from the standard parades to lure tourists to visit the city. Until 1969, there really wasn't much going on the weekend before Mardi Gras. There were a few parades here and there, but they were kind of insignificant parades. So once Bacchus starts, and it is people within the tourist industry who created this, then you have a new tourist attraction that in effect is creating a three-day weekend— Sunday, Monday, and Tuesday—and justification for tourists staying here longer than they normally would. 1969 is a real watershed in the history of Mardi Gras just as Rex was in 1872. Prior to Rex in 1872, you had two parades, Twelfth Night Revelers and Comus. Those were mainly local parades for locals. Rex obviously had a mission to draw visitors into the community. Bacchus, same thing. I think the guys who started Bacchus and the guys who started Rex earlier are pretty much the same. It is young men who wanted to do something to boost the community.[12]

As a leader of Bacchus told me:

> Back in the 1960s, I helped form a krewe called Bacchus. The whole idea behind Bacchus was to increase the number of tourists to come to Mardi Gras. We saw at Carnival that there weren't quite as many people coming to New Orleans, and we thought of Bacchus as a way to

fill up hotel rooms and the restaurants. We wanted people to come. So, we founded a club that was open to everyone. It was a pretty radical thought at the time. We built the large animated floats, and it was a tremendous success. Our idea was that Mardi Gras could draw in people with wealth and money that could afford the good restaurants, the hotels, and to go back home and sing praises for New Orleans.[13]

These interviews suggest that the super krewe of Bacchus was a new cultural invention to further the development of a tourist-dominated economy. The dramatic and spectacular nature of the parades, combined with the active recruitment of nonlocal and celebrity riders, reflected concerted efforts to rationalize Mardi Gras while creating new avenues for commodifying the celebration. Unlike the old-line krewes, the leaders of Bacchus and later super krewes worked explicitly and systematically with the Greater New Orleans Tourist and Convention Commission (GNOTCC) to attract visitors to the city, thus shifting from accommodating tourists to actively and methodically recruiting tourists. Rather the using literary themes or motifs drawn from traditional Western culture, the super krewes of Bacchus, Endymion, and Orpheus adopted well-known and popular themes such as Disney characters, rock music, Hollywood movies, and television shows as the major themes of their parades (fig. 8.2). The ability of the super krewes and their promotions to increase visitors and deliver entertainment became a major benchmark to judge the "fun factor" of later parades and a formula for evaluating the "success" of New Orleans's Mardi Gras. What was significant was not the originality of super krewes per se but the coherence and concentration of glitz, spectacle, and entertainment in the parade experience. The use of themes drawn from mass culture was a mechanism to achieve the goals of appealing to adults as well as children, distinguishing the super krewes from the old-line krewes, and, more broadly, associating the Mardi Gras "experience" with mass entertainment and consumer culture.

We can interpret the rise of the super krewes as an example of the growth of a touristic culture in New Orleans where tourism imagery and motifs increasingly permeate local culture and provide a symbolic code that different groups use to define and assess local authenticity. Like the formation of the Krewe of Rex in 1872, the super krewes of Bacchus, Endymion, and Orpheus were bellwethers of cultural change that presaged a major transformation in the production and promotion

A

B

Fig. 8.2. The super krewes of (A) Bacchus (formed in 1969) and (B) Endymion (1975) are huge parades containing double-decker and tandem floats. Today, the super krewes together have thousands of members and dozens of super floats in their parades. From the beginning, Bacchus and the other super krewes spent enormous sums of money on their parades, bucking the entrenched old-line krewes, and revolutionizing Carnival. In 1999, Endymion debuted its five tandem float "Captain Eddie's S.S. *Endymion*," containing more than 200 riders and weighing 250 tons. To put this in perspective, there are more riders on one Endymion float today then there used to be in an entire Comus parade in the 1960s. (Reproduced by permission of Marc Pagani Photography)

of Carnival. As forces of cultural innovation, the super krewes usurped the longstanding dominance of the old-line krewes as the cultural authorities and authenticators of Carnival. Critics of the old-line krewes argued that the upper-class pretentiousness and exclusivity of Comus, Momus, and Proteus locked out new entrepreneurs from elite society and culture, and therefore hampered New Orleans's economic development. By providing a new mode of integration and set of relationships —celebrity riders, open dances and balls, and an ideology of nonexclusivity—the super krewes provided a new set of collective representations and vocabulary for understanding and reinterpreting Carnival. The super krewes also became corporate recruiting tools to persuade wealthy business owners to invest in New Orleans. Tourism boosters maintained that Mardi Gras was the "world's greatest free show," while Endymion and other super krewes claimed that they "democraticized" Carnival. Yet the super krewes opened access to Carnival for visitors while denying it to locals who could not afford the exorbitant membership fee and high cost of attending the krewe's ball. In addition, the much heralded democraticization process was really about reinforcing the class insularity and exclusivity of Carnival while creating a new mechanism for the cultural reproduction of class inequality.

The super krewes of Bacchus, Endymion, and Orpheus are major cultural organizations that further enmesh Mardi Gras within an expanding global tourism industry dominated by enhanced spatial flows of people, capital, and new forms of chain entertainment and consumption. Before the 1970s, Mardi Gras was a discrete tourist attraction that the city celebrated for approximately two weeks. By the 1980s, however, Mardi Gras had become a year-round "industry," with hundreds of local residents employed in float building, museums, and the mass production of souvenirs. During these decades, we see the development of a new global network of supply houses and factories to produce and distribute Mardi Gras–themed T-shirts, videos, music, flags, hats, and coffee and beer mugs, among many other products displaying the official Mardi Gras colors of purple, green, and gold. The maturation of this industry takes place in the 1990s as the internet opens a burgeoning market for buying and selling Mardi Gras memorabilia, as well as other New Orleans paraphernalia, commemorative souvenirs, and various trinkets. Today, a handful of factories in China produce most of the Mardi Gras beads imported to the United States. While no official statistics are available, estimates suggest that the bead industry sells $500 million of beads each year worldwide. Workers in China sew the plastic beads for $4.25 a day, or about $85 a month. Local krewes contract with U.S. bead distributors to order customized beads to sell to individual members, who toss the beads from the parade floats.[14] In short, the production of Mardi Gras beads, products, souvenirs, and memorabilia is no longer the province of local craft skills geared toward local consumption; it has been appropriated, reimagined, and retooled for mass production and mass consumption.

The rise of the super krewes and the mobilization of business elites to promote tourism through Carnival are the catalysts for transformation of the local float-building market into a global industry. Today, the New Orleans–based Kern Company is the largest float builder for Mardi Gras and Carnival celebrations throughout the world, netting $20 million in annual revenues from building and maintaining more than 300 floats for forty parades. Once a seasonal business, Kern Studios is now busy year-round, not only for designing floats but also for renting its facilities for Mardi Gras–themed parties. Kern Studios creates sculptures, themed environments, and visual signage for such clients as Paramount Park, Harrah's Casino, MGM Casino, and Circus Casino, among others. Other projects include parades for Disney World in Orlando, Florida; Euro Disney in Paris; Warner Bros.' Movie World theme park in Madrid, Spain; Universal Studios in Barcelona, Spain; Samsung Corp.'s Everland Theme Park in Seoul, South Korea; Parque Espana outside Osaka, Japan; and Disneyland, Tokyo. In the United States, Kern Studios has signed deals to produce parades at the Gasparilla Pirate Fest in Tampa, Florida, Fiesta San Antonio, and Mardi Gras in Galveston, Texas.[15] In 1989, New Orleans float builder Blaine Kern opened Mardi Gras World, which allows people to view costumes, shop for gifts, dress up in Carnival costumes, and "experience Mardi Gras year round" rather than just during a delimited season.

Together, the Kern Companies—Kern Studios, Mardi Gras World, and Blaine Kern Artists—earn about half their annual revenue outside New Orleans. Float building, sculpture, and other art production facilities are now found in Orlando, Florida; Valencia, Spain; and Las Vegas, Nevada. "Mardi Gras has opened up all these doors to us all over the world," according to Barry Kern. "It's our calling card. It's allowed our company to keep getting better people, allowing us to build better facilities, and therefore making Mardi Gras better at home."[16] In short, a key strategy for the Kern Company and other New Orleans tourism businesses is to "globalize the local," which involves exporting Mardi Gras images and New Orleans cultural resources to other areas of the world, creating demand for Mardi Gras products, and stimulating travel to New Orleans to experience the city.

In sum, the transformation of Carnival provides insight into how tourism from above processes are localized and how tourism from below processes are globalized. Arjun Appadurai and Ulf Hannerz suggest that global-level forces do not stand in opposition to local cultural elements but engender selectivity, and agency, creating localized forms of globalization.[17] The mechanisms of this selectivity are local organizations, groups, and social networks that appropriate, redefine, and anchor capital flows and commodity images. Transplanting the global to the local does not involve a wholesale transfer of a coherent and closed system of social relations. Instead, local groups and networks of individuals select partial pieces of the global and adapt extralocal processes such as commodification and rationalization to local contexts. Early Bacchus leaders were embedded in tourism institutions such as the GNOTCC and worked to frame and define Carnival using tourism discourse and visual representations. Yet Bacchus and other super krewe leaders did not adopt tourism modes of visualization and staging in their entirety; instead, they negotiated a compromise between global and local frameworks.

Over the years, leaders and supporters of Bacchus, Endymion, and Orpheus have attempted to authenticate themselves as expressions of local culture by defining their cultural inventions as complements of other Carnival traditions already in place in New Orleans. The combination of a long history of grassroots control over Carnival, antipathy toward overt advertising and commercialization, and a strong network of other neighborhood-based krewes are the local frameworks that have filtered and shaped the local implementation of tourism from above in Carnival. On the one hand, we can view super krewes as institutions of localization and hybridization that embrace and emplace tourism practices to reinforce existing local sentiments and create new meanings of the local. On the other hand, super krewe leaders have worked to reframe Carnival as part of the world of globalized entertainment and tourism consumption, thereby redefining the parameters of local authenticity. In this way, the localization of the tourism from above processes of commodification and rationalization nurtures and promotes the growth of a touristic culture in which tourism discourses and imagery

Fig. 8.3. A woman attempts to expose her breast to persuade a person on a French Quarter balcony to give her beads. Nudity, disrobement, and exhibitionism can be common sights in New Orleans during Mardi Gras, especially in the French Quarter. While some people contend that the practice of "baring breasts for beads" has "always existed" in New Orleans, there is little evidence to suggest that it was a widespread practice before the 1970s. Signs and displays such as "show your tits" and "show your penis" and other sexual slogans have become commercialized on T-shirts, buttons, and a variety of Mardi Gras paraphernalia. The increasing ubiquity and commercialization of nudity and exhibitionism at Mardi Gras mirror the telecasting of the celebration worldwide. Entertainment Tonight, MTV, and the Playboy Channel telecast live reports from New Orleans every year, and camera crews from the BBC, Japan, the Travel channel, and other countries showcase the festivities to a worldwide audience. (Reproduced by permission of Marc Pagani Photography)

increasingly structure and define meanings and assertions of local authenticity (fig. 8.3).

Who Owns Carnival?

The public's desire to leave the old-timers alone may point to the current irrelevance of nineteenth-century caste rituals. Today an increasingly important issue is class. Participating in a krewe is expensive, as is belonging to any private business club in any city. If elite white krewes integrate, they will likely admit people from the black elite of New Orleans. As a member of Rex told me anonymously, "Hell, the [black] guys they'd admit would be better than the whites." Social problems rooted in the city's economic crisis have been increasing since it lost its industrial base in the 1970s. Like the politics of David Duke, another famous product of Louisiana, the Mardi Gras controversy evokes many submerged conflicts in its focus on race.

—*Nation*, April 13, 1992[18]

Over the past few decades, as tourism has come to dominate more areas of social life within New Orleans, Mardi Gras has become a festival of contention, where various residents, elite groups, and city leaders claim to represent the "spirit" and "culture" of the city and duel over competing and contradictory meanings of the city's signature celebration. Exemplary of the conflictual and contested nature of Carnival is the rancorous debate that took place in the early 1990s over efforts to pass an anti-discrimination law that would prohibit Mardi Gras krewes and other Carnival organizations from excluding membership to anyone based on "race, color, sex, sexual orientation, national origin, ancestry, age, physical condition, or disability."[19] Debate began in late 1991, when local civil rights activists and City Council members proposed a bill modeled on a New York City law that banned discrimination in business-oriented private clubs that received public monies and subsidies. In December, the New Orleans City Council voted unanimously to approve an anti-bias law that would deny city services and parade permits, and would require jail time and fines, for krewes and marching clubs that discriminated.[20]

For decades, according to proponents of the ordinance, the old-line krewes of Comus, Momus, and Proteus had been receiving police, fire, and sanitation services during the parades, despite their explicitly segregated and discriminatory policies. "We can't support discrimination or the perception of discrimination," according to Mayor Sidney Barthelemy. Councilwoman Dorothy Mae Taylor, the bill's author and an African American civil rights activist noted, "We close off streets. We deny the taxpayer the right to drive down the street to give a segregated club the opportunity to parade. Now that's unbelievable in 1991."[21] African American leaders celebrated the passage of the ordinance as an important step toward eliminating racism in Mardi Gras, undoing the long-segregated Carnival structure, and democratizing the celebration. Broadly, Mayor Barthelemy and other supporters lauded the passage of the new law for sending a clear message to the world "that New Orleans is an open town and everyone is recognized."[22]

After the passage of ordinance, leaders of sixty-five Carnival krewes and clubs joined to condemn the ordinance, calling the law a "tragic mistake" that would lead to the end of Mardi Gras and the demise of tourism in New Orleans. City Council member Jackie Clarkson complained that the proposal would "kill Mardi Gras" by forcing Carnival krewes to cancel their parades or move them to the suburbs.[23] As debate ensued during 1992, Clarkson and other council members, including Peggy Wilson, recanted their initial support for the ordinance and argued that the law was undermining the fragile black-white coalition that had recently defeated David Duke's racially divisive campaign for Louisiana governor. A *Times-Picayune* editorial lambasted the ordinance as injecting a "new racial anger" that was disastrous for tourism and race relations in city.[24] Opponents of the anti-bias law questioned the timing and motivations of the ordinance, accusing councilwoman Dorothy Mae Taylor and her allies for diverting attention from more pressing social problems such as the eroding economy, poverty, crime, and urban disinvestment. "The city's falling apart, and they go after one of the few things that are still really working," complained float designer Henri Schindler. For Carnival historian Errol Laborde, "We were just getting over the David Duke mess, and this hits. This has turned brother against brother for no good reason at al."[25] Two of the old-line krewes that had been parading since the nineteenth century, the Krewe of Comus and the Knights of Momus, canceled their parades in 1992 rather than comply with the anti-discrimination statute. The Krewe of Proteus later announced that it was canceling its parade in 1993.[26] In response, the African American Krewe of Zulu mocked the decisions of the old-line krewes by displaying banners on its floats such as "Momus Quit, Comus Quit, Zulu's Too Legit to Quit."[27]

The racial animosity and enmity displayed in the heated reaction over the anti-bias law reflected larger political and cultural struggles in the city over meanings and definitions of Mardi Gras and the role of Carnival in challenging and reinforcing social inequalities. These struggles fed into racial debates over who owned Mardi Gras and who had legitimate access to and control over the public space of the parades. African American leaders championed the discrimination ordinance for its potential to expand tourism under a banner of anti-racism and openness.

Members of the old-line krewes argued that the contributions they made to the economic development of the city through tourism and other activities effectively exempted them from government intrusion into their private affairs.[28] These arguments had no legitimacy for African American leaders. "Why is there a need to discriminate," asked Dorothy Mae Taylor in the debate over the passage of the ordinance. "It really saddens me to hear [opponents of the law] boasting of how much money is generated through discriminatory practices."[29] Critics of the anti-bias law maintained that the decision of the three old-line Carnival organizations to cease parading was about maintaining a tradition of anti-commercialism in Mardi Gras and resisting government efforts to control private social clubs. The anti-discrimination ordinance "has opened the way for Carnival becoming a totally commercialized festival rather than an expression of native ethnic culture," lamented *New Orleans Magazine*.[30] "We have lost three old-line organizations in Proteus, Momus, Comus and these were the ones that established tradition and the way things were done," according to Carnival historian Errol Laborde. "They really clung to the tradition of non-commercialism."[31]

The controversy over racial discrimination in Carnival stoked the flames of racial protest and animosity while evoking submerged conflicts over class power in New Orleans. For more than a century, many of the old-line Mardi Gras krewes had been all-white, all-male organizations composed of wealthy business owners who explicitly excluded blacks, women, Jews, and other groups from their membership. For the old-line krewes, the anti-bias law threatened to undermine their power not just to racially discriminate but to meet privately to make decisions about the economic development of the city. These krewes had direct ties to powerful organizations such as the Louisiana and Pickwick Clubs, where important business deals were often planned and decided. *The Nation* reported that the ordinance was an attempt to "crack the code of the old boys' clubs, the private groups controlling much of the decision making" in New Orleans. Critics of New Orleans's elite social clubs argued that their meetings were "the places where the real power in the city is preserved and bestowed."[32]

Proponents of the anti-discrimination ordinance interpreted the measure as a political tool to dismantle the private and secretive nature of the old-line krewes and compel them to divulge their membership lists for public scrutiny. Gaining access to the private spaces and institutions of elite New Orleans society required legal measures to undo class and racial segregation. Marc Morial, son of the city's first black mayor, and himself mayor from 1994 to 2002, noted that the anti-bias ordinance was an outgrowth and extension of the public integration laws of the 1960s. "Thirty years ago, people made arguments that it didn't matter that black people couldn't sit at the same lunch counter as whites," according to Morial. "When people join country clubs, they don't just play golf or go swimming. They discuss business, they discuss politics. They build relationships."[33] More broadly, African American proponents of the law argued that it had a dual purpose of ending racism and challenging the entrenched class power of the white economic elite. "The Mardi Gras issue is only a smoke screen," according to Councilwoman Dorothy Mae Taylor; "there are no crowds of blacks waiting to jump on floats, but they are waiting for a cut of the economic pie."[34]

The acrimonious debate over race and class intersected with gender, raising the question of whether all-male and all-female krewes would be forced to relinquish their gender homogeneity and exclusivity in order to dismantle racial segregation. The longstanding all-female krewes of Iris and Venus vehemently opposed any discrimination ordinance because they recognized that it would undermine their power to exclude men. "We're an all woman krewe, and we want to stay that way," exclaimed Joy Oswald, head of the Krewe of Iris, the oldest of New Orleans's female parading organizations. "This should have just been left alone."[35] For the all-male and all-female krewes, the racial discrimination ordinance was an affront to New Orleans culture and identity. As reported in the *New York Times,* float builder Blaine Kern favored the racial desegregation of the krewes, but as for women, "we don't want them, pure and simple."[36] While the African American Krewe of Zulu supported the anti-discrimination ordinance for its potential to eliminate segregation and racism, members were divided on whether women should be allowed as members. City Councilman James Singleton, a proponent of the law, noted that "I'm in Zulu and I'm still undecided on my feelings about having women in the group."[37]

After two months of intense and divisive debate, in February 1992, the City Council voted to remove the jail sentence provision in the ordinance and shifted the burden of proof onto individuals who maintained that they had been discriminated against if they attempted to join a krewe.[38] In addition, the City Council allowed krewes to remain all-male or all-female and softened the enforcement by requiring the council to dismiss any discrimination complaint against a krewe if the club submitted an affidavit pledging that it did not discriminate. Yet even these watered-down changes could not survive court challenge. In subsequent years, two federal courts declared the ordinance an unconstitutional infringement on First Amendment rights of free association and an unwarranted government interference into the privacy of krewes and other organizations subject to the ordinance. Later, the U.S. Supreme Court refused to hear the city's appeal of the federal court decisions.[39]

The failure of the anti-discrimination ordinance in Mardi Gras provides insight into the intersection of race, class, and gender in investing cultural phenomena with meaning and significance. In previous chapters I have used the concept of racialization to refer to a process of constructing racial identities, meanings, and signification. Racialization is neither uniform nor homogeneous but refers to a range of historically changing ways in which structures and ideas become endowed with racial meanings and significations. In the sociology of race, the work of Michael Omi and Howard Winant, among others, points to the notion of *rearticulation* as representing the construction of new racial ideologies and practices that "both build upon and break away from their cultural and political predecessors."[40] In the case of Carnival, this building upon and breaking away happened through the rearticulation of race with the categories of class and gender. The all-male old-line krewes and all-female krewes formed a powerful alliance that cultivated and disseminated an ideology that defined racial segregation and exclusion as unimportant and irrelevant. A longstanding tradition of philanthropy and support for womens' concerns formed the basis of the female krewes' claims that they had a political "right" to exempt themselves from the anti-discrimination ordinance. Supporters of the all-male elite krewes of Comus, Momus, and Proteus argued that the racial ordinance was a prelude to commercialization that would undermine the longstanding tradition of tableaux balls. Supporters of the anti-discrimination ordinance were divided along gender lines and failed to build cross-race alliances to effectively press their claims and neutralize counterarguments that racism was a non-issue in Carnival. More important, in attending to the racial dimensions of their experience as African Americans, black supporters of the anti-discrimination ordinance allowed blackness to occlude the other axes of identity and experience including gender and class, which opponents tapped into and exploited to control the debate and defeat the ordinance.

As this example illustrates, racialization was coupled with class and gender and involved a rearticulation of race with culture. The exclusive focus on race obscured how racial identities were inflected by and permeated with other experiences and inequalities. In addition, the case of the debate over the anti-bias law shows the hybrid and fragmented meanings of whiteness and blackness in New Orleans. Thus, unlike the period before the1960s, there is not one, fixed ideology of race pivoting along the black-white divide, but a complex spectrum of structures and discriminations that become racialized in different situations and conjunctures. In subsequent years, many krewes opened their membership to women and other krewes, including the Krewe of Rex, invited blacks and other groups to join their ranks. In 1993, jazz musician and local resident Harry Connick Jr. formed the super krewe Orpheus as a gender- and race-mixed krewe. Today, many krewes are integrated and contain both men and women. At the same time, the high cost of joining a krewe and becoming a rider in a parade effectively locks out lower-class people and those who cannot afford to be members.[41] These developments reflect the fluidity and permeability of racial boundaries in New Orleans while also highlighting the multiple and contradictory nature of racial and class inequalities in the city.

Antinomies of Commodification

Mardi Gras has a deep-rooted tradition against commercialization. It goes back many decades, and it is the source of the preservation of Mardi Gras over time. If it was commercial, it would die. Everything else is so corporate these days—Disney, Universal, you name it, it is probably corporate; there is no getting around it. The other major events in the nation, the Macy's Parade, the Rose Bowl, the Super Bowl, all these are inundated with advertising and corporate sponsorship. We actually have something very rare that people can be and are proud of. It is a celebration by the people and for the people, put on by the participants, without commercialization.

—Carnival historian and editor of a local magazine [42]

One of the unique features of Mardi Gras in New Orleans is the prevalence of longstanding cultural traditions that discourage corporate sponsorship and advertising within parades. The City of New Orleans bans advertising on Mardi Gras floats, and the city code stipulates: "No parade shall be of a commercial nature or convey or contain a commercial message, corporate or commercial sign, logo, or symbol. . . . No advertising of any kind shall be displayed or used in any parade." The ordinance also prohibits the throwing of beads that have corporate logos.[43]

Despite New Orleans's ban on advertising, more subtle forms of commodification have emerged in recent years in the city, developments that have generated vehement protest and widespread opposition. In December 1993, Mayor Sidney Barthelemey announced he had hired an Atlanta-based marketing firm, Primedia, to recruit corporate sponsors to license and sell "official" Mardi Gras products. The announcement unleashed a storm of controversy as opponents derided Mayor Barthelemy for attempting to commercialize a local festival and transform it into a corporate-driven tourist attraction.[44] While Barthemey's plan was never implemented, future mayors and political leaders continued to work to license "official" Mardi Gras products, develop marketing and merchandising programs, and sign up corporate Mardi Gras sponsors. In 2005, in response to the devastation of Hurricane Katrina, Mayor C. Ray Nagin and the City Council joined to seek an "official sponsor of Mardi Gras 2006" to pay $2 million to underwrite the cost of police overtime, fire protection, and sanitation during Carnival. Two months later, in February 2006, the city government announced that the trash bag maker Glad Products Company had donated 100,000 trash bags and an unspecified six-figure money donation to assist in hosting Mardi Gras and providing for Hurricane Katrina cleanup efforts. While the city was unable to land a "presenting sponsor" for 2006, the city government is making plans to recruit interested companies to become corporate sponsors in later years.[45]

It is important to recognize the blurred boundaries between commodification and sponsorship in Mardi Gras and the limitations and problems of trying to "market" and "sell" Carnival to corporate sponsors. Unlike festivals that take place in ticketed venues, Mardi Gras is an amorphous celebration that takes place all over the city of New Orleans. No corporation can be the sole or "official" sponsor of Mardi Gras because it is legally impossible to assign them exclusive rights to the event. As a multifaceted and widespread festival, Mardi Gras gives all companies the freedom to be "unofficial" or de facto sponsors and to use public space to sell any type of commodity, souvenir, or item. In addition, the fact that Mardi Gras takes place in public space means that local activities cannot be as thoroughly commodified as festivals that require an admission fee. The logic and success of commodification depend on the rationalization of space, product standardization and packaging, and promotion of economies of scale. Those festivals that lack distinctive local ties and cultural connections are more likely to be transformed into generic spectacles that are dominated by corporate sponsors and the selling of "official" merchandise. As a relatively localized festival, Mardi Gras' complexity and idiosyncratic nature are countervailing forces to the strictly rational and utilitarian pursuit of profit maximization that governs tourism from above. In addition, the lack of predictability and standardization in public space complicates efforts to commodify Mardi Gras and sell the celebration to corporate sponsors.

One subtle form of commodification that has penetrated Mardi Gras is the business of selling memberships and riderships on floats. For many years, local companies have extended invitations to business associates to join their executives, riding in a parade at the company's expense. In recent years, however, non-local businesses have begun organizing special Carnival travel packages for employees, customers, and business prospects that culminate with riding in a parade. The idea is that Mardi Gras can be a site for corporate entertaining to foment or strengthen business relationships and cultivate profit opportunities with other executives. In the Orpheus parade, for example, American Express typically has at least one float, though they do not advertise it. The Sheraton New Orleans Hotel pays all the expenses for an entire float of meeting planners, and the Hotel Inter-Continental owns four slots in Orpheus for corporate entertaining. Companies that sponsor the bands and children's entertainment at the Zulu Social Aid and Pleasure Club Lundi Gras Festival typically are rewarded with spots in the parade.[46] The rise of the internet has established a new means of advertising and soliciting corporate riders. In 2006, internet sites such as www.Mardi GrasNewOrleans.com and www.MardiGrasUnmasked.com, for example, listed parading organizations—Mid-City, Morpheus, Okeanos, Orpheus, Pegasus, Pontchartrain, Pygmalion, Tucks, and Zulu—and the cost to ride in each parade.[47]

The practice of selling float positions has caused much local controversy in recent years, with critics contending that it is an indicator of "creeping commercialism" that prefigures a gradual corporate takeover of the Mardi Gras celebration. Some charge that the practice is a threat to Carnival tradition and that krewes are starting to look more like businesses than social clubs. One long-time Mardi Gras enthusiast and historian laments the marketing and selling of memberships and riderships. As this person put it:

> The term "krewe" has been traditionally applied to social and cultural organizations, clubs in which people were members, and they met frequently throughout the year. But to me some krewes are not really krewes; they are more like businesses and less like social organizations, which is antithetical to everything that Mardi Gras stands for. Some of these krewes are really just profit centers that exist to make money; they are not real krewes, which were created and maintained not for profit but for solidarity, camaraderie, and cheer. You should not have to advertise for riders if you are a real krewe. Krewes that advertise are culturally backward.[48]

Others contend that while some krewes may allow "tourists" to ride on floats, this is not a regular feature, and these "outsiders" typically do not become full-fledged members of the krewes. So, for example, while the Zulu Social Aid and Pleasure Club's parade on Mardi Gras morning includes some 1,200–2,000 riders, only about 200 out of 500 members actually ride. Inviting nonmembers to ride Zulu floats is a common practice for the Zulu Krewe: "Every year our parade is comprised mainly of nonmembers," according to 2006 Zulu President Charles Hamilton. In February 2006, due to the hardship imposed by Hurricane Katrina, Zulu presented a scaled-down version of their parade with about 600 riders, including about 100 members on Fat Tuesday, February 28. In an effort to finance their parade, the krewe offered the general public—men and women—the opportunity to ride in the Zulu parade for a fee of $1,500.[49]

Before Hurricane Katrina, some of the larger krewes argued that they needed corporate riders to fill their positions because the population of New Orleans was not growing and there were not enough people living in the city who were willing to pay the high costs of riding in a parade. This argument has become more compelling with the massive displacement of people by Hurricane Katrina. For the krewes, the advantage of selling riderships to companies is not to find a sponsor to subsidize local riders but to fill all the positions on the floats. Beyond that, companies tend to spend lavishly on beads and buy more tables at a ball. As one person I interviewed put it:

> I don't see corporate involvement in Mardi Gras as an evil, as long as that is not the purpose of the krewe. It should not be a money-making venture. Selling riderships helps to underwrite a spectacular parade. But it has to be done in balance and in good taste. I don't think anyone on the street knows or really cares if the person behind the mask on the float is from New York representing American Express or if they live right down the street. Corporate sponsorship and corporate advertising on floats is an affront to all that is special about Mardi Gras. Corporations have been involved in Mardi Gras for a long time, and it has never been a problem, as long as it is discrete.[50]

Despite complaints against commodification and corporate riders, the residents I interviewed draw a firm distinction between the practice of corporate advertising and the practice of corporate riders. For some residents, corporate advertising on floats is an exploitative practice that portends the erosion of Mardi Gras as an indigenous festival for residents. Indeed, the growth of tourism and the spread of commodification in Mardi Gras have caused some krewes and Mardi Gras traditionalists to call for even more stringent enforcement of anti-commercial statutes to combat trends toward the commercialization of the celebration. This sentiment has become more vocal and widespread in recent years with the legalization of corporate sponsorship and advertising on floats in suburban Jefferson Parish. According to one Mardi Gras historian and publisher of a popular tourist guide book,

> Mardi Gras in Orleans Parish goes back 150 years but the suburban parishes have only existed over the last 30 years. There is a completely different mind set. Jefferson Parish argues that without advertising then some parades would not be able to roll. They say that there is a great need to fund parades through corporate advertising. In New Orleans, we have long had a view, understanding, and philosophy that Mardi Gras is not a corporate affair, it is not about advertising, and it should not be a corporate opportunity. The citizens are the shareholders in

Mardi Gras. And it is a party we pay for and give to ourselves and our guests. There is too much resistance and opposition to the commercialization of Mardi Gras in New Orleans. This resistance is based more on tradition than by law.[51]

Another Mardi Gras enthusiast and author of several books on Carnival had similar feelings. As this person put it:

I think that when most people think of the commercialization of Mardi Gras, they think of parades that have corporate signs and explicit advertising on them. In New Orleans, this is illegal and, to the city's credit, this is fairly well enforced. There have been a lot of groups that have tried to get around it. There was one year where Zulu had cups with a beer logo. There was one year when the Krewe of Ponchartrain had tractors with advertisements from Casino Magic. Jefferson Parish, on the other hand, has just rolled over in the face of commercialization. The suburban parades are just total corporate buyouts. Some of these parades claim they need to have corporate advertisements on the floats to survive. I say this is the subversion of Mardi Gras. I hate to hear what people from out of town think when they see the suburban parades. I say any parade that needs to resort to commercialism to survive should die.[52]

A local artist and float designer views New Orleans culture and tradition as a bulwark against commodification and reflects on the problems some cities have had with hosting Mardi Gras celebrations. As this person sees it,

A couple of years ago a couple of cities tried to stage a Mardi Gras and they had all kinds of trouble, violence and rioting and looting. And a reporter from the *New York Times* called me and he asked, "why do you think these cities had these troubles," and I said, "well, that is easy, because it is not part of their culture." I said, "you cannot just graft on a Mardi Gras." Many of these cities hosted a Mardi Gras to just make money. It was staged and not about the culture of the city. And what they don't understand, especially beer sellers who organized this in different cities, is that Mardi Gras is the culminating day of an entire season that lasts up to two months. It has a momentum of its own. It has a cultural context. I mean we have Ash Wednesday in the city. Mardi

Gras is part of our tradition, part of our culture, and not just a money-making operation.[53]

These quotations express a powerful message of anti-commercialism and resistance to corporate advertising and sponsorship within Mardi Gras. Respondents contrast the anti-commercial tradition of New Orleans's Mardi Gras with the pro-commercial sentiment of suburban parades and Mardi Gras celebrations in other U.S. cities. The persistence and strength of anti-commercialization is also evident in the vehement opposition to the Krewe of America, which openly advertised a $5,500 travel package to New Orleans to ride in a parade in 1998. The parade rolled in 1998 but ceased parading the following year because of public opposition and inability to attract corporate sponsors and riders.[54] The Krewe of America example and my interview data suggest that the critique of corporate influence and advertising in Mardi Gras is less about commodification or commercialism per se and more about how people construct a sense of place and cultural authenticity. Residents view direct and explicit corporate influence as the antithesis of their constructed notions of place and culture. While images of Mardi Gras are advertised in corporate and tourism promotions, they are also used by local people as symbolic representations of New Orleans as a whole. Thus, the opposition to corporate influence in Mardi Gras is part of a broader community effort to reinforce the local specificity of Mardi Gras that, in turn, supports the web of group affiliations that constitute urban culture.[55]

Generally, we can view local attacks against corporate influence in Mardi Gras as organizational strategies for civic action and cultural politics. The elaboration and dissemination of anti-commercial sentiments through local networks and organizations creates a powerful means of group solidarity and motivation for collective action. To discourage corporate influence in Mardi Gras, in 2000, the all-female Krewe of Muses formed with an explicitly local agenda to hold a competition in New Orleans high schools for the design of their annual cups. The case of the Muses signature cup reveals the process of localization whereby local groups and organizations commandeer commodity images, objects, and relations and transform them into expressions of local culture and authenticity. The presentation of "local" in a plastic cup or other souvenirs is not simply a residual, something that has defied global processes. Instead, it is in large part hybrid and emergent and reflects local efforts to rework the tourism from above processes of commodification and standardization to produce new and locally distinctive expressions of culture. Like other forms of regionalism or localism, assertions of the local are not opposed to but are characteristic of the global circulation of commodities and images that define tourism from above. More important, Carnival krewes like Muses are embedded within local aesthetic networks and heritage networks that transmit knowledge, information, and other expressive resources to reinforce local sentiments and enhance place distinctiveness. In addition, local Carnival customs—tableaux balls, krewes, walking clubs, and informal street processions and parades—are the very practices that comprise New Orleans's cultural repertoire or "tool kit" that feed into and support tourism from above.[56]

While some residents castigate the commercialization that tourism has brought to Mardi Gras, others have attempted to appropriate tourism images and practices to maintain old Mardi Gras traditions and create new traditions as a means of preserving local culture and heritage. Many local traditions remain central to New Orleans's Mardi Gras, including the tableaux balls and the Mardi Gras Indians. Other long-standing traditions include the walking or marching clubs that parade on foot throughout the city. These clubs include the Jefferson City Buzzards (founded in 1890), Pete Fountain's Half-Fast Walking Club, Lyons Carnival Club, Corner Carnival Club, Mondo Kayo Social and Marching Club, and the Westbank Social and Marching Club. New traditions that have emerged since the 1980s include the streetcar ride of the Phunny Phorty Phellows, the pet dog Krewe of Barkus, and the satirical Krewe du Vieux, both of which parade in the French Quarter.

Another tradition that has emerged in the past two decades is the tradition of Lundi Gras (Fat Monday). For most of the twentieth century, only one parade (Proteus) rolled on the day before Mardi Gras. In 1987, the City of New Orleans formed a three-way partnership with the Krewe of Rex and the Riverwalk Shopping Mall, created by the Rouse Corporation, to stage a Monday river arrival for the Rex parade. From 1874 to 1917, the leader of Rex arrived in the city by boat, on the Mississippi River. Local residents and the city government revived this tradition in 1987, and in 1993, the Zulu Social Aid and Pleasure Club joined in the tradition with its own celebration in a local park. In the 1990s, the Krewe of Orpheus augmented the Lundi Gras tradition by being the first super krewe to include women, feature local musical talent combined with national celebrities, and have a supper dance open to the public. One local resident claimed credit for helping to establish Lundi Gras, while noting the role of local people in using tourism to build new traditions:

> In 1987, I helped start a new tradition, Lundi Gras, to complement and benefit tourism in the city. Lundi Gras is where the leaders of the Rex parade arrive on the Mississippi River and there are fireworks and celebration. In 1984, we have the World's Fair and we create this infrastructure for future tourism development, including the building where the Rouse Company created the Riverwalk, which was the international pavilion of the World's Fair. So, I went to the Rouse Company and I said, if I can get the Rex people to start arriving again, will you stage the event? They saw the opportunity to advertise with music and fireworks, and they said OK. And then I went to Rex, and I said, look Rouse is going to do all these things, and they agreed to the idea of creating a new Mardi Gras tradition. I said we are going to call it Lundi Gras, which means Fat Monday. This was a new tradition that was added to the tourist package. Then all of a sudden the Orpheus super krewe comes in, and now we have super krewes on Saturday, Sunday, and Monday, and then Rex on Tuesday. So you see, all these parades are designed and staged to attract tourists to New Orleans and to keep them in New Orleans for the weekend and longer.[57]

This comment is illustrative of the nexus of tourism from above and below and draws our attention to the importance of understanding tourism practices and activities as providing opportunities and resources for localized cultural creation, innovation, and hybridization. In this interpretation, the processes of commodification and rationalization that distinguish tourism from above can expand the range of local expressive possibilities and help stimulate the creation of new traditions. The assumption here is that local people and groups can dramatically reconfigure the standardized, banal, and commodified products of the tourism industry in aesthetic practices of tourism from below, in the everyday actions that govern the construction of works of art and culture. To paraphrase sociologist Pierre Bourdieu, tourism is not just a global force but a set of local cultural activities that help frame the *habitus* of social life—the "ensemble of dispositions" and internalized schemes through which people perceive, understand, and evaluate the social world.[58] As a product of individual and collective practices, the *habitus* is the source of regulated cultural improvisation.

In short, the development of tourism has generated new conflicts and struggles over meanings and definitions of Mardi Gras, over who owns and controls Mardi Gras, and how people should advertise and promote the city's signature celebration. The processes of commodification and rationalization that have spread through tourism and culture have motivated local actors and groups to improvise on past traditions and create new ones to fit the constraints and opportunities of the present, the "invention of tradition" in Eric Hobsbawm's classic formulation.[59] Rather than viewing tourism as eroding indigenous cultures, we can view tourism as a set of social practices and images that local groups can put to the service of enhancing Carnival and local culture. What this interpretation suggests is that tourism may offer positive functions in enhancing the resources available for local people and groups to create new definitions of place character and transform meanings of authenticity.

9

Conclusion
The Future of New Orleans

In the conclusion to this book, I return to the three future scenarios introduced in the first chapter and reflect on the role of tourism in the aftermath of Hurricane Katrina and the rebuilding of New Orleans. The following excerpt from the *Times-Picayune* newspaper reveals the striking contrasts between elite perceptions of the recovery process versus ordinary people's struggles to rebuild their homes and neighborhoods. While one group hosts a laudatory reception with fine wine and cuisine, the other group suffers with the misery of devastated homes and neighborhoods:

> New Orleans' recovery from Hurricane Katrina is proceeding on many different tracks. Two sharply contrasting ones were on display Tuesday afternoon at the Sheraton Hotel on Canal Street. On the third floor, scores of residents lined up to tell Mayor Ray Nagin how increasingly hard it is to try to put their lives back together in the ravaged city. Two floors below, an opening reception was under way for the New Orleans Tourism Media Center, a project of the New Orleans Tourism Marketing Corp. designed to help persuade the world that the Crescent City once again is ready for tourists. Back on the third floor, voices rose in anger or cracked with sobs as speaker after speaker told of being unable to find a job at a living wage, of facing imminent eviction from an apartment, of waiting week after week for electricity or gas or a trailer or a return call from a city official. Two floors below, local tourism executives sipped wine and sampled raw oysters, crabmeat, and pumpkin soup, gumbo, shrimp remoulade, and other treats from Galatoire's, Restaurant August, Redfish Grill, and other top local dining spots.[1]

The different meanings and pressures of "recovery" and "rebuilding" are not distributed equally but signify entrenched inequalities and power relations. A variety of opposing constituencies, local as well as national groups, now struggle to frame conditions and shape meanings of "New Orleans" in an effort to legitimate their views of how rebuilding should proceed. As I pointed out in chapter 1, one version of the future views New Orleans as a cultural wasteland, a twenty-first-century Pompeii whose past charm and vibrancy have been lost forever. This interpretation connects the massive displacement of people with an erosion or diminution of culture and heritage. Socially, the networks, organizations, and relationships that used to support cultural improvisation and innovation have been destabilized, and it is not clear what the future holds. Physically, massive flooding of neighborhoods has raised the specter of historically significant homes and buildings facing the wrecking ball as the city attempts to clear land for new development. A second version of post-Katrina New Orleans views the rebuilt city as containing an amalgam of "tourist bubbles" that incorporate the standardized entertainment features of a Disney theme park or Las Vegas–style entertainment destination. In this vision of the future, large corporations will supply the capital to help resurrect a new city of discrete tourist destinations and entertainment spaces to accommodate tourists. Flooded neighborhoods like the Ninth Ward will become commercial centers to anchor the building of new cruise ship terminals, while other neighborhoods will be converted into culturally and ethnically homogenous spaces. A third interpretation views post-Katrina rebuilding as undergirding the creation of new structures and networks to support a phoenix-like rebirth of local culture and identity. In this scenario, networks of grassroots organizations will mobilize people to create new authenticities, reinvent culture, and foster new conceptions of place identity.

Overall, these differing views of New Orleans's future are built on fragmentary and selective interpretations of the past and reflect current struggles over meanings and definitions of race, culture, and authenticity. Indeed, present New Orleans, like all cities, takes on meanings in comparison to what has come before and what might occur in the future. The future scenarios are not complete or coherent but are replete with contradictions and tensions, and they resist unequivocal interpretation. Each view presents competing and conflicting choices, suggests causes and consequences, and prescribes courses of action. Moreover, these three future scenarios are neither exhaustive nor mutually exclusive. The future New Orleans will incorporate elements of all three scenarios and other interpretations, and not be reducible to any one interpretation. Currently, partial combinations of all three scenarios are unfolding in New Orleans, albeit in uneven and paradoxical ways. Asking questions about recovery and rebuilding in the aftermath of Hurricane Katrina means rejecting sweeping generalizations and absolute conclusions about New Orleans's future.

A Cultural Wasteland?

It is unlikely that a future New Orleans will resemble a cultural wasteland of widespread neighborhood abandonment and economic collapse. In the days and weeks following Hurricane Katrina, pundits across the United States foretold of the death of New Orleans and the end of the city as we know it. Yet New Orleans's longstanding status as a major port city along the Mississippi River mitigates against complete disinvestment by the public and private sectors. In addition, a strong national movement and grassroots desire to maintain the distinctive role New Orleans plays in African American politics, culture, and education has overcome early commentary that New Orleans should not be rebuilt.

Nevertheless, Katrina has aggravated conflicts over neighborhood authenticity and social inequality. Several planning commissions and groups have initiated studies and held meetings to identify goals and strategies to rebuild New Orleans. The Urban Land Institute's (ULI) November 2005 report, "A Strategy for Rebuilding," drew intense local criticism for recommending that rebuilding be organized according to "investment zones," based on measures such as historical significance, topography, home ownership, and flood inundation. The Bring New Orleans Back (BNOB) Commission led by Mayor Ray Nagin and a panel of developers and business people formulated recovery recommendations based on the premise that neighborhoods should have to prove themselves self-sufficient and viable to win building permits and city services.[2] Both the ULI and the BNOB reports have exacerbated community tensions, as neighborhoods resisted elite efforts to reinforce patterns of class segregation by deciding in advance where to allocate public resources and channel private investment. The recommendations of the ULI and BNOB did not offer remedies for undoing the deleterious effects of past patterns of class and racial segregation but were proactive in offering suggestions on how to reinforce the status quo.

In addition, planners have adopted a market-centered view that the rebuilding "process is going to define itself" as the repopulation of the city will be left to private choices and individual decisions.[3]

The contested nature of the post-Katrina rebuilding planning process is not confined to the city of New Orleans but spans the region, as racial animosity and class conflict divide the metropolitan area. All neighborhoods have become battlefields of contention as unflooded neighborhoods face new challenges, such as denser population and over-taxed infrastructure, while many flooded areas remain in a state of disrepair. Fears that government agencies will locate substance abuse clinics, homeless shelters, and low-income housing in neighborhoods on higher ground is sparking not-in-my-backyard (NIMBY) movements.[4] In October 2006, the Greater New Orleans Fair Housing Action Center filed a federal lawsuit to overturn a recently enacted suburban St. Bernard Parish ordinance that prohibits homes from being rented to anyone who is not a blood relative of the owner, a measure the suit condemns will "perpetuate segregation" and reinforce the predominantly white character of the parish.[5] That same month, the suburban Jefferson Parish Council passed a resolution objecting to any applications by developers to use federal tax credits to build government-subsidized low-income housing.[6] The U.S. Department of Housing and Urban Development (HUD) has proposed not to rebuild the city's aging public housing developments, thus making it difficult for low-wage earners to return to the city.[7]

Broadly, the discourse of cultural wasteland is an integral component of the urban rebuilding process that reflects diverse efforts to construct New Orleans as a place of unique culture and authenticity, claims that are rooted in a romanticized and idealized conception of the past. Symbols of authentic New Orleans such as ethnically diverse and historic neighborhoods, creole cuisine, rich architecture, and a tradition of musical improvisation are coordinating devices to focus public sentiment on the potential loss of local character and urban distinctiveness. New Orleans boosters and other advocates deploy these and other signs of authenticity to represent a nostalgic New Orleans that is in need of preserving. More important, the rhetoric of cultural wasteland emphasizes the severe threat that neighborhood disinvestment and abandonment poses, not just to New Orleans but to local African American identity and collective memory. Mayor C. Ray Nagin's controversial speech on January 17, 2006 (that God intended New Orleans to rise again as a "chocolate city," which he defined as a "black-majority city") taped into and expressed widespread insecurities that New Orleans was losing its African American culture and racial heritage.[8] At the same time, Nagin's "chocolate city" imagery employed during his Martin Luther King Jr. Day address drew on the themes of melancholy and sentimentality to fabricate a uniform African American authenticity located in a mythical idyll of community solidarity. By defining future New Orleans as an African American city, Nagin attempted to minimize class differences and inequalities within and between racial groups. This community building speech followed earlier attacks against Hispanic workers who had migrated to the city to help in the rebuilding effort: "How do I ensure that New Orleans is not overrun by Mexican workers?"[9]

Nagin's points express broader conflicts and disagreements over meanings of culture and authenticity and reflect underlying inequalities of race and class in New Orleans. Just as Hurricane Katrina revealed and displayed these inequalities, the rebuilding process embodies race and class conflicts, as different groups struggle to reinforce and contest dominant power relations in the Crescent City. Thus, the narrative of cultural wasteland accentuates and arranges situations and events in a larger discourse of nostalgia for the past and illusory community solidarity. Like authenticity, the notion of cultural wasteland may be a fabrication, but in moments of its articulation, it becomes meaningful to people as part of their reality.

A Disneyized New Orleans?

A second interpretation of the future suggests that post-Katrina New Orleans will be sanitized of its past charm and rebranded as a Disneyized city devoid of authenticity and cultural value. Disneyization implies the serial reproduction of themed and controlled entertainment spaces that contain ersatz traditions and simulated cultures. While it is unlikely that New Orleans will be converted into a totally contrived tourist destination, past trajectories of development combined with Katrina-induced problems imply that the future of New Orleans is toward more corporate control over tourism development, increased emphasis on security and surveillance in tourist spaces, and greater use of themes and theming strategies in tourism rebuilding.

In chapter 6, I discussed the mobilization of tourism organizations to rebrand New Orleans as the "most authentic city" in the United States. Over the past year, the New Orleans Metropolitan Convention and Visitors Bureau (NOMCVB) and the New Orleans Tourism Marketing Corporation (NOTMC) have elaborated on their past branding campaigns and created new campaigns to alter people's perceptions and images of New Orleans using brand elements such as new slogans and logos. In chapter 7, I noted recent efforts by Harrah's New Orleans Casino to use its 450-room hotel near the convention center to create an entertainment district to link the French Quarter with the convention center. As pointed out in chapter 8, the city of New Orleans has recently hired a marketing firm to seek sponsors for future Mardi Gras celebrations and to contract with television networks to broadcast Carnival parades nationwide. In September 2006, The U.S. Department of Housing and Urban Development (HUD) approved $28.5 million to distribute to seventeen tourism offices and organizations in Louisiana to promote their venues. State and local tourism officials have earmarked this money to finance a national tourism campaign similar to one used by New York City after the September 11, 2001, disaster.[10] All these developments complement the $185 million that has been spent to repair and improve the Superdome stadium, which reopened in September 2006.

Much of the impetus for the development of tourism in post-Katrina New Orleans involves planning for highly regulated, commodified, and privatized spaces to maximize consumption. On the one hand, urban rebranding and tourism rebuilding aim to present an image of "authentic" New Orleans as clearly demarcated, disconnected, and segregated from flooded neighborhoods. Indeed, promotional efforts depict the French Quarter and other tourist spaces as hermetically sealed enclaves that are safe and crime-free. Tourism officials are seeking to attract new visitors, especially those like Dorothy Washington from Philadelphia, who told a wire-service reporter in July 2006, "Really, I haven't seen any sign of the hurricane or crime. The French Quarter's a whole world to itself."[11]

On the other hand, Katrina has inspired a new industry of "disaster tourism" that involves the circulation of people to flooded neighborhoods in the safety and security of a guided tour bus. Beginning in January 2006, Gray Line New Orleans Bus Tours began offering its "Hurricane Katrina: America's Worst Catastrophe!" tour through devastated neighborhoods. The bus tour presents flooded neighborhoods as spectacular and entertaining sites to visit. Like other tours and place marketing efforts, Gray Line invests ordinary places with the status of tourist attractions that have historical and cultural significance, thereby mobilizing travelers to visit them. New Orleans neighborhoods affected by Katrina are remade into abstract representations, with viewers constituted as consumers and disaster constructed as a consumable spectacle. What is important is that the constitution of flooded neighborhoods as tourist sites reflects conscious and organized efforts to capitalize on the tourist's desire for the dramatic, spectacular, and unusual. Disaster tourism depends on the commodification of leisure and the transformation of tragic events into what John Urry calls objects of the "tourist gaze," where otherwise ordinary places are transformed into exotic attractions that can deliver extraordinary experiences.[12] Katrina bus tours compose New Orleans's urban landscape into a collage of fixed and static images that are marketed and interpreted for tourists.

New Orleans's long history of tourism development, along with the novel pressures of post-Katrina rebuilding, suggests a continuation of past trends toward the blurring of boundaries between tourism and other social activities. Diverse scholars including Chris Rojek, John Urry, Mark Gottdiener, Sharon Zukin, Richard Lloyd, and Terry Nichols Clark have all drawn attention to the centrality of cultural concerns in the transformation of urban economies in the past several decades.[13] I have used the concept "touristic culture" to suggest that tourism modes of visualization, staging, and discourse are now a central part of understanding New Orleans and cannot be bounded off as a discrete activity. On the one hand, touristic culture involves enhanced spatial flows of people, commodities, capital, and cultures. On the other hand, touristic culture is a set of codes or repertoires that structure people's ability to think of places as objects of tourism and to see themselves "as if tourists," who use tourist practices to affirm identities and construct culture.[14]

Indeed, in the coming years, post-Katrina New Orleans may become an exemplary case for the implosion of tourism, culture, and other activities. Katrina did little damage to the extralocal networks, corporations, and chain firms that make up tourism from above. While the hurricane temporarily disrupted flows of people and capital, tourism organizations and entertainment corporations are now working diligently to rebuild their casinos and tourism venues along the Gulf Coast. In addition, local and state tourism officials are capitalizing on the idea of "voluntourism," a term that integrates voluntary service experiences with entertainment-based tourist activities, to attract energetic volunteers from around the world to help with demolition and rebuilding. While the combination of volunteerism and tourism has a long history, tourism organizations are using voluntourism as a major strategy not only to attract volunteer labor to help in the rebuilding effort but also to re-image and brand New Orleans as a resilient city. In this sense, the combination of tourism practices with volunteer activities complicates binary distinctions between "residents" and "tourists" and reflects blurrings between migration processes and tourism.

These points draw attention to the multidimensional and complicated role that tourism practices are playing in the rebuilding process and provide a corrective to the one-sided and reductive conceptions of tourism posited by the Disneyization thesis. As I have shown throughout this book, tourism is an amalgam of conflictual processes that can disempower some groups of people, empower other interests, transform meanings of local authenticity, and create new pressures for local autonomy. On the one hand, the Disneyization thesis draws our attention to tourist attractions and other commodified spectacles as expressions of powerful corporate interests and ideologies that seek to transform the built and social environment of the city into an aesthetic product symbolizing consumption, leisure, and entertainment. The increasing ubiquity of corporate entertainment in the production of urban space provokes fears of standardized sameness and cultural homogenization. Yet these trends are neither inexorable nor unambiguous. Indeed, tourism practices have the potential for creative encounters and can engender a host of unforeseen consequences, including period manifestations of social revolt and political challenge, as we saw with the 1984 Louisiana World Exposition and continue to see with Mardi Gras.

In addition, the tourism from above processes such as Disneyization, urban branding, commodification, and rationalization are not monolithic forces that incapacitate local people, nor do these processes necessarily undermine the capacities for local cultural invention and innovation. Despite the globalized nature of tourism, it is important to remember that entertainment firms, tourism institutions, and social processes are embedded in specific locations, plugged into locally constituted social relationships, networks, and cultural ties. This local embeddedness of tourism suggests that corporate actors and other tourism firms and interests are not free agents to impose their modes of operation on passively accepting cities. In most cases, they are forced to confront local idiosyncracies and long-standing customs and traditions. Such a perspective suggests that the interaction of local actions with tourism from above processes produces unique social phenomena that are not reducible to either the global or the local.

Rather than condemn the processes associated with tourism from above as a threat to authenticity, I have argued for a more complex and nuanced understanding of people's relationship to tourism. Over the years, researchers have eschewed a conception of authenticity as immutable and primordial and examined the process of authentication, focusing on how and under what conditions people make claims for authenticity and the interests that such claims serve.[15] Richard Peterson illustrated the idea of authenticity as a "renewable resource" in his study of the historical development of country music.[16] David Grazian's study of Chicago blues music suggests that authenticity is a fabricated category that people construct and reconstruct all the time to convey the credibility and sincerity of a performance.[17] For Grazian, Chicago's claim as the home of blues music is embedded within the active production of blues culture as a major pillar of the tourist economy. These perspectives are important for their sophisticated examinations of how social structural forces shape and frame assertions of authenticity in the production of culture and tourism.

In the case of New Orleans, authenticity has always been a fluid and hybrid category that is constantly being created again and again as social movements, cultural authorities, and other groups struggle to legitimate selective and idealized perceptions of the city as fixed and immutable. All authenticities are potential victims of what Joseph Schumpeter called "creative destruction."[18] That is, while some past cultural forms have faded and disappeared (the Krewe of NOR children's parade of the 1930s and 1940s), others have emerged in recent decades (African American heritage organizations), and still others remain rich in distinctive content and have undisputed credibility as authentic expressions of local culture (Mardi Gras Indians). Going further, the example of the super krewes revels how a cultural form that was initially viewed as inauthentic by some segments of the local population has, over time, become redefined and recognized as an authentic expression of Carnival.[19]

Broadly, the chapters of this book show that the commodification of local customs, traditions, and cultures through tourism from above transmits symbols, imagery, and discourses that local people can interpret and integrate into their tactics of invention to produce new expressions of local authenticity. From this nuanced point of view, a dynamic feedback relationship exists between tourism and culture, whereby tourism practices and discourses can expand and enrich understandings of particular locales that, in turn, can help stimulate cultural invention that the tourism industry then goes on to commodify. In chapter 3, I note how the planning and staging of the 1884 World's Industrial and Cotton Centennial Exposition mobilized a variety of firms, writers, and grassroots organizations to raise interest in local culture and build global awareness of New Orleans as a place of unique character and charm. In the 1960s, the GNOTCC inaugurated a new era of enhanced place promotion and greater standardization of image production to rationalize the process of tourism development. As I point out in chapter 6, in recent decades, New Orleans tourism organizations have developed a triad of food, music, and history—the holy trinity of New Orleans tourism—to simplify the complexity of urban culture and attract tourists to visit the city.

Moreover, the history of Carnival and Mardi Gras provides an instructive case on how the very activity of the tourism industry in commodifying images and symbols of the celebration can serve to stimulate the reinvention of local traditions. As I discuss in chapter 8, the invented traditions of the Phunny Phorty Phellows, the Krewe of Barkus, the Krewe du Vieux, and Lundi Gras are not arbitrary, capricious, or spontaneous creations. Neither are these cultural traditions planned, strategic, and intentional acts of organized resistance against tourism. To paraphrase Karl Marx, local people create their own traditions but not under circumstances chosen by themselves.[20] On the level of the capacities of local actors, the homogenizing and standardizing forces of tourism from above are embedded in the practical consciousness of residents and provide the stocks of knowledge they draw on to produce new cultural forms.

In this book, I point out that the ability to create and deploy images of New Orleans through advertising and tourist promotions are mechanisms of asserting cultural and political power: "the power to impose a visual frame becomes the power to define a public culture," as sociologist Sharon Zukin argues.[21] Specifically, the triad of food, music, and history that constitutes the holy trinity of New Orleans tourism is part of a larger tourism discourse of "diversity talk" that trumpets multiculturalism and ethnic heterogeneity, recognizing ethnic differences in a formal and abstract manner, but denying the specificity of social inequality and marginalized group experiences. Here terms such as "diversity," "culture," and "ethnicity" have a great deal of symbolic value and utility for New Orleans and other cities. Their use does not rule out any particular group, and they can refer to almost any artistic or entertaining activity associated with tourism.

More important, the terms "culture" and "ethnicity" are not actively resisted by consumers and tourists, and, at the same time, they do not carry the negative connotation that the term "race" has for many people. Indeed, "race" signifies inequality, oppression, domination and subordination. In contrast, place marketers deploy the terms "diversity," "ethnicity," and "culture" to create the impression that New Orleans is both nonhierarchical and egalitarian. Indeed, the proliferation of these terms, combined with the absence of race in tourism discourse suggests a political logic to the practice of tourism marketing. What the local tourism industry seeks to promote is a simulated or ersatz culture and ethnicity of no offense.[22] Tourism discourses highlight ethnic differences and diversity while ignoring social divisions, conflicts, and struggles. Thus, whether ethnic and cultural differences are "authentic" or not is irrelevant, for tourism marketing seeks to efface social categories and identities of all meaning except the signification of pleasure. The decontextualization of ethnicity and culture in tourism promotion is not accidental or happenstance. Which cultures or ethnic identities are marketed, how they are marketed, and who the promotional images are targeted to reflect profit considerations and elite conceptions of urban reality and life.

The themes of food, music, and history so prevalent in urban branding and niche marketing aim to project an image of cohesion and harmony among the disparate (and potentially divisive) classes and races, while at the same time enshrining local authenticity in a colorblind discourse that eradicates critical readings of the urban landscape. Moreover, this colorblind tourism discourse and marketing strategy operates to promote an image of African Americans as a multifarious category composed of diverse and hybrid cultures. We see this hybridization process in the decisions by city leaders in 1999 to change the name of the New Orleans Black Tourism Network (BTN) to the New Orleans Multicultural Tourism Network (NOMTN). This name change follows a decision made in 1997 by the Preservation Resource Center (PRC),

New Orleans's main historic preservation organization, to rename the African American Heritage Preservation Council to the Ethnic Heritage Preservation Program. These transformations continue the longstanding promotion of "diversity" in tourism images and discourses about New Orleans culture by characterizing New Orleans's African American people as an ethnic group.

Although multiculturalism and diversity bring narrative coherence to tourism discourses and practices by celebrating ethnic pluralism, these same themes symbolize larger contradictions and tensions over race and culture. Several points are important. First, the increasing prevalence of multiculturalism and diversity talk reflects the erosion of explicit and legally sanctioned racism and the emergence of a less stable and less rigid system of racial classification. Second, the language of multiculturalism reflects profiteering motives to expand the range of images and meanings of local culture and tap into more and more niche markets of tourists and consumers. Third, the tendency to define all ethnic and cultural differences as equal, horizontal, and plural obscures the continuing significance of class and race as major organizing principles of cities. The objective is to affirm in the minds of tourists (and residents) the harmonious mix of races, classes, and ethnic groups in New Orleans so as to make internal class and racial divisions less apparent. As a result, the themes of diversity and multiculturalism are a polite and euphemistic way of affirming and reinforcing unequal power relationships.

A Cultural Renaissance?

A third future scenario suggests that post-Katrina rebuilding will help to foster a new appreciation and rebirth of local culture to mobilize people to create new bases of urban authenticity. Despite appearances of disarray and confusion in the rebuilding process, many local cultural organizations have mobilized and joined together to re-create a sense of local identity and to fashion new repertoires of authenticity. The New Orleans Jazz and Heritage Foundation continues to be active in working with other grassroots cultural organizations and neighborhood coalitions to build a nationally based network of jazz-presenting organizations to commission new works, provide support for artists' residences, and build endowments that support and build jazz programming.[23] These efforts complement the foundation's longstanding efforts to organize Neighborhood Free Street Festivals, which use proceeds from the Jazz and Heritage Festival to produce free mini-jazzfests in communities across New Orleans throughout the year.

Other organizations such as the Urban Conservancy and local businesses have banded to launch "Stay Local!," a city-wide initiative for enhancing the local economy by creating a network of locally owned and operated businesses in New Orleans. The Urban Conservancy partners with local community radio stations like WWOZ to encourage consumers to shop locally, support independent businesses through an online directory, and provide information to people to build public awareness and interest in local culture.[24] Groups like the Urban Conservancy do not view tourism as an ancillary concern in their activist efforts to rebuild New Orleans. As one member told me, "I guess I think anything that helps maintain a certain authenticity of the culture could be linked into the tourism industry. But our focus is for the people who live here and making viable communities and neighborhoods. Of course, that would benefit tourists and anyone that comes to visit."[25]

Cultural organizations like the New Orleans Jazz and Heritage Foundation and the Urban Conservancy are embedded within a variety of information flows and resource networks—aesthetic, residential, heritage, and media—that circulate different collective representations of New Orleans that people use to construct notions of place identity and urban distinctiveness. Other organizations such as the Arts Council of New Orleans, the Preservation Resource Center, Save Our Cemeteries, and the different Carnival krewes, among other local groups, are agents of localization and hybridization. As noted in past chapters, the networks associated with tourism from below contain a multiplicity of local meaning-making agents that construct different local authenticities. Since the 1980s, for example, African American leaders have established specialized tourism organizations and historic preservationist groups to bring awareness to the African American community as an important contributor to the development of New Orleans culture. Organizations such as the New Orleans Multicultural Tourism Network (NOMTN) and the Preservation Resource Council's (PRC) Ethnic Heritage Preservation Program construct notions of ethnic heritage that frame New Orleans's black community as populated by cultural innovators, unconstrained by past forms of racial discrimination, and economically and culturally independent of white control.

Ethnic heritage tourism aims to fabricate an idealized vision of local history and culture, distract visitors from the city's less appealing qualities, and distinguish New Orleans's African American heritage from rival cities.[26] In addition, these organizations and programs work to portray African Americans and other ethnic groups as essential to the process of post-Katrina reconstruction and frame heritage tourism as important to every member of New Orleans's minority community. In these and other cases, tourism boosters and others draw on a deep historical reservoir of narratives and cultural imagery, collective memories, and mnemonic devices to construct an "authentic" New Orleans, motivate a sense of belonging, and define a common purpose.

Social constructions and discourses about "authentic" New Orleans are always multivocal and mix up different themes, narratives, and vocabularies, a process that reflects what Gerald Suttles called the "cumulative texture of local urban culture."[27] As an interpretive system, urban culture designates the belief systems, art, music, customs, and traditions that constitute local notions of authenticity. Yet present constructions of local culture are not simply a historical residual, a set of meanings and traditions inherited from the past. Rather, people construct culture by appropriating images and symbols from the past, discarding others, and adding new ones. Such a perspective resonates with Ann Swidler's cultural tool kit imagery and Joane Nagel's shopping cart metaphor, while drawing attention to how constructions of culture and authenticity are an integral component of doing tourism. Swidler argues that people use the cultural tools in their tool kits to fashion identities and create social bonds.[28] For Nagel, we not only use tools already in the kit but we also determine its contents by "picking and choosing items from the shelves of the past and present."[29] Culture becomes the things we put into the cart, including symbols, myths, customs, dress, norms, beliefs, and rituals.

Much of what appears in New Orleans's cultural tool kit or shopping cart has been created and transformed through people's engagement with tourism practices, imagery, and discourses. Doing tourism involves an array of practices, including the production of nostalgia; the mobilization of collective memories and heroic imagery; the asetheticization and theming of space; and the circulation of people to particular places to consume culture, history, nature, and otherness. Today, tourism, culture, and authenticity are all blurred, with similar vocabularies, symbols, imagery, and interpretive systems. Indeed, researchers are missing a large part of the picture if they attempt to analyze urban culture as a clearly bounded entity that is conceptually separate and analytically distinct from tourism.

Overall, the historical account I offer in this book suggests that the dramatic expansion of tourism and the intensification of government and corporate efforts to commodify place and culture in New Orleans have triggered an explosion of authenticities over the past several decades.[30] These authenticities are embedded within discourses about racial and ethnic identities, culture and heritage, and struggles over access to and control over political and economic resources. Culture and history are the substance of tourism and are often intertwined in people's constructions of "authentic" New Orleans. As I suggest in other chapters, constructions of authenticity can serve as a bridge not only to sustain current network connections but also to create new ones. This is because the creation and reproduction of different networks facilitates the social interactions and information exchanges necessary for the formation of social identities and localized cultural creations (e.g., cuisine, music, art).

Today, different networks associated with tourism from below are the incubators, storehouses, and transmitters of different meanings of "authentic" New Orleans. Networks are regularized and patterned interactions between different actors and organizations that reflect and reproduce the "connective tissues" through which people make contact, create cultural meanings, and convey information—including flows of information and symbols embedded in tourism discourses—to reinforce place differences, maintain local character, and create new forms of local uniqueness.[31] As the demographic consequences of the displacement of tens of thousands of people unfold, different groups and organizations will likely appropriate a variety of nostalgic myths, symbols, and images about New Orleans to create new meanings of local culture and authenticity.[32] These discourses and information flows will be the cultural raw material that will feed tourism from below and provide the expressive resources that local people will draw on to enhance place distinctiveness, contest marginalization, and challenge dominant power relations.

Rather than providing the reader with a series of answers, I end this book by elaborating starting points and questions to guide future research on the connections among culture and tourism in post-Katrina New Orleans. The tourism from above and below heuristic suggests that the creation of a multiplicity of authenticities and urban representations reflects a symbolic world of meanings about tourism and its positive features and negative consequences. As in the past, collective struggles over meanings and definitions of local authenticity will shape and constrain the development of tourism in the New Orleans. At the same time, the conflicts over the development of tourism in the post-Katrina years will pressure local actors and groups to improvise on past conceptions of authenticity and create new ones to fit the constraints and opportunities of the present. More generally, I suggest that future constructions of authentic New Orleans will emerge not as indicators of a cultural renaissance or symbols of community solidarity but as collective representations that seek to make more lucid and comprehensible a city's conflicting conceptions of itself and its past.

Will we see the emergence of new forms of racial animosity, signification, and authentication? Will racial categories fade in importance as new ethnic groups migrate into the city, or will race continue to operate as a system of social stratification? How will tourism practices shape the production of local knowledge, including revisions of the past, the mobilization of collective memories, and the construction of new cultural forms? How will assertions of place identity, including those that make claims about a primordial and immutable New Orleans under assault from a feared global homogeneity, configure with a broad-based touristic culture? Is it possible that present-day objects and sites deemed as culturally perverse and inauthentic (chain entertainment firms, French Quarter T-shirt shops, etc.) may someday be redefined as authentic expressions of New Orleans? How will the unique mobilities, immobilities, and diasporas generated by Hurricane Katrina alter interpretations of New Orleans's history and culture? Will displaced individuals and groups construct new meanings and assertions of "authentic" New Orleans in other places? Finally, how will new migrations of people and groups transform New Orleans as they create new social relations, new ways of living, and new assertions of place distinctiveness?

Notes

NOTES TO CHAPTER I

1. John Logan, "The Impact of Katrina: Race and Class in Storm Damaged Neighborhoods," at http://www.s4.brown.edu/katrina/report.pdf (accessed May 10, 2006).

2. Anne Rice, "Do You Know What It Means to Lose New Orleans?" *New York Times* (September 4, 2005), 11.

3. Quoted in Jeff Turrentine, "A City's Heritage, Reflected at Home; Creole Cottages, Shotgun Doubles," *Washington Post* (September 8, 2005), 1.

4. Kirk Johnson, "Where Musical Refugees Can Thicken the Gumbo," *New York Times* (September 15, 2005), E1; John Schwartz, "Archeologist in New Orleans Finds a Way to Help the Living," *New York Times* (January 3, 2006), 1.

5. Eugene Robinson, "Requiem for the Crescent City," *Washington Post* (January 13, 2006), A21.

6. Quoted in William Porter, "Resurrecting a City's Spirit," *Denver Post* (September 23, 2005), 1.

7. Quoted in Manuel Roig-Franzia, "A City Fears for Its Soul: New Orleans Worries That Its Unique Culture May Be Lost," *Washington Post* (February 3, 2006), A1.

8. Quoted in Porter, "Resurrecting a City's Spirit," 1.

9. Ibid.

10. Quoted in Jeff Donn, "La. Evacuation May Weaken Gumbo Flavor," *Times-Picayune* (November 7, 2005), B7.

11. "Welcome to New Orleans," *Times-Picayune* (March 20, 2002), 6.

12. Quoted in Porter, "Resurrecting a City's Spirit," 2–4.

13. Dean MacCannell, *Empty Meeting Grounds: The Tourist Papers* (New York: Routledge, 1992); Dean MacCannell, *The Tourist: A New Theory of the Leisure Class* (New York: Schocken, 1976); Dean MacCannell, "Staged Authenticity: Arrangements of Social Space in Tourist Settings," *American Journal of Sociology* 79 (1973) 3: 589–603.

14. For analyses and overviews of the socially constructed nature of race and ethnicity, see Kevin Fox Gotham, *Race, Real Estate, and Uneven Development: The Kansas City Experience, 1900–2000* (Albany: State University of

New York Press, 2002); Joane Nagel, *Race, Ethnicity, and Sexuality: Intimate Intersections, Forbidden Frontiers* (New York: Oxford University Press, 2003); Michael Omi and Howard Winant, *Racial Formation in the United States: From the 1960s to the 1980s*, second edition (New York: Routledge, 1994); Eduardo Bonilla-Silva, *White Supremacy and Racism in the Post-Civil Rights Era* (Boulder, Colo.: L. Rienner, 2001).

15. For insightful analyses of the socially constructed nature of authenticity, see David Grazian, *Blue Chicago: The Search for Authenticity in Urban Blues Clubs* (Chicago: University of Chicago Press, 2003); Richard Peterson, *Creating Country Music, Fabricating Authenticity* (Chicago: University of Chicago Press, 1997).

16. I use the term "discourse" to refer to combinations of collective representations, narratives, ideologies, stories, and other signifying practices that people use to construct and reproduce reality, understand their situation, and enact those understandings through behavior and action. Discourses guide social actions and are realized through social practices. Tourism "practices" can include the socialization of locals to view their hometown as a tourist site, the aestheticization of space, the construction and production of nostalgia, and the idealization of place. In this sense, tourism discourses and practices are multidimensional and can include forms of migration and mobility, flows of people and commodities, and different modes of consumption. In addition, tourism discourses and practices are about the production of cultural difference and the valorization of local authenticity to stimulate people to visit a place to consume its distinct characteristics including, for example, history, cuisine, music, culture, identities, and so on. For overviews of tourism discourses and practices, see Jane C. Desmond, *Staging Tourism: Bodies on Display from Waikiki to Sea World* (Chicago: University of Chicago Press, 1999); Adrian Franklin and Mike Crang, "The Trouble with Tourism and Travel Theory," *Tourist Studies* 1 (2001): 5–22; Mimi Sheller and John Urry (editors), *Tourism Mobilities: Places to Play, Places in Play* (New York: Routledge, 2004).

17. Catherine Cocks, *Doing the Town: The Rise of Urban Tourism in the United States, 1850–1915* (Berkeley: University of California Press, 2001); Desmond, *Staging Tourism*; Harvey Newman, *Southern Hospitality: Tourism and the Growth of Atlanta* (Tuscaloosa: University of Alabama Press, 1999); Hal Rothman, *Devil's Bargains: Tourism in the Twentieth-Century American West* (Lawrence: University Press of Kansas, 1998); John F. Sears, *Sacred Places: American Tourist Attractions in the Nineteenth Century* (Oxford: Oxford University Press, 1989); Marguerite S. Shaffer, *See America First: Tourism and National Identity, 1905–1930* (Washington, D.C.: Smithsonian Institution, 2001).

18. The view that tourism contaminates or degrades a "pure" and "authentic" culture and place is shared by many scholars in a variety of disciplines. For oft-cited classical works, see Daniel Boorstin, *The Image: A Guide to Pseudo-*

Events in America (New York: Harper and Row, 1964); Guy Debord, *The Society of the Spectacle,* translated by Donald Nicholson-Smith (New York: Zone Books, 1994). For more recent discussions and overviews of the connection between tourism and cultural erosion, see Gerry Kearns and Chris Philo (editors), *Selling Places: The City as Cultural Capital, Past and Present* (Oxford: Pergamon, 1993); Nezar Alsayyad (editor), *Consuming Tradition, Manufacturing Heritage: Global Norms and Urban Forms in the Age of Tourism* (London: Routledge, 2001); G. Llewellyn Watson, and Joseph P. Kopachevsky, "Interpretations of Tourism as Commodity," *Annals of Tourism Research* 21 (1994): 643–60; D. Greenwood, "Culture by the Pound: An Anthropological Perspective on Tourism as Cultural Commoditization," in *Hosts and Guests: The Anthropology of Tourism,* edited by V. Smith (Philadelphia: University of Pennsylvania, 1997), 129–39. For critical evaluations of the cultural degradation argument in tourism, see Robert Shepherd, "Commodification, Culture, and Tourism," *Tourist Studies* 2 (2002): 183–201; Susan S. Fainstein and David Gladstone, "Evaluating Urban Tourism," in *The Tourist City,* edited by Dennis R. Judd and Susan S. Fainstein (New Haven, Conn.: Yale University Press, 1999), 21–34.

19. The celebratory account of tourism as enhancing cultural awareness of diverse peoples, promoting democracy, and discouraging ethnocentrism is shared by scholars in a variety of disciplines but is most apparent in tourism industry-sponsored research. To the extent that tourism studies tend to internalize industry priorities and approaches, existing research does not have the theoretical tools or conceptual devices to adequately investigate or analyze the complex socioeconomic and cultural processes that have evolved in recent decades. For critiques and overviews, see Kevin Meethan, *Tourism in Global Society: Place, Culture, and Consumption* (New York: Palgrave, 2001); C. Michael Hall, Allan M. Williams, and Alan A. Lew (editors), *A Companion to Tourism* (New York: Blackwell, 2004).

20. The literature on the growth of Disneyization is vast. For general overviews, see essays in Michael Sorkin (editor), *Variations on a Theme Park: The New American City and the End of Public Space* (New York: Hill and Wang, 1992); Alan Bryman, "Disneyization of Society," *Sociological Review* 47 (1999): 25–47; Alan Bryman, *The Disneyization of Society* (Thousand Oaks, Calif.: Sage, 2004); Alexander J. Reichl, *Reconstructing Times Square: Politics and Culture in Urban Development* (Lawrence: University Press of Kansas, 1999). "Theming" refers to the increasing dominance of entertainment venues across the world according to a scripted theme or idea, such as an Irish pub, a jazz club, or a Las Vegas–style casino. For overviews and critical analyses of theming, see Mark Gottdiener, *Theming of America: Dreams, Visions, and Commercial Spaces,* second edition (Boulder, Colo.: Westview, 2001); Paul Chatterton and Robert Hollands, *Urban Nightscapes: Youth Cultures, Pleasure Spaces, and Corporate Power* (London: Routledge, 2003).

21. Like research on Disneyization, the literature on urban branding is vast and growing. For a critical overview and analysis, see Miriam Greenberg, "Branding Cities: A Social History of the Urban Lifestyle Magazine," *Urban Affairs Review* 36(2) (November 2000): 228–262; Miriam Greenberg, "The Limits of Branding: The World Trade Center, Fiscal Crisis, and the Marketing of Recovery," *International Journal of Urban and Regional Research* 27(22) (June 2003): 386–416; Miriam Greenberg, *Branding New York* (New York: Routledge, forthcoming, 2008).

22. For overviews of glocalization and related terms, see Arjun Appadurai, *Modernity at Large: Cultural Dimensions of Globalization* (Minneapolis: University of Minnesota Press, 1996); John Tomlinson, *Globalization and Culture* (Chicago: University of Chicago Press, 1996); Roland Robertson, *Globalization: Social Theory and Global Culture* (Thousand Oaks, Calif.: Sage, 1996); George Ritzer, *The Globalization of Nothing* (Thousand Oaks, Calif.: Pine Forge, 2004).

23. N. G. Canclini, *Hybrid Cultures: Strategies of Entering and Leaving Modernity* (Minneapolis: University of Minneapolis Press, 1995); Ulf Hannerz, *Cultural Complexity* (New York: Columbia University Press, 1992); Mike Featherstone, Scott Lash, and Roland Robertson (editors), *Global Modernities* (Thousand Oaks, Calif.: Sage, 1995); Marwan M. Kraidy, *Hybridity, or the Cultural Logic of Globalization* (Philadelphia: Temple University Press, 2005).

24. "Structures" refer to norms, rules, and laws that constrain and enable individual behavior and collective action; define informal and informal activity; and coordinate the movement of commodities, money, people, and information across space and time. "Networks" refer to regularized patterned interactions and resource flows between different groups and organizations, government agencies, corporate firms, and forms of activity. The different networks listed under "tourism from above" are extralocal networks that have national and global reach through flows of information, capital, and commodities. *Public-private networks* draw our attention to policies, government agencies, and corporate structures that mobilize tourism investment and regulate tourism flows at the local, national, and international levels. The networks listed under "tourism from below" tend to be regionally or locally based networks that create and transmit cultural representations, local knowledge, and information and coordinate financial flows. *Aesthetic networks*, for example, aim to create and reinforce values and meanings about local cultural products, preserve existing modes of cultural expression, and foster new expressions of authenticity. Cultural organizations and schools of art, music, and cuisine, for example, seek to involve people in cultural activities, secure recognition and funds to achieve cultural goals, and increase access to cultural opportunities. *Neighborhood networks* are comprised of neighborhood coalitions and other resident associations dedicated to raising awareness of local culture and forging a community identity. *Heritage networks* work to represent and reconstruct local history and

identify places, people, and practices deemed historically significant. *Media networks* are amalgams of media organizations that are involved in the production and transmission of images, symbols, and representations of local traditions, norms, and sensibilities. Structures, networks, and organizations shape the actions and decisions of specific actors as they seek to accommodate, challenge, contest, and implement the processes of tourism from above and below. For overviews of network analysis, see Manuel Castells, *The Rise of the Network Society* (Cambridge, Mass.: Blackwell, 1996); Manuel Castells, "Materials for an Exploratory Theory of the Network Society," *British Journal of Sociology* 51 (January/March 2001): 5–24; Barry Wellman, "Network Analysis: Some Basic Principles," *Sociological Theory* 1 (1983): 155–200; Barry Wellman, "The Community Question: The Intimate Networks of East Yonkers," *American Journal of Sociology* 84 (March 1979): 1201–31.

25. To be sure, not all organizations listed under tourism from below stand in opposition to tourism from above. Some nonprofit art organizations like the Community Arts Center, the Arts Council of New Orleans, and the Jazz and Heritage Foundation rely on corporate support and view themselves as agents that leverage local culture for economic development and tourism growth. City government agencies and departments that specialize in tourism promotion stand at the nexus of tourism from above and below. While some agencies seek to encourage the commodification and rationalization of culture and space for tourist consumption, others help promote localization and cultural hybridization through their sponsorship of festivals and institutional links with local music clubs. In recent years, for example, the New Orleans Mayor's Office of Economic Development and Office of Music Business Development have sponsored the MO' Fest and established formal connections with Tipitina's music club to promote local music (see http://www.cityofno.com). Just as extralocal organizations and networks associated with tourism from above can encourage localization and hybridization, grassroots groups from below can promote commodification and embrace rationalized organization and technology to achieve their goals. Moreover, even as cultural products (like jazz music and Mardi Gras beads) have become globalized and rationalized commodities, they still retain their deep cultural meaning for local people as signifiers of local authenticity.

26. In addition, I explore the ways in which local groups and individuals have appropriated tourist images and representations to promote the "invention of tradition." According to Eric Hobsbawm, "invented traditions" are created through rituals, rules, activities, and the use of historically loaded symbols, imagery, and motifs that "establish continuity with a suitable past." Such a conception breaks with the view that traditions are abstract ideologies that venerate the past. Traditions are not just passed down or created spontaneously. Traditions are a mode of organizing action in terms of present-day problems and shared collective understandings of social reality (Eric Hobsbawm, "Introduction: In-

venting Traditions," in *The Invention of Tradition,* edited by Eric Hobsbawm and Terence Ranger [Cambridge: Cambridge University Press, 1992], 1–14).

27. Harvey Molotch, William Freudenberg, and Krista E. Paulsen," History Repeats Itself, But How? City Character, Urban Tradition, and the Accomplishment of Place," *American Sociological Review* 65 (2000): 791–823; Wendy Griswold and Nathan Wright, "Cowbirds, Locals, and the Endurance of Regionalism," *American Journal of Sociology* 109 (2004): 1411–51; Thomas Hylland Eriksen, "Creolization and Creativity," *Global Networks* 3 (2003): 223–37; Ulf Hannerz, *Cultural Complexity* (New York: Columbia University Press, 1992); Ulf Hannerz, *Transnational Connections* (London: Routledge, 1996).

28. "Crescent City" alludes to the crescent-shaped course of the Mississippi River around and through the city.

29. For overviews of the changing makeup of the New Orleans metropolitan economy, see Pierce F. Lewis, *New Orleans: The Making of an Urban Landscape,* second edition (Charlottesville: University of Virginia Press, 2005); Mickey Lauria, Robert K. Whelan, and Alma H. Young, "Revitalization of New Orleans," in *Urban Revitalization: Policies and Programs,* edited by Fritz W. Wagner, Timothy E. Joder, and Anthony J. Mumphrey Jr. (Thousand Oaks, Calif.: Sage, 1995), 102–27; Robert K. Whelan and Alma Young, "New Orleans: The Ambivalent City," in *Big City Politics in Transition,* edited by H. V. Savitch and John Clayton Thomas (Newbury Park, Calif.: Sage, 1991), 132–48.

30. For an overview of socioeconomic changes affecting New Orleans in the 1960s and 1970s, see Michael Peter Smith and Marlene Keller, " 'Managed Growth' and the Politics of Uneven Development in New Orleans," in *Restructuring the City: The Political Economy of Urban Redevelopment,* edited by Susan Fainstein, Norman I. Fainstein, Richard Child Hill, Dennis Judd, and Michael Peter Smith (New York: Longman, 1986), 126–66.

31. Figures on the growth in number of hotel rooms and conventions come from the New Orleans Metropolitan Convention and Visitor Bureau (NOMCVB), the Ernest N. Morial Convention Center, the New Orleans Aviation Board, the Louisiana Office of Tourism, the U.S. Travel Data Center, and the Louisiana Hotel-Motel Association.

32. Figures come from Brookings Institution, *New Orleans after the Storm: Lessons from the Past, a Plan for the Future* (Washington, D.C.: Brookings Institution, 2005).

33. "Hotel Workers March," *Progressive* 63 (October 1999): 15.

34. Association of Community Organizations for Reform Now (ACORN), "Supreme Court Rejects Landslide Living Wage Victory in New Orleans," press release, at www.acorn.org (September 4, 2002).

35. John Urry, *The Tourist Gaze,* second edition (Thousand Oaks, Calif.: Sage, 2002); Dean MacCannell, *The Tourist*; MacCannell, *Empty Meeting Grounds: The Tourist Papers* (New York: Routledge, 1992).

36. Mark Gottdiener, Claudia C. Collins, and David R. Dickens, *Las Vegas: The Social Production of an All-American City* (Malden, Mass.: Blackwell, 1999); Richard Lloyd, *Neo-Bohemia: Art and Commerce in the Postindustrial City* (New York: Routledge, 2006); Christopher Mele, *Selling the Lower East Side: Culture, Real Estate, and Resistance in New York City* (Minneapolis: University of Minnesota Press, 2002); Grazian, *Blue Chicago.*

37. Susan S. Fainstein and Dennis R. Judd, "Global Forces, Local Strategies, and Urban Tourism," in *The Tourist City,* edited by Dennis R. Judd and Susan S. Fainstein (New Haven, Conn.: Yale University Press, 1999), 16.

NOTES TO CHAPTER 2

1. Sir Charles Lyell, *A Second Visit to the United States of North America,* volume 2 (London: John Murray, 1849), 112.

2. For scholarly overviews of the history of Carnival and Mardi Gras in New Orleans, see Samuel Kinser, *Carnival, American Style: Mardi Gras at New Orleans and Mobile* (Chicago: University of Chicago Press, 1990); Reid Mitchell, *All on a Mardi Gras Day: Episodes in the History of New Orleans Mardi Gras* (Cambridge: Harvard University Press, 1995); Munro Edmonson, "Carnival in New Orleans," *Caribbean Quarterly* 4 (1956): 233–45.

3. "The Carnival," *New Orleans Daily Delta* (February 22, 1855), 1.

4. Kinser, *Carnival, American Style,* 60. For insights on early cultural production at Congo Square, see Gary A. Donaldson, "A Window on Slave Culture: Dances at Congo Square in New Orleans, 1800–1962," *Journal of Negro History* 69 (1984): 63–72.

5. Kinser, *Carnival, American Style,* 25

6. Official Proceedings of the New Orleans City Council, February 2, 1805, New Orleans Public Library, City Archives: 1984 Louisiana Exposition Collection.

7. Randal R. Couch, "The Public Masked Balls of Antebellum New Orleans: A Custom of Masque outside the Mardi Gras Tradition," *Louisiana History* 34 (1994): 403–31.

8. Mitchell, *All on a Mardi Gras Day,* 12–13.

9. Benjamin Henry Latrobe, *Impressions Regarding New Orleans: Diaries and Sketches, 1818–1820* (New York: Columbia University Press, 1951), 32; Karl Bernard, *Travels through North America during the Years 1825 and 1826* (Philadelphia: Carey, Lea and Carey, 1828), 61; Louis Fitzgerald Tasistro, *Random Shots and Southern Breezes Containing Critical Remarks on the Souther States and Southern Institutions with Semi-Serious Observations on Men and Manners* (New York: Harper Brothers, 1842), 51; Lyell, *Second Visit to the United States of North America,* 112.

10. Carnival street celebrations organized by small groups of young men

had European origins and reflect the influence of French Carnival processions from the sixteenth century on. For overviews, see Kinser, *Carnival, American Style,* 3–15; Mitchell, *All on a Mardi Gras Day,* 19–22.

11. N.t., *New Orleans Picayune* (February 8, 1937), sec. 1, p. 13.

12. N.t., *New Orleans Commercial Bulletin* (February 28, 1838).

13. Tasistro, *Random Shots and Southern Breezes,* 48–50.

14. Kinser, *Carnival, American Style,* 65.

15. For population figures on growth of New Orleans during the nineteenth century, see Campbell Gibson, *Population of the 100 Largest Cities and Other Urban Places in the United States: 1790–1990,* U.S. Bureau of the Census, Population Division Working Paper No. 27 (Washington, D.C.: U.S. Bureau of the Census, 1998).

16. For descriptions of New Orleans's ethnic diversity, see Roger A. Fischer, "Racial Segregation in Ante Bellum New Orleans," *American Historical Review* 74 (1969): 926–57; John W. Blassingame, *Black New Orleans, 1860–1880* (Chicago: University of Chicago Press, 1976).

17. For overviews, see Sybil Kein (editor), *Creole: The History and Legacy of Louisiana's Free People of Color* (Baton Rouge: Louisiana State University Press, 2000); Arnold Hirsch and Joseph Logsdon (editors), *Creole New Orleans: Race and Americanization* (Baton Rouge: Louisiana State University Press, 1992), 9–10.

18. For overviews of racial segregation in antebellum New Orleans, see Grace Elizabeth King, *New Orleans: The Place and the People* (New York: Macmillan, 1895); Fischer, "Racial Segregation in Ante Bellum New Orleans"; Blassingame, *Black New Orleans.*

19. Joseph Tregle, "Early New Orleans Society: A Reappraisal," *Journal of Southern History* 18 (1952): 20–36; Joseph Tregle, "Creoles and Americans," in *Creole New Orleans: Race and Americanization,* edited by Arnold R. Hirsch and Joseph Logsdon (Baton Rouge: Louisiana State University Press, 1992), 131–88.

20. During the eighteenth and nineteenth centuries, "creole" meant indigenous to Louisiana or New Orleans. For overviews of the historically changing meanings of this term, see Hirsch and Logsdon, *Creole New Orleans;* Kein, *Creole;* Virginia R. Domínguez, *White by Definition: Social Classification in Creole Louisiana* (New Brunswick, N.J.: Rutgers University Press, 1986); Gwendolyn Midlo Hall, *Africans in Colonial Louisiana: The Development of Afro-Creole Culture in the Eighteenth Century* (Baton Rouge: Louisiana State University Press, 1992); Kimberly S. Hanger, *Bounded Lives, Bounded Places: Free Black Society in Colonial New Orleans, 1769–1803* (Durham, N.C.: Duke University Press, 1997).

21. Labor struggles and industrial unrest at mid-century are discussed in Robert C. Reinders, *End of an Era: New Orleans, 1850–1860* (New Orleans:

Pelican, 1964), 21–22; Steve Wells and Jim Stodder, "A Short History of New Orleans Dockworkers," *Radical America* 10 (1976): 43–69.

22. Karl Marx, *Capital*, volume 1, translated by Ben Fowlkes (New York: Vintage, [1867] 1978), 79.

23. Giles Vandal, "Nineteenth-Century Municipal Responses to the Problem of Poverty: New Orleans' Free Lodgers, 1850–1880, as a Case Study," *Journal of Urban History* 19 (1992): 33, 36–37, 51.

24. N.t., *New Orleans Daily Delta* (March 4, 1851), 2.

25. N.t., *New Orleans Daily Crescent* (February 8, 1853), 1; N.t., *New Orleans Bee* (February 8, 1853), 1; N.t., *New Orleans Daily Delta* (February 6, 1856), 1.

26. Fred Davis, *Yearning for Yesterday: A Sociology of Nostalgia* (New York: Free Press, 1979); Melinda Milligan, "Displacement and Identity Discontinuity: The Role of Nostalgia in Establishing New Identity Categories," *Symbolic Interactionism* 26 (2003): 381–403; David Hummon, *Commonplaces: Community, Ideology, and Identity in American Culture* (Albany: State University of New York Press, 1990); Herbert Gans, *The Urban Villagers: Group and Class in the Life of Italian-Americans* (New York: Free Press, 1962).

27. Quoted in Kenneth E. Snewmaker and Andrew K. Prinz (editors), "A Yankee in Louisiana: Selections from the Diary and Correspondence of Henry R. Gardiner, 1862–1866," *Louisiana History* 5 (1964): 271.

28. I refer to "rationalization" as a process by which the spontaneous, impulsive, and relatively unorganized aspects of Carnival became increasingly subject to planned control, regulation, and management by groups, organizations, and networks of actors. This definition draws on the work of Max Weber, *The Protestant Ethic and the Spirit of Capitalism* (New York: Scribner's, [1902] 1958).

29. For descriptive overviews of the history of the Krewe of Comus and the transformation of Mardi Gras, see James Gill, *Lords of Misrule: Mardi Gras and the Politics of Race in New Orleans* (Jackson: University Press of Mississippi, 1997); Henri Schindler, *Mardi Gras, New Orleans* (Paris: Flammarion, 1997). For the official history of the Krewe of Comus, see Perry Young, *Carnival and Mardi Gras in New Orleans* (New Orleans: Harmanson's, 1939).

30. Ann Swidler, "What Anchors Cultural Practices," in *The Practical Turn in Contemporary Theory*, edited by Theodore R. Schatzki, Karin Knorr-Cetina, and Eike von Savigny (London: Routledge and Kegan Paul, 2001); 74–92; Ann Swidler, "Culture in Action: Symbols and Strategies," *American Sociological Review* 51 (1986): 273–86.

31. For a discussion of the private-public division in Carnival, see Karen Trahan Leathem, "'A Carnival According to Their Own Desires': Gender and Mardi Gras in New Orleans, 1870–1941," Ph.D. dissertation, University of North Carolina at Chapel Hill, 1994.

32. Anonymous writer to his wife, 1872, in Williams Research Center, Historic New Orleans Collection, MS 2001-70-L.

33. For example, King, *New Orleans*, 390–92; Kinser, *Carnival, American Style*, 88–89; Arthur Burton La Cour and Stuart Omer Landry, *New Orleans Masquerade: Chronicles of Carnival* (New Orleans: Pelican, 1957), 16–17; Mitchell, *All on a Mardi Gras Day*, 23, 25; Joseph Roach, *Cities of the Dead: Circum-Atlantic Performance* (New York: Columbia University Press, 1996), 257–58.

34. N.t., *New Orleans Daily Crescent* (February 14,1861), 1.

35. Roach, *Cities of the Dead*, 257.

36. Tristine Lee Smart, "Prestige Symbol Manipulation: Controlling Form and Meaning—Prestige Symbols, Carnival, Louisiana, Earthwork Complexes, Ohio," Ph.D. dissertation, University of Michigan, Ann Arbor, 1999, 92–96.

37. Errol Laborde, "The Men Who Made Mardi Gras," *New Orleans City Business* (February 2002), 45–50; Errol Laborde, *Marched the Day God: A History of the Rex Organization* (New Orleans: School of Design, 1999).

38. John Hannigan, *Fantasy City: Pleasure and Profit in the Postmodern Metropolis* (New York: Routledge, 1998), 16.

39. Emile Durkheim, *Elementary Forms of Religious Life*, translated by Karen E. Fields (New York: Free Press, [1912] 1995), 420–21.

40. N.t., *New Orleans Commercial Bulletin* (February 22, 1871), 1; Editorial, *New Orleans Daily Picayune* (February 8, 1874), 11.

41. N.t., *New Orleans Republican* (February 11, 1872), 1. For discussions and debates on the origin and motivation for the establishment of the Krewe of Rex, see Laborde, "Men Who Made Mardi Gras"; Laborde, *Marched the Day God*; Lee A. Farrow, "Grand Duke Alexei and the Origins of Rex, 1872: Myth, Public Memory, and the Distortion of History," *Gulf South Historical Review* 18 (2002): 6–30.

42. J. Curtis Waldo, *The History of the Carnival in New Orleans from 1857–1882* (New Orleans: Chicago, St. Louis, and New Orleans Railroad, 1882); Southern Pacific Lines, *The Carnival* (N.p.: Southern Pacific Lines, 1917), 5, in Tulane University, Howard-Tilton Memorial Library, Special Collections, Vertical File: Carnival History.

43. George Soule, *The Carnival in New Orleans: Its Story and Its Sentiment* (1887), 2–3, 16, in Tulane University, Howard-Tilton Memorial Library, Special Collections, Vertical File: Carnival.

44. Gill, *Lords of Misrule*, 30–46, 86; Laborde, *Marched the Day God*, 11–13, 17.

45. Farrow, "Grand Duke Alexei and the Origins of Rex," 15.

46. Mark Twain, *Life on the Mississippi* (Harper and Brothers, 1896), at http://www.mardigrasunmasked.com/mardigras/carnival_quotes.htm (accessed April 15, 2007).

47. For an overview of New Orleans race and ethnic relations during the nineteenth century, see Hirsch and Logsdon, *Creole New Orleans*; Paul Lachance, "The Formation of a Three-Caste Society: Evidence from Wills in Antebellum New Orleans," *Social Science History* 18 (1994): 211–42.

48. Joseph Logsdon and Caryn Cosse Belle, "The Americanization of Black New Orleans, 1850–1900," in *Creole New Orleans: Race and Americanization*, edited by Arnold R. Hirsch and Joseph Logsdon (Baton Rouge: Louisiana State University Press, 1992), 208; Reinders, *End of an Era*, 24.

49. For figures on the changing racial population, see table 2, "State of Louisiana," in U.S. Census Bureau, Ninth Census, volume 1: *The Statistics of the Population of the United States: Population by Counties 1790–1870* (Washington, D.C.: U.S. Government Printing Office, 1872), 34.

50. Giles Vandal, "The Origins of the New Orleans Riot of 1866, Revisited," *Louisiana History* 22 (Spring 1981): 135–65.

51. New Orleans's streetcars would remain desegregated until 1902 when the Louisiana legislature passed a law mandating racially segregated streetcars (Roger A. Fischer, "A Pioneer Protest: The New Orleans Streetcar Controversy of 1867," *Journal of Negro History* 53 [1968]: 219–33).

52. W. E. B. Dubois, *Black Reconstruction in America, 1860–1880* (New York: Free Press, 1935).

53. The literature on racial conflict and struggle in Louisiana and the U.S. South during the Reconstruction years is vast. For analyses and overviews, see Dan T. Carter, *When the War Was Over: The Failure of Self-Reconstruction in the South, 1865–1867* (Baton Rouge: Louisiana State University Press, 1985); Eric Foner, *Reconstruction: America's Unfinished Revolution, 1863–1877* (New York: Harper and Row, 1988); William Gillette, *Retreat from Reconstruction, 1869–1879* (Baton Rouge: Louisiana State University Press, 1979); Louis R. Harlan, "Desegregation in New Orleans Public Schools during Reconstruction," *American Historical Review* 68 (April 1962): 663–75; Joe Gray Taylor, *Louisiana Reconstructed, 1863–1877* (Baton Rouge: Louisiana State University Press, 1974); Ted Tunnel, *Crucible of Reconstruction: War, Radicalism, and Race in Louisiana, 1862–1877* (Baton Rouge: Louisiana State University Press, 1984).

54. Mitchell, *All on a Mardi Gras Day*, 66–67; Roach, *Cities of the Dead*, 261–62; Gill, *Lords of Misrule*, 104–8; Richard Rambuss, "Spenser and Milton at Mardi Gras: English Literature, American Cultural Capital, and the Reformation of New Orleans Mardi Gras," *Boundary* 27 (Summer 2000): 61–62.

55. For an overview and insightful analysis of the Battle of Liberty Place, see Jacob A. Wagner, "The Myth of Liberty Place: Race and Public Memory in New Orleans, 1874–1993," Ph.D. dissertation, University of New Orleans, 2004.

56. Young, *Carnival and Mardi Gras in New Orleans*, 34.

57. Mystick Krewe of Comus, *One Hundred Years of Comus* (New Orleans: Mystick Krewe of Comus, 1956), 23.

58. Augustin Advertising and Information Bureau, *Mardi Gras in New Orleans 1798–1908* (New Orleans: Augustin Advertising Bureau, 1908), 1, in Tulane University, Howard-Tilton Memorial Library, Special Collections, Vertical File: Carnival.

59. N.t., *New Orleans Republican* (February 11, 1872), 1; ibid. (February 14, 1872), 1.

60. Editorial, *New Orleans Times* (March 6, 1881), 1.

61. Rand, McNally and Company, *The World's Industrial and Cotton Centennial Exposition at New Orleans* (Chicago: Rand, McNally, 1885), 64–65.

62. Julian Ralph, "New Orleans, Our Southern Capital," *Harper's New Monthly Magazine* 86 (February 1893): 365–66.

63. Mikhail Bakhtin, *Rabelais and His World*, translated by Helene Iswolsky (Bloomington: Indiana University Press, 1984).

NOTES TO CHAPTER 3

1. "The World's Exposition: The Attendance Yesterday Greater Than for Some Time Past," *New Orleans Times-Democrat* (January 19, 1885), 1.

2. Georg Simmel, "Metropolis and Mental Life," in *Georg Simmel: On Individuality and Social Forms*, edited by Donald N. Levine (Chicago: Chicago University Press, [1903] 1971), 325.

3. Thomas D. Watson, "Staging the 'Crowning Achievement of the Age': Major Edward A. Burke, New Orleans, and the Cotton Centennial Exposition," *Louisiana History* 25 (1984): 341–66.

4. Samuel C. Shepard, "A Glimmer of Hope: The World's Industrial and Cotton Centennial Exposition, New Orleans, 1884–1885," *Louisiana History* 26 (1985): 271–90.

5. Joy Jackson, *New Orleans in the Gilded Age: Politics and Urban Progress, 1880–1896* (Baton Rouge: Louisiana State University Press, 1969).

6. Total building coverage for the 1884 Exposition was 81 acres, 20 acres more than the U.S. Centennial Exposition held in Philadelphia in 1876 (http://www.earthstation9.com/index.html?1884_new.htm [accessed October 1, 2005]).

7. Quoted in "The Exposition Opened: New Orleans Happy with Its World's Fair; President Arthur Starts the Great Engine by Electricity—A Great Throng in Attendance," *New York Times* (December 17, 1884).

8. "The World's Exposition: Attendance Yesterday Greater," 1.

9. Quoted in Herbert Fairall, *World's Industrial and Cotton Centennial Exposition, New Orleans, 1884–1885* (Iowa City: Republican Publishing, 1885), 20.

10. Benjamin Moore Norman, *Norman's New Orleans and Environs* (New Orleans: B. M. Norman, 1845).

11. For the significance of photography for tourism, see John Urry, *The Tourist Gaze,* second edition (Thousand Oaks, Calif.: Sage. 2002), 128–29. Broadly, the invention of photography helped support the expansion of a vast literature on American cities, from booster literature, travel sketches, guidebooks, tourism itineraries, and other illustrated brochures (Catherine Cocks, *Doing the Town: The Rise of Urban Tourism in the United States, 1850–1915* [Berkeley: University of California Press, 2001]; Marguerite Shaffer, *See America First: Tourism and National Identity, 1905–1930* [Washington, D.C.: Smithsonian Institution, 2001]).

12. N.t., *New Orleans Times-Democrat* (January 14, 1885), 1.

13. Eric Hobsbawm, *Industry and Empire: An Economic History of Britain since 1750* (London, Weidenfeld and Nicolson, 1968), 56.

14. Ellis L. Tuffly, "The New Orleans Cotton Exchange, the Formative Years, 1870–1880," *Journal of Southern History* 39 (1973): 545–64; Gary Bolding, "Change, Continuity, and Commercial Identity of a Southern City: New Orleans, 1850–1950," *Louisiana Studies* 14 (1975): 161–78.

15. On the connection between railroads and time zones, see Eviatar Zerubavel, "The Standardization of Time: A Sociohistorical Perspective," *American Journal of Sociology* 88 (1982): 1–23.

16. For a general discussion of the organization of exposition planning in the United States, see Robert W. Rydell, "The Culture of Imperial Abundance: World's Fairs in the Making of American Culture," in *Consuming Visions: Accumulation and Display of Goods in America, 1880–1920,* edited by Simon J. Bronner (New York: Norton, 1989), 204–10.

17. "The New Orleans Exposition," *New York Times* (August 15, 1884), 4.

18. "The World's Cotton Centennial," *New York Times* (December 17, 1882), 1; "The New Orleans Exposition," *New York Times* (October 22, 1883), 5.

19. "The New Orleans Exposition," *New York Times* (February 17, 1884), 7; "The Cotton Centennial," *New York Times* (September 24, 1884), 4.

20. Official foreign participation included Belgium, Brazil, British Honduras, China, Colombia, Costa Rica, El Salvador, France, Great Britain, Guatemala, Honduras, Jamaica, Japan, Mexico, Nicaragua, Russia, Thailand (then Siam), and Venezuela. Many other countries sent displays to New Orleans, including Austria-Hungary, Germany, Hawaii (then the Sandwich Islands), Italy, San Salvador, and Spain ("Matters in Washington: The Government at the New Orleans Exposition—The Interesting and Instructive Exhibits to Be Contributed by the Various Departments," *New York Times* [May 19, 1884], 5).

21. "The World's Fair: A Change in the Date for the Opening Ceremonies," *New York Times* (November 2, 1884), 2; "The New Orleans Exposition," *New York Times* (November 11, 1884), 4.

22. Lydia Strawn (compiler), *World's Industrial and Cotton Centennial Exposition* (Chicago: General Passenger Department, Illinois Central Railroad, n.d.), 3, 11.

23. "The World's Exposition: The Attendance Yesterday Greater Than for Some Time Past," *New Orleans Times-Democrat* (January 19, 1885), 1.

24. "The World's Exposition: All Ready for the Opening on Tuesday Next," *New York Times* (December 12, 1884), 2.

25. Eugene Smalley, "In and Out of the New Orleans Exposition," *Century Magazine: A Popular Monthly* 30 (June 1885): 194, at http://cdl.library.cornell .edu (accessed May 1, 2005).

26. Georg Simmel, "The Berlin Trade Exhibition," in *Simmel on Culture: Selected Writings,* edited by David Frisby and Mike Featherstone (London: Sage, [1896] 2000), 257, 255, 256.

27. The display of the Sioux Indian is reported in "1884 World's Industrial and Cotton Centennial Exposition," World's Fair and Exposition Information and Reference Guide, at http://www.earthstation9.com/index.html?1884_new .htm (accessed December 15, 2006).

28. Anne C. Goater, "What Jean and Joe Saw at the New Orleans Exposition," in Williams Research Center, Historic New Orleans Collection: World's Industrial and Cotton Centennial Exposition Collection, 1883–1885, Folder 9, MS 214.

29. Excerpt from the *New York Commercial Advisor* appears in the *New Orleans Times-Democrat* (December 22, 1884), 1.

30. William H. Coleman, *Historical Sketch Book and Guide to New Orleans and Environs* (New York: N.p., N.d.).

31. For an overview of Lafcadio Hearn's writings, see S. Frederick Starr (editor), *Inventing New Orleans: The Writings of Lafcadio Hearn* (Jackson: University Press of Mississippi, 2001).

32. Christine M. Boyer, *The City of Collective Memory: Its Historical Imagery and Architectural Entertainments* (Cambridge, Mass.: MIT Press, 1994), 325.

33. For descriptions of the Women's Exhibit, see Shepard, "Glimmer of Hope, 285; Smalley, "In and Out of the New Orleans Exposition," 188.

34. The *New York Times* reported that a "large percentage" of the 3,000 visitors from Nebraska and Minnesota "are school teachers" ("Visitors from the Northwest" [December 23, 1884], 1). Later, the *New York Times* reported that "three hundred school teachers" from Texas were in town ("The New Orleans Fair: Exhibitors' Spaces Rapidly Filling up and the Attendance Increasing" [December 27, 1884], 1).

35. Grace Elizabeth King, *Memories of a Southern Woman of Letters* (New York: Macmillan, 1932), 55.

36. "The World's Exposition: All Ready for the Opening on Tuesday Next,"

New York Times (December 12, 1884), 2; Rand, McNally, *World's Industrial and Cotton Centennial Exposition*, 66–67. See also Richmond and Danville Railroad, Piedmont Airline, and Atlantic Coast Line, *Our Great All Around Tour for the Winter of '84–'85* (New York: Leve and Alden Printing, 1884–1885), 23; Vandercock and Company, *Illustrated Guide to the Winter Resorts for Health and Pleasure in the Southern States and Florida: The World Exposition at New Orleans, La.* (Chicago: Vandercock, 1884), 6.

37. "Visitors from the Northwest: Things Beginning to Assume a Business Aspect at the Fair," *New York Times* (December 24, 1884), 5.

38. Rand, McNally, *World's Industrial and Cotton Centennial Exposition*, 61.

39. Richmond and Danville Railroad et al., *Our Great All Around Tour*, 28.

40. Strawn, *World's Industrial and Cotton Centennial Exposition*, 15.

41. The description of New Orleans as the "Paris of America" is found in Rand, McNally, *World's Industrial and Cotton Centennial Exposition*, 51. The description of New Orleans as "City of Progress, Beauty, Charm, and Romance" is the title of a travel guide (n.d.) published by the Louisville and Nashville Railroad, Folders 218 and 219 in Williams Research Center, Historic New Orleans Collection, William Russell Jazz Collection, Series: William Russell Pamphlet Collection, MSS 527.

42. Rand, McNally, *World's Industrial and Cotton Centennial Exposition*, 87.

43. "The World's Fair: The Colored People's Exhibit," *Cleveland Gazette* (December 9, 1884); Ohio Historical Center Archives Library, Newspaper Roll no. 4427, sec. 2, p. 17, at http://dbs.ohiohistory.org/africanam/page.cfm?ID=14449 (accessed May 1, 2005).

44. Quoted in Dale A. Somers, "Black and White in New Orleans: A Study in Urban Race Relations, 1865–1900," *Journal of Southern History* 40 (1974): 33.

45. Charles Dudley Warner, "Impressions of the South," *Harper's New Monthly Magazine* 71 (September 1885): 550, at Cornell University, "Making of America," http://cdl.library.cornell.edu/ (accessed May 1, 2005).

46. For overviews of racial mixing in New Orleans institutions during the second half of the nineteenth century, see Jerah Johnson, "Jim Crow Laws of the 1890s and the Origins of New Orleans Jazz: Correction of an Error," *Popular Music* 19 (2000): 243–51; Somers, "Black and White in New Orleans."

47. Quoted in Robert W. Rydell, *All the World's a Fair: Visions of Empire at American International Expositions, 1876–1916* (Chicago: University of Chicago Press, 1984), 80–81.

48. Quoted in Shepard, "Glimmer of Hope," 287.

49. Quoted in Vandercock and Company, *Illustrated Guide to the Winter Resorts*, 1.

50. Warner, "Impressions of the South," 551.

51. Smalley, "In and Out of the New Orleans Exposition," 193, 194.

52. Ibid., 193.

53. John Smith Kendall, *History of New Orleans* (Chicago: Lewis, 1922), 464.

54. For an overview and critical discussion, see Rydell, *All the World's a Fair.*

55. Ibid., 81.

56. Smalley, "In and Out of the New Orleans Exposition," 193.

57. "The Colored People at the New Orleans Exposition," *American Missionary* 39 (July 1885): 189.

58. For discussions of the intensification of racial discrimination and the effect of Jim Crow segregation on New Orleans life and culture, see Johnson, "Jim Crow Laws of the 1890s," and Somers, "Black and White in New Orleans." On the rise of segregation within Protestant and Catholic Churches in New Orleans, see James B. Bennett, *Religion and the Rise of Jim Crow in New Orleans* (Princeton, N.J.: Princeton University Press, 2005).

59. Reported in Jackson, *New Orleans in the Gilded Age,* 318.

60. Ibid., 20.

61. Daphne Spain, "Race Relations and Residential Segregation in New Orleans: Two Centuries of Paradox," *Annals of the American Academy of Political and Social Science* 441 (1979): 88–89.

62. Quoted in Strawn, *World's Industrial and Cotton Centennial Exposition*; emphasis in original.

63. *New York Times* (February 19, 1890), 1; *New York Times* (February 12, 1893), 1; James B. Townsend, "The New Orleans Carnival of 1896," *Illustrated American* 19 (March 14, 1896): 326.

64. Illinois Central Railroad, *New Orleans for the Tourist* (Chicago: Illinois Central Railroad, 1903); Louisville and Nashville Railroad Company, Passenger Department, *New Orleans and Her Carnival* (Chicago: Corbett, 1904); Southern Pacific Company, *The Winter in New Orleans: Carnival, Racing, French Opera* (New Orleans: Southern Pacific Company, 1899), in Williams Research Center, Historic New Orleans Collection: William Russell Jazz Collection, William Russell Pamphlet Collection, Folder 356, MSS 527.

65. William Leach, *Land of Desire: Merchants, Power, and the Rise of a New American Culture* (New York: Pantheon, 1993), xiii.

66. Walter Benjamin, *Reflections, Essays, Aphorisms, Autobiographical Writing* (New York: Harcourt Brace, 1978).

67. For insights on railroads and broad changes in time and space in the decades after the Civil War, see George A. Douglas, *All Aboard! The Railroad in American Life* (New York: Paragon House, 1992); Stephen Kern, *The Cul-*

ture of Time and Space, 1880–1918 (Cambridge: Harvard University Press, 1983); Zerubavel, "Standardization of Time."

NOTES TO CHAPTER 4

1. "Favorable Opinion of New Orleans," in Monthly Report of the General Manager to the President and Board of Directors of the New Orleans Association of Commerce, September 8, 1916, volume 17 (MSS 66, NOCC, UNO). Reports and minutes of meetings are contained in the volumes of the New Orleans Chamber of Commerce Collection at the University of New Orleans (cited as MSS 66, NOCC, UNO).

2. Annual Report of the Convention and Visitors' Bureau, November 30, 1937, volume 49 (MSS 66, NOCC, UNO).

3. Louis C. Hennick, *The Streetcars of New Orleans* (Gretna, La.: Pelican, 1965), 211–12, 367.

4. Mark Gottdiener, *Theming of America: Dreams, Visions, and Commercial Spaces,* second edition (New York: Westview, 2001); Sharon Zukin, "Urban Lifestyles: Diversity and Standardization in Spaces of Consumption," *Urban Studies* 35 (1998): 825–39; William Leach, *Land of Desire: Merchants, Power, and the Rise of a New American Culture* (New York: Pantheon, 1993).

5. For an overview of the rise of jazz music, voodoo ceremonies, and other attractions in late-nineteenth-century New Orleans, see Joy Jackson, *New Orleans in the Gilded Age: Politics and Urban Progress, 1880–1896* (Baton Rouge: Louisiana State University Press, 1969), 23–24, 63, 255–57, 273–82.

6. Hearn is discussed in ibid., chap. 11; see also S. Frederick Starr (editor), *Inventing New Orleans: The Writings of Lafcadio Hearn* (Jackson: University Press of Mississippi, 2001).

7. Lawrence H. Larsen, *The Rise of the Urban South* (Lexington: University of Kentucky Press, 1985), 140.

8. Alecia P. Long, *The Great Southern Babylon: Sex, Race, and Respectability in New Orleans, 1865–1920* (Baton Rouge: Louisiana State University Press, 2004).

9. Reid Mitchell, *All on a Mardi Gras Day: Episodes in the History of New Orleans Mardi Gras* (Cambridge: Harvard University Press, 1995), 132–33.

10. Young Men's Business League of New Orleans, *New Orleans of 1894: Its Advantages, Its Conditions, and Its Prospects* (New Orleans: Young Men's Business League of New Orleans, n.d.), in Tulane University, Howard-Tilton Memorial Library, Special Collections, Vertical File: Descriptions, New Orleans, 1880–1899.

11. "Chamber History," n.d., Box 652, Folder 5 (MSS 66, NOCC, UNO).

12. For a historical overview of tourism promotion efforts in New Orleans

during the early twentieth century, see Anthony J. Stanonis, *Creating the Big Easy: New Orleans and the Emergence of Modern Tourism, 1918–1945* (Atlanta: University of Georgia Press, 2006).

13. Bruce Raeburn, "Early New Orleans Jazz in Theaters," *Louisiana History* 43 (2002): 41–52.

14. Patricia Rosendahl, "New Orleans' Own Silent Films," *Southern Quarterly* 23 (1984): 40–46.

15. Wayne H. Schuth, "The Image of New Orleans on Film," *Southern Quarterly* 19 (1981): 240–45; Wayne H. Schuth, "The Images of Louisiana in Film and Television," *Southern Quarterly* 23 (1984): 5–17.

16. Argument of W. B. Thompson on behalf of the City of New Orleans in the Matter of the World's Panama Exposition before the House Committee on Industrial Arts and Expositions, Washington D.C., January 1911, in Tulane University, Howard-Tilton Memorial Library, Special Collections, Vertical File: Fairs and Festivals: 1915 Panama Exposition.

17. Gary A. Bolding, "New Orleans Commerce: The Establishment of the Permanent World Trade Mart," *Louisiana History* 8 (1967): 351–52.

18. Annual Report of the Secretary-Manager of the New Orleans Progressive Union, January 9, 1911, volume 4, p. 11 (MSS 66, NOCC, UNO).

19. Catherine Cocks, *Doing the Town: The Rise of Urban Tourism in the United States, 1850–1915* (Berkeley: University of California Press, 2001), 134.

20. Quotes come from a pamphlet titled "San Francisco, the Exposition City, 1915," N.a., N.d., N.p., in Tulane University, Howard-Tilton Memorial Library, Special Collections, Vertical File: World's Fair, International Exposition, 1915, Panama-Pacific Exposition.

21. "Racialization" refers to the ways in which racial categories sort people, society distributes resources along racial lines, and state policy shapes and is shaped by the racial contours of society. In this conception, race has an emergent and variable quality rather than a fixed or immutable group characteristic. Racial groups are socially and politically constructed and exist as the outcome of diverse historical practices (programmatic organization of social policy, modes of political participation, etc.) that are continually subject to challenge over definition and meaning. For example, Kevin Fox Gotham, *Race, Real Estate, and Uneven Development: The Kansas City Experience, 1900–2000* (Albany: State University of New York Press, 2002); Steve Martinot, *The Rule of Racialization: Class, Identity, Governance* (Philadelphia: Temple University Press, 2002); Karim Murji and John Solomos (editors), *Racialization: Studies in Theory and Practice* (Oxford: Oxford University Press, 2005); Michael Omi and Howard Winant, *Racial Formation in the United States: From the 1960s to the 1980s* second edition (New York: Routledge, 1994).

22. Michele Lamont (editor), *The Cultural Territories of Race: Black and White Boundaries* (Chicago: University of Chicago Press, 1998); Matthew Frye

Jacobson, *Whiteness of a Different Color: European Immigrants and the Alchemy of Race* (Cambridge: Harvard University Press, 1998); Daniel Bernardi (editor), *The Birth of Whiteness: Race and the Emergence of U.S. Cinema* (New Brunswick, N.J.: Rutgers University Press, 1996).

23. The literature on the racialization of white Europeans and the social construction of whiteness is vast. For example, Theodore Allen, *The Invention of the White Race* (New York: Verso, 1994); Tomas Almaguer, *Racial Fault Lines: The Historical Origins of White Supremacy in California* (Berkeley: University of California Press, 1994); Karen Brodkin, *How Jews Became White Folks: and What That Says about Race in America* (New Brunswick, N.J.: Rutgers University Press, 1998); Nicholas M. Evans, *Writing Jazz: Race, Nationalism, and Modern Culture in the 1920s* (New York: Garland, 2000); Grace Elizabeth Hale, *Making Whiteness: The Culture of Segregation in the South, 1890–1940* (New York: Pantheon, 1998); Ian Haney-Lopez, *White by Law: The Legal Construction of Race* (New York: New York University Press, 1996); Noel Ignatiev, *How the Irish Became White* (New York: Routledge, 1995).

24. Minutes of Executive Committee of the Association of Commerce, April 2, 1930, volume 34, p. 2 (MSS 66, NOCC, UNO).

25. Daphne Spain, "Race Relations and Residential Segregation in New Orleans: Two Centuries of Paradox," *Annals of the American Academy of Political and Social Science* 441 (1979): 88–89. See also Adam Fairclough, *Race and Democracy: The Civil Rights Struggle in Louisiana, 1915–1972* (Athens: University of Georgia Press, 1995).

26. Daniel Rosenberg, *New Orleans Dockworkers: Race, Labor, and Unionism, 1892–1923* (Albany: State University of New York Press, 1988).

27. Roger Biles, "The Urban South in the Great Depression," *Journal of Southern History* 56 (1990): 71–100.

28. Arnold R. Hirsch, "Simply a Matter of Black and White: The Transformation of Race and Politics in Twentieth Century New Orleans," in *Creole New Orleans: Race and Americanization,* edited by Arnold R. Hirsch and Joseph Logsdon (Baton Rouge: Louisiana State University Press, 1992), 268.

29. Minutes of Regular Monthly Meeting of the Board of Directors of the New Orleans Association of Commerce, November 12, 1915, volume 20, p. 2 (MSS 66, NOCC, UNO).

30. "Colored Auxiliary to A. of C.," in Minutes of Regular Weekly Meeting of Executive Committee of the Association of Commerce of the New Orleans Area, October 14, 1926, volume 22a, p. 1 (MSS 66, NOCC, UNO).

31. "Use of Auditorium by Colored People," in Minutes of Executive Committee, February 19, 1930, volume 33 (MSS 66, NOCC, UNO).

32. Minutes of Meeting of the Convention and Visitors Bureau, Committee of Management, April 25, 1940, volume 55, pp. 1–2 (MSS 66, NOCC, UNO).

33. "Contemplated Opening of Crescent Theater Exclusively for Colored

People," in Minutes of Executive Committee Meeting, April 2, 1930, volume 33 (MSS 66, NOCC, UNO).

34. Minutes of Regular Semi-Monthly Meeting of the Board of Directors of the New Orleans Association of Commerce, April 9, 1946, volume 66, p. 5 (MSS 66, NOCC, UNO).

35. Louisiana Hotel Clerks Association, "Guide Book of New Orleans," November 21, 1915, in Tulane University, Howard-Tilton Memorial Library, Special Collections, Vertical File: Descriptions, New Orleans, 1903–1018.

36. Arnold R. Hirsch and Joseph Logsdon (editors), *Creole New Orleans: Race and Americanization* (Baton Rouge: Louisiana State University Press, 1992).

37. Edwin L. Jewell, *Jewell's Crescent City Illustrated: The Commercial, Social, Political and General History of New Orleans — Including Biographical Sketches of Its Distinguished Citizens, Together with a Map and a General Strangers' Guide* (New Orleans: Edwin L. Jewell, 1873), 15.

38. Alcee Fortier. "The French Language in Louisiana and the Negro-French Dialect," *Transactions* 1 (1884–1885): 98.

39. Virginia R. Dominguez suggests that blacks later cultivated the creole label to refer to their French and Spanish descendants (*White by Definition: Social Classification in Creole Louisiana* [New Brunswick, N.J.: Rutgers University Press, 1986]). Gwendolyn Midlo Hall gives a historical sketch of the various meanings of the term "creole" and offers a current definition of the word: "A person of non-American ancestry, whether African or European, who was born in the Americas" (*Africans in Colonial Louisiana: The Development of Afro-Creole Culture in the Eighteenth Century* [Baton Rouge: Louisiana State University Press, 1992], 157). See also Sybil Kein (editor), *Creole: The History and Legacy of Louisiana's Free People of Color* (Baton Rouge: Louisiana State University Press, 2000), 157.

40. Mary Morrison, "Problems of the Vieux Carre," speech before the board of directors of St. Mark's Community Center, January 23, 1950, in Williams Research Center, Mary Meeks Morrison and Jacob Morrison Papers, Box 89, MSS 553.

41. For a discussion of formation of art clubs and other cultural organizations in the French Quarter, see Laura Clark Brown, "New Orleans Modernism: The Arts and Crafts Club in the Vieux Carre, 1919–1939," *Louisiana History* 41 (2000): 317–43.

42. Lyle Saxon, draft for *Fabulous New Orleans*, Tulane University, Howard-Tilton Memorial Library, Special Collections, Lyle Saxon Papers.

43. Quoted in Brown, "New Orleans Modernism," 327.

44. "Inventory of the Vieux Carre Property Owners, Residents, and Associates. "Historical Background,"University of New Orleans, Earl K. Long Li-

brary, Louisiana Collection: Vieux Carre Property Owners, Residents, and Associates, MS 247, p. 4.

45. Minutes of Meeting of Executive Committee, Association of Commerce, September 25, 1925, volume 28, p. 1 (MSS 66, NOCC, UNO).

46. "Preservation of Buildings in the Vieux Carre," in Minutes of Meeting of the Board of Directors, Association of Commerce, July 20, 1938, volume 50, p. 6 (MSS 66, NOCC, UNO).

47. Minutes of Meeting of the Committee of Management of the Convention and Visitors Bureau, October 7, 1940, volume 55 (MSS 66, NOCC, UNO).

48. For insights on authenticity, representational struggles, and collective memory, see Gary Allen Fine, *Difficult Reputations: Collective Memories of the Evil, Inept, and Controversial* (Chicago: University of Chicago Press, 2001); Michael Schudson, *Watergate in American Memory* (New York: Basic Books, 1992); Barry Schwartz, *Abraham Lincoln and the Forge of National Memory* (Chicago: University of Chicago Press, 2000); Eviatar Zerubavel, *Time Maps: Collective Memory and the Social Shape of the Past* (Chicago: University of Chicago Press, 2003).

49. Minutes of Special Meeting of the Committee of Management of the Convention and Visitors Bureau, May 30, 1933, volume 41, pp. 1–2 (MSS 66, NOCC, UNO).

50. Minutes of Meeting of the Committee of Management of the Convention and Visitors Bureau, December 18, 1930, volume 35 (MSS 66, NOCC, UNO).

51. Minutes of Meeting of the Publicity Committee, March 3, 1938, volume 51 (MSS 66, NOCC, UNO).

52. Letter from P. J. Rinderle, Publicity Secretary, to Mr. Ben Williams, President, and Members, Board of Directors, New Orleans Association of Commerce, March 4, 1938, volume 50 (MSS 66, NOCC, UNO).

53. Minutes of Meeting of the Publicity Committee of the Association of Commerce, March 6, 1941, volume 57 (MSS 66, NOCC, UNO).

54. Institutional connections and organized networks between hotels, railroads, and other tourism organizations and interests are described in the minutes of meetings of the Publicity Bureau and the Convention and Visitors Bureau of the Chamber of Commerce of the New Orleans Area. These minutes of meetings are contained in the volumes of the Chamber of Commerce collection at the University of New Orleans Library (MSS 66, NOCC, UNO).

55. "Children's Carnival Parade," in Minutes of Special Meeting of the Committee of Management of the Convention and Visitors Bureau, May 30, 1933, volume 41, p. 2 (MSS 66, NOCC, UNO).

56. Semi-Annual Report of the Convention and Visitors' Bureau, January 1 to June 30, Inclusive, 1934, volume 43, p. 2 (MSS 66, NOCC, UNO). The Krewe or NOR paraded from 1934 to 1940 and again in 1948 and 1949.

57. Public Relations Office, November 6, 1947, "History and Background of Mardi Gras," City Hall, in Tulane University, Howard-Tilton Memorial Library, Special Collections, Vertical File: Carnival; Minutes of Board of Directors Meeting of the Association of Commerce, February 15, 1934, volume 42 (MSS 66, NOCC, UNO).

58. Perry Young, *Carnival and Mardi-Gras in New Orleans* (New Orleans: Harmanson's, 1939), 50–51.

59. Quoted in Mitchell. *All on a Mardi Gras Day*, 166.

60. Ibid., 174.

NOTES TO CHAPTER 5

1. Tourist Planning Committee, *Tourist Planning Report* (New Orleans: Tourist Planning Committee, 1960), volume 98 (MSS 66, NOCC, UNO).

2. For a historical overview of the rise of tourism between World War I and World War II in New Orleans, see Anthony J. Stanonis, *Creating the Big Easy: New Orleans and the Emergence of Modern Tourism, 1918–1945* (Atlanta: University of Georgia Press, 2006).

3. Annual Report, Publicity Department for 1924, submitted by Wilson S. Callender, Secretary, Publicity Department of the New Orleans Association of Commerce, volume 26 (MSS 66, NOCC, UNO).

4. "Revised List" of stories, from P. J. Rinderle, Editor, Bureau of New Orleans News, 1938, volume 50 (MSS 66, NOCC, UNO).

5. Passage of the International Travel Act of 1961 created the U.S. Travel Service (USTS), the first official federal government travel office to "promote increased and more effective investment in international tourism by the States, local governments, and cooperative tourism marketing programs." See International Travel Act of 1961, Title 22, Chapter 31, Subchapter I, Section 2121, at http://www.thecre.com/fedlaw/lega127q/uscode22-2121.htm (accessed August 3, 2005).

6. For overviews of the "going global" ideology in tourism and other fields, see T. C. Chang, "Renaissance Revisited: Singapore as a 'Global City for the Arts," *International Journal of Urban and Regional Research* 24 (December 2000): 818–31; J. Eade (editor), *Living the Global City: Globalization as Local Process* (London: Routledge, 1997); Gerry Kearns and Chris Philo (editors), *Selling Places: The City as Cultural Capital, Past and Present* (Oxford: Pergamon, 1993); David Harvey. "From Space to Place and Back Again: Reflections on the Condition of Postmodernity," in *Mapping the Future: Local Cultures, Global Change*, edited by J. Bird, B. Curtis, T. Putnam, G. Robertson, and L. Tucker (London: Routledge, 1993), 3–29.

7. From the *Louisiana Weekly* newspaper, July and August 1963, quoted in

Arnold R. Hirsch and Joseph Logsdon, *Creole New Orleans: Race and Americanization* (Louisiana State University Press, 1992), 287.

8. Figures on the changing racial population of New Orleans come from U.S. Census Bureau, Census of Population and Housing, 1940–1960.

9. Minutes of Meeting of the Executive Committee of the Chamber of Commerce of the New Orleans Area, June 1, 1959, volume 96 (MSS 66, NOCC, UNO).

10. Harris, Kerr, Forster and Company, *Trends in the Hotel-Motel Business: Twenty-Eighth Annual Review* (Atlanta: Harris, Kerr, Forster, 1964).

11. Reports about the lack of hotel space and constrained convention situation are repeated time and again in reports and minutes of meetings of the Convention and Visitors Bureau (CVB), the Board of Directors, and the Executive Committee of the Chamber of Commerce during the 1940s and 1950s. For example, "Local Hotel Situation," in Minutes of Meeting of the Executive Committee of the Chamber of Commerce, January 26, 1948, volume 70, p. 7; Minutes of Regular Semi-Monthly Meeting of the Board of Directors, New Orleans Chamber of Commerce, May 8, 1951, volume 76, p. 2; Minutes of Meeting of the Board of Directors, Chamber of Commerce of the New Orleans Area, July 26, 1955, volume 86, p. 15 (MSS 66, NOCC, UNO).

12. Minutes of Meeting of the Executive Committee, January 26, 1948, volume 70 (MSS 66, NOCC, UNO).

13. Minutes of Meeting of the Board of Directors, Chamber of Commerce of the New Orleans Area, July 26, 1955, volume 86, p. 15 (MSS 66, NOCC, UNO).

14. Civic Affairs Committee Letter from Leonard V. Huber, Chairman to Mr. C. C. Walther, President, and Members, Board of Directors, New Orleans Association of Commerce, February 9, 1949, volume 72, p. 2 (MSS 66, NOCC, UNO).

15. Minutes of Meeting of the Board of Directors of the Chamber of Commerce, April 26, 1949, volume 72, p. 2 (MSS 66, NOCC, UNO).

16. "HB 1412 Prohibiting Interracial Social and Athletic Activities," Minutes of Executive Committee Meeting of the Chamber of Commerce, July 16, 1956, volume 90, pp. 14–18 (MSS 66, NOCC, UNO).

17. Minutes of Meeting of the Executive Committee, Chamber of Commerce of the New Orleans Area, March 16, 1959, volume 96, p. 2 (MSS 66, NOCC, UNO).

18. Morton Inger, *Politics and Reality in an American City: The New Orleans School Crisis of 1960* (New York: Center for Urban Education, 1969), 61–62; Joseph Luders, "The Economics of Movement Success: Business Responses to Civil Rights Mobilization," *American Journal of Sociology* 111 (January 2006): 980.

19. From the *Louisiana Weekly* newspaper, July and August 1963, quoted in Hirsch and Logsdon, *Creole New Orleans*, 287.

20. Michael J. Flynn and Linda Kephart Flynn. *The Evolution of CVBs: Serving Exhibitions for More Than a Century,* 1999, at http://expoweb2.pubdyn .com/Show_Management_101/feature436.htm (accessed April 29, 2006).

21. A summary of the Commerce Department's 1957 booklet, "Your Community Can Profit from the Tourist Business," is contained in "Findings of Chamber of Commerce Subcommittee on Tourism," 1960, Box 7, Folder 5 (MSS 66, NOCC, UNO).

22. Quote from *Tourist Planning Report,* 1960, volume 98 (MSS 66, NOCC, UNO).

23. Ibid; emphasis in original.

24. Minutes of Meeting of the Executive Committee of the Chamber of Commerce, April 4, 1952, volume 78, p. 6 (MSS 66, NOCC, UNO).

25. Discussion of the groups and organizations in favor and opposed to the creation of an autonomous tourist bureau is found in "Proposal to Raise Funds for Convention Promotion through Chamber's Convention and Visitor's Bureau: Proposal to Promote Tourist Trade through Formation of Separate Agency," in Minutes of Meeting of the Executive Committee, March 16, 1959, volume 96; Minutes of Special Meeting of the Executive Committee of the Chamber of Commerce of the New Orleans Area, March 18, 1959, volume 96 (MSS 66, NOCC, UNO).

26. Letter from deLesseps S. Morrison, Mayor, City of New Orleans, to Lawrence A. Molony, President, Chamber of Commerce of the New Orleans Area, October 20, 1954, volume 85 (MSS 66, NOCC, UNO).

27. The purpose of the GNOTCC is quoted in "Tourist Group Set up for N.O.," *Times-Picayune* (April 5, 1960), 1.

28. "Report of Tourist Planning Committee; Formation of Independent Visitors Development Commission; Transfer of Activities of Chamber's Convention and Visitors Bureau to New Agency" in Minutes of Meeting of the Board of Directors of the Chamber of Commerce, March 22, 1960, volume 98 (MSS 66, NOCC, UNO); "CC Directors OK Tourism Report," *Times-Picayune* (March 23, 1960); "Tourist Group Is 'In Business,'" *Times-Picayune* (July 1, 1960).

29. "Report of U.S. Chamber Covering Analysis of Operation and Activities of New Orleans Chamber; Consolidation of Convention Commission with Chamber; Program of Work" in Minutes of Meeting of the Board of Directors, June 11, 1963, volume 104, p. 13 (MSS 66, NOCC, UNO).

30. Quote from *Tourist Planning Report,* 1960, volume 98 (MSS 66, NOCC, UNO).

31. Greater New Orleans Tourist and Convention Commission (GNOTCC), *Annual Report,* 1973–74 (New Orleans: GNOTCC, 1974).

32. "Ceremony Marks Start of Hotel," *New Orleans States Item* (May 20, 1969); Frank Schneider, "1971 Is Recalled as Year They Built Those Hotels," *Times-Picayune* (January 23, 1972); Greater New Orleans Tourist and Convention Commission (GNTOCC), "Greater New Orleans Tourism Goals," GNOTCC *Annual Report* (New Orleans: GNTOCC, 1970–1971).

33. Greater New Orleans Tourist and Convention Commission (GNOTCC), *Ten-Year Report, 1960–1970* (New Orleans: GNOTCC, 1970); Don Lee Keith, "City Still Attracting Throngs," *Times-Picayune* (January 23, 1972), sec. 7, p. 11.

34. "N.O. to Get Regular Cruise Service," *Times-Picayune* (January 15, 1974), 1.

35. Quoted in Walter Gallas, "Neighborhood Preservation and Politics in New Orleans: Vieux Carré Property Owners, Residents and Associates, Inc. and City Government, 1938–1983," M.A. thesis, University of New Orleans, 1996, 55–56.

36. GNTOCC, "Greater New Orleans Tourism Goals," 1.

37. "Market Study and Economic Analysis of Proposed Exhibition Convention Facility for New Orleans as Part of International Trade Mart Complex," in Minutes of Meeting of the Board of Directors, August 8, 1961, volume 101, p. 3 (MSS 66, NOCC, UNO); "City Exhibition Hall Need Seen as Urgent in Report," *Times-Picayune* (August 8, 1961).

38. Real Estate Research Corporation, *Economic Survey of the Central Area of New Orleans* (Chicago: Real Estate Research Corporation, 1960), 7.

39. Quoted in Minutes of Special Meeting of the Executive Committee of the Chamber of Commerce of the New Orleans Area, March 18, 1959, volume 96, p. 4 (MSS 66, NOCC, UNO).

40. Tourist Planning Committee, 1960, Report of Subcommittee No. 2, volume 98, p. 4 (MSS 66, NOCC, UNO).

41. "VC Group Demands Probe to Place Disaster Blame," *Times-Picayune* (September 22, 1966).

42. Gallas, "Neighborhood Preservation and Politics in New Orleans," 66.

43. Quoted in ibid., 55–56.

44. For an overview of the Riverfront Expressway controversy, see Richard O. Baumbach and William Borah, *The Second Battle of New Orleans: A History of the Vieux Carre Riverfront Expressway Controversy* (Birmingham: University of Alabama Press, 1981).

45. Interview with W. H. B., New Orleans, June 15, 2003.

46. "Hotelville," *Vieux Carre Courier* (July 5, 1968), 4

47. Interview with B. C. C., New Orleans, May 12, 2003.

48. "Hotelville," 4.

49. Baumbach and Borah, *Second Battle of New Orleans*; "Quarter Hotel Ban Voted By Council," *New Orleans States Item* (January 3, 1969).

50. "Suit Attacks Son et Lumiere," *Times-Picayune* (August 18, 1973). Mayor Landrieu quoted in "Son et Lumiere Show in Square," *Times-Picyaune* (April 26, 1973). "Sound and Light: Final Bout?" *Times-Picayune* (June 7, 1975), sec. 1, p. 12; "Turn Off Sound and Light," *Times-Picayune* (July 16, 1975).

51. Sally K. Reeves, "Making Groceries: Public Markets and Corner Stores in Old New Orleans," *Gulf South Historical Review* 16 (2000): 40–43.

52. French Market Corporation, *French Market District: America's Oldest Market,* at: www.frenchmarket.org/history.htm (accessed July 3, 2004).

53. Stella Pitts, "French Market Controversy Is Nothing New," *Times-Picayune* (April 13, 1975), sec. 2, p. 2; J. E. Bourgoyne, "Vieux Carre Commission Too Strong or Too Weak?" *Times-Picayune* (December 30, 1975).

NOTES TO CHAPTER 6

1. Letter from Frank S. Craig, Jr., President, Council for a Better Louisiana, to the Honorable Secretary of Commerce, Washington, D.C., 31 January 1977, in New Orleans Public Library, City Archives: 1984 Louisiana Exposition Collection.

2. "N.O. Fair Designer Promises a Temporary Magic Kingdom," *Times-Picayune* (November 7, 1981).

3. "Master Plan: Visitors at '84 Fair Will Find Water, Water Everywhere," *Times-Picayune* (November 15, 1981), sec. 1, p. 20; Mitchell Osborne, *1984 World's Fair, New Orleans: The Official Guidebook,* edited by Linda C. Delery (New Orleans: Picayune, 1984); *Annual Reports of the Louisiana World Exposition, Inc.,* 1981, 1982, 1983; *Exposition World* 1, (March 1982), in Williams Research Center, Historic New Orleans Collection: Mary Meeks Morrison and Jacob Morrison Papers, MS 553, Box 26.

4. "World's Fair in Financial Bind as Bills Come Due, Sources Say," *Times-Picayune* (January 24, 1984); "Fair Passes Deadline with Large Bills Unpaid," *Times-Picayune* (April 21, 1984); "House Oks Bailout for World's Fair," *Times-Picayune* (April 24, 1984); "Contractors, Fair Officials Try Again to Work out Millions in Overdue Bills," *Times-Picayune* (June 8, 1984); "Fair Seeks Bankruptcy Protection," *Times-Picayune* (September 7, 1984).

5. Quoted in Wayne King, "Failed Fair Gives New Orleans a Painful Hangover," *New York Times* (November 12, 1984), 16.

6. Quoted in William E. Schmidt, "Doubts Are on Exhibit Also as Fair Nears Opening Day in New Orleans," *New York Times* (May 6, 1984), 23.

7. Patricia Gay, "The 1984 World's Fair, the Warehouse District, and the Preservation Industry," *Preservation in Print* (June/July 2004), 6; "Residuals May Sweeten Taste of Fair," *Times-Picayune* (November 12, 1984); "Big Losses Paved Way for Growth," *Times-Picayune* (May 12, 1994); Rebecca Mowbray

and Greg Thomas, "That Was Then, This Is Now: The 1984 World's Fair—20 Years Later," *Times-Picayune* (May 9, 2004).

8. Paul Goldberger, "There's Fun in the Fair's Architecture, but Not Quite Enough," *New York Times* (May 13, 1984), 24.

9. Mowbray and Thomas, "That Was Then, This Is Now," F1.

10. For discussions of touristic culture, see Michel Picard, *Bali: Cultural Tourism and Touristic Culture* (Singapore: Archipelago Press, 1996); Adrian Franklin and Mike Crang, "The Trouble with Tourism and Travel Theory," *Tourist Studies* 1 (2001): 5–22.

11. "Residuals Real Reason for '84 Fair," *Times-Picayune* (January 25, 1983); "New Convention Center Called 98% Complete," *Times-Picayune* (November 10, 1983); "New Center Locks in Tourism as Bulwark of New Orleans Economy," *Times-Picayune* (December 5, 1983); "Developers Deal for Fair Site," *Times-Picayune* (January 28, 1984); "Residuals May Sweeten Taste of Fair," *Times-Picayune* (November 12, 1984); "New Orleans Fair Get a Boat-Whistling, Specifying Start," *New York Times* (May 13, 1984).

12. "Shop Rents in Quarter Skyrocket: Businesses Are Forced Out, Merchants Say," *Times-Picayune* (July 30, 1983); "Thousands Line up for Fair Jobs," *Times-Picayune* (November 10, 1983), 15; "Rescue Mission at the Fair," *New York Times* (June 24, 1984); Wayne King, "Failed Fair Gives New Orleans a Painful Hangover," *New York Times* (November 12, 1984); "New Orleans Fair Is Fun but Too Few Are Going," *New York Times* (June 18, 1984), 12.

13. Arnold R. Hirsch, "New Orleans: Sunbelt in the Swamp," in *Sunbelt Cities: Politics and Growth since World War II*, edited by Richard M. Bernard and Bradley R. Rice (Austin: University of Texas Press, 1983), 100–37; Beverly Wright. "Black New Orleans: The City That Care Forgot," in *In Search of the New South: The Black Urban Experience in the 1970s and 1980s*, edited by Robert Bullard (Tuscaloosa: University of Alabama Press, 1989), 45–74; Robert K. Whelan and Alma Young, "New Orleans: The Ambivalent City," in *Big City Politics in Transition*, edited by H. V. Savitch and John Clayton Thomas (Newbury Park, Calif.: Sage, 1991), 132–48; Nan Perales, "Hotels Trying to Ride out Slump," *Times-Picayune/States Item* (June 19, 1985), sec. 1, p. 4; Nan Perales, "Hotels: Slump Is Hitting Workers Too; Number of Jobs Trails Expansion," *Times-Picayune/States Item* (July 21, 1985); Nan Perales, "New Orleans's Conventions: Is the Money There?" *Times-Picayune/States Item* (March 3, 1985), sec. 1, p. 10.

14. Michael Demarest, "The Worldliest World's Fair," *Time Magazine* (May 27, 1984).

15. Local newspapers began to document the revenue problems of New Orleans as early as 1966, and media coverage continued throughout the decade. For example: "4 Researchers Here to Study Financial Crisis," *New Orleans States Item* (July 19, 1966); "City Revenues Short," *New Orleans States Item*

(September 30, 1967); "Trouble Seen for City's 1968 Budget Plans," *Times-Pic-ayune* (July 11, 1967); "Financial Outlook Dim," *New Orleans States Item* (April 30, 1968); "City Is Facing Fund Shortage," *Times-Picayune* (June 21, 1968); "More Fiscal Hot Water for City," *New Orleans States Item* (August 23, 1968); "City Spending Frozen; Budget Slash Blamed," *New Orleans States Item* (January 6, 1969); "$1,947,812 Budget Deficit Is Cited," *Times-Picayune* (March 27, 1969); Office of Policy Planning and Analysis, Majorie Fox Larson (compiler), "The New Orleans Economic Outlook, 1976–1981," April 26, 1976, in Loyola University Archives, Mayor Moon Landrieu Collection, Box 121, Folder 5, MS 2.

16. The changing ratio of tax revenue is reported in "City of New Orleans Operating Budget, 1964 and 1984," calculations by the Commission on the Future of the City, April 1985, in "Recommendations for the Future of New Orleans," Tulane University, Howard-Tilton Memorial Library, Louisiana Collection, Blanche F. Mysing Papers, Box 3, Folder 86, MS 804-A, p. 44.

17. These fiscal constraints included (a) a reduction in the ability of local governments to collect income taxes, thereby increasing their reliance on revenue from sales taxes; (b) a statute that two-thirds of both houses of the state legislature had to approve any increase in an existing local tax; and, (c) an expanded exemption on homeowners' property taxes. The state legislature increased this homestead exemption from $50,000 of assessed valuation in 1974 to $75,000 in 1982 (Michael Peter Smith and Marlene Keller, " 'Managed Growth' and the Politics of Uneven Development in New Orleans," in *Restructuring the City: The Political Economy of Urban Redevelopment,* edited by Susan Fainstein, Norman I. Fainstein, Richard Child Hill, Dennis Judd, and Michael Peter Smith [New York: Longman, 1986], 150–54). On the local level, New Orleans's long tradition of elected assessors who owned their assessor data bases, and distribution of assessed property values, meant that assessors appraised few homes over $75,000 (Lawrence Knopp, "Exploiting the Rent Gap: The Theoretical Significance of Using Illegal Appraisal Schemes to Encourage Gentrification in New Orleans," *Urban Geography* 11 [1990]: 48–64; Lawrence Knopp, "Some Theoretical Implications of Gay Involvement in an Urban Land Market," *Political Geography Quarterly* 9 [1990]: 337–52; Mickey Lauria, "The Implications of Marxian Rent Theory for Community-Controlled Redevelopment Strategies," *Journal of Planning Education and Research* 4 [1984]: 16–24).

18. "Mayor Seeks Bigger Role for City in Fair Planning," *Times-Picayune* (August 7, 1981); "World's Fair May Hurt City, Morial Says," *Times-Picayune* (September 16, 1981); "Morial's Skepticism Putting Treen on the Hot Seat," *Times-Picayune* (September 20, 1981); "Is Morial Being Unfair to the Fair? Depends on Who's Talking," *Times-Picayune* (September 20, 1981).

19. "Hire Residents for Jobs with Fair, Morial Asks," *Times-Picayune* (February 19, 1983). The Louisiana State Legislature also attacked exposition plan-

ners and organizers for awarding a disproportionate number of contracts to out-of-state firms ("House Panel Attacks World's Fair Contracts," *Times-Picayune* [January 6, 1983]).

20. "Morial: Fair's Backers Lack Concern for the City," *Times-Picayune* (September 25, 1981), 7.

21. "Council Warns Fair Officials to Cooperate with City," *Times-Picayune* (January 7, 1983).

22. Editorial, "World's Fair—Some Questions," *Times-Picayune* (September 20, 1981), 22.

23. "World's Fair Feels Squeeze," *Times-Picayune* (September 16, 1981); "Treen Threatens to Abandon Fair," *Times-Picayune* (September 17, 1981).

24. "Council Delays Vote on Fair Audit," *Times-Picayune* (February 17, 1982); Frank Donze, "Giarrusso Seeking World's Fair Records," *Times-Picayune* (March 15, 1984).

25. Quoted in Nicolas Lemann, "Hard Times in the Big Easy," *Atlantic* 259 (1987).

26. "Jackson Warns of '84 Fair Rights Fight," *Times-Picayune* (July 7, 1982).

27. "Fair's Black Hiring Unfair," *Times-Picayune* (September 12, 1982).

28. "Selling World's Fair to Legislature No Easy Task," *Times-Picayune* (January 9, 1983), 33.

29. "Women and Blacks at Fair," *Times-Picayune* (January 9, 1983); "Fair Wants Blacks, Women, Boggs Says," *Times-Picayune* (January 18, 1983).

30. Letter from John T. Scott et al. to Honorable Ernest N. Morial, Mayor, et al., February 10, 1984; Letter from Mrs. Jo Griffin Web to Mrs. Noelle LeBlanc et al., February 10, 1984, in New Orleans Public Library, City Archives: 1984 Louisiana Exposition Collection, Box 72, Folder 2.

31. Quoted in Joe Massa, "Fair Is Expected to Bring Significant Economic Boom," *Times-Picayune/States Item* (September 20, 1980), 1.

32. For descriptions of world's fairs, Disney theme parks, and tourist attractions as "bread and circuses," see David Harvey, *The Condition of Postmodernity: An Enquiry into the Origins of Cultural Change* (New York: Blackwell, 1987); David Harvey, "Voodoo Cities." *New Statesman and Society* 1 (September 30, 1988): 33–35; Gerry Kearns and Chris Philo (editors), *Selling Places: The City as Cultural Capital, Past and Present* (Oxford: Pergamon, 1993).

33. Mary-Kate Tews (preparer), "Artworks '84: An Arts and Cultural Affairs Program for the 1984 Louisiana World Exposition," presented to the LWE Arts Consortium, January 12, 1983, in New Orleans Public Library, City Archives: 1984 Louisiana Exposition Collection. For the history of the Arts Council of New Orleans, see http://www.artscouncilofneworleans.org/ (accessed April 20, 2006).

34. Clifford Geertz, *The Interpretation of Cultures* (New York: Basic Books, 1973), 89.

35. Jeffrey K. Olick (editor), *States of Memory: Continuities, Conflicts, and Transformations in National Retrospection* (Durham, N.C.: Duke University Press, 2003).

36. Diane Barthel, *Historic Preservation: Collective Memory and Historical Identity* (New Brunswick, N.J.: Rutgers University Press, 1996); Robin Wagner-Pacifici and Barry Schwartz, "The Vietnam Veterans Memorial: Commemorating a Difficult Past," *American Journal of Sociology* 97 (September 1991): 376–420; John Walton, *Storied Land: Community and Memory in Monterey* (Berkeley: University of California Press, 2001).

37. Gay, "1984 World's Fair, Warehouse District, and Preservation Industry."

38. Grace Elizabeth King, *Memories of a Southern Woman of Letters* (New York: Macmillan, 1932), 55.

39. Arjun Appadurai, *Modernity at Large: Cultural Dimensions of Globalization* (Minneapolis: University of Minnesota Press, 1996); Ulrich Beck, *What Is Globalization?* (Cambridge: Polity, 1999); Mike Featherstone, Scott Lash, and Roland Robertson (editors), *Global Modernities* (Thousand Oaks, Calif.: Sage, 1995); Roland Robertson, *Globalization: Social Theory and Global Culture* (Thousand Oaks, Calif.: Sage, 1996); John Urry, *The Tourist Gaze*, second edition (Thousand Oaks, Calif.: Sage, 2002).

40. Brand Strategy, Inc., *The BrandScience Guide for Destination Research: The Handbook to Help Convention and Visitors Bureaus Manage Tourism Research for Destinations* (N.p.: Brand Strategy, October 2004), at http://www.destinationmarketing.org (accessed September 6, 2006).

41. For reports and discussions of New Orleans's fiscal problems and growing poverty during 1980s and 1990s and beyond, see the citations in note 13; see also Mickey Lauria, Robert K. Whelan, and Alma H. Young, "Revitalization of New Orleans," in *Urban Revitalization: Policies and Programs,* edited by Fritz W. Wagner, Timothy E. Joder, and Anthony J. Mumphrey Jr. (Thousand Oaks, Calif.: Sage, 1995), 102–27.

42. New Orleans Tourism Marketing Corporation (NOTMC), *Annual Report* (New Orleans: NOTMC, 2003).

43. The phrase "as if tourists" comes from Terry Nichols Clark, Richard Lloyd, Kenneth K. Wong, and Pushpam Jain, "Amenities Drive Urban Growth," *Journal of Urban Affairs* 24 (2002): 493–515.

44. Around the world, Convention and Visitor's Bureaus (CVBs) have embraced and implemented branding strategies to clearly define their local attractions, differentiate them from competitors in the minds of visitors, and create a "promise" that frames the destination experience for visitors. Slogans like "Live Large, Think Big" (Dallas), "City of Angels" (Los Angeles), and "Country Mu-

sic Capital of the World" (Nashville) are part of the repertoire of local urban branding and represent strategic efforts to identify a city's image and establish a singular personality (Special Report from the International Association of Convention and Visitor Bureaus [IACVB], "Developing a Genuine Destination Brand," *Nation's Cities Weekly* [May 9, 2005], at http://www.iacvb.org/ (accessed May 21, 2006); Leon Stafford, "Las Vegas: Gambling. Orlando: Disney. New Orleans Bourbon Street. Atlanta: Hmmm . . ." *Atlanta Journal-Constitution* [May 10, 2005]; Nick Miroff, "Taking a Tip from Madison Avenue, Towns Buy into Branding," *Washington Post* [July 17, 2005], B1).

45. New Orleans Tourism Marketing Corporation (NOTMC), *Annual Report* (New Orleans: NOTMC, 2002).

46. New Orleans Tourism Marketing Corporation (NOTMC), *Annual Report* (New Orleans: NOTMC, 2003).

47. Ibid.

48. Paul Chatterton and Robert Hollands, *Urban Nightscapes: Youth Cultures, Pleasure Spaces, and Corporate Power* (London: Routledge, 2003); John Hannigan, *Fantasy City: Pleasure and Profit in the Postmodern Metropolis* (New York: Routledge, 1998); Allen J. Scott, *The Cultural Economy of Cities: Essays on the Geography of Image-Producing Industries* (London: Sage, 2000).

49. George Ritzer, *Enchanting a Disenchanted World: Revolutionizing the Means of Consumption*, second edition (Thousand Oaks, Calif.: Pine Forge, 2005); George Ritzer, *The Globalization of Nothing* (Thousand Oaks, Calif.: Pine Forge, 2004); Scott Lash and John Urry, *Economies of Signs and Space* (London: Sage, 1994).

50. Interview with T. S. R., New Orleans, May 4, 2003.

51. Interview with S. T. U., New Orleans, June 12, 2003.

52. New Orleans Multicultural Tourism Network, at www.soulofneworleans .com (accessed January 21, 2003).

53. New Orleans Jazz Orchestra, at http://www.thenojo.com/mission.html (accessed December 12, 2005).

54. C. Ray Nagin, "Mayor Builds Music Industry," City of New Orleans, Mayor's Office of Communications, press release, August 9, 2004.

55. The quote "re-image and re-brand" is from Stephen Perry, president and CEO of the NOMCVB, quoted in Rebecca Mowbray, "$30 Million for Tourism OK'd: It's a Good Start, Visitors Bureau Says," *Times-Picayune* (April 22, 2006).

56. "Hyatt-Superdome Area to Be Redeveloped into New Hyatt Jazz District: Finished Site to Generate More Than 6,500 Permanent Jobs," City of New Orleans, press release, May 30, 2006, at http://www.thenojo.com/ (accessed July 28, 2006); Rebecca Mowbray, Michelle Krupa, and Greg Thomas, "Plan Would Reshape Downtown to Build Jazz Center," *Times-Picayune* (May 30, 2006).

NOTES TO CHAPTER 7

1. J. E. Bourgoyne, "Is the Emphasis on Tourism Ruining the Vieux Carre?" *Times-Picayune* (December 23, 1973), 4.

2. James Nolan, "We Watch as the Quarter Is Drained of Its Soul," *Times-Picayune* (May 20, 2001), B7.

3. Interview with H. S. L., New Orleans, July 19, 2003.

4. Walter Gallas, "Neighborhood Preservation and Politics in New Orleans: Vieux Carré Property Owners, Residents and Associates, Inc. and City Government, 1938–1983," M.A. thesis, University of New Orleans, 1996; John Foley, "Neighborhood Movements, Identity, and Change in New Orleans's French Quarter" (Ph.D. dissertation, University of New Orleans, 1999); John Foley and Mickey Lauria, "Historic Preservation in New Orleans French Quarter: Unresolved Racial Tensions," in *Knights and Castles: Minorities and Urban Regeneration,* edited by Huw Thomas and Francesco L. Piccolo (Burlington, Conn.: Ashgate, 2003); John Foley and Mickey Lauria, "Plans, Planning, and Tragic Choices," *Planning Theory and Practice* 1 (2000): 219–33.

5. National Trust for Historic Preservation, "11 Most Endangered Historical Places," at http://www.nationaltrust.org/11Most/list.asp?i=62 (accessed April 11, 2006).

6. University of New Orleans, College of Urban and Public Affairs, *Changing Land Use in the Vieux Carre: Managing Growth to Preserve a National Landmark District* (University of New Orleans, 1992); Randi Kaufman, "The Social Impacts of Condominium Conversion in the Vieux Carre Neighborhood" (M.A. thesis, University of New Orleans, 1999); Catherine Vesey, "Tourism Impacts in the Vieux Carre: An Analysis of Cultural Issues, Residential Perspectives, and Sustainable Tourism Planning," Ph.D. dissertation, University of New Orleans, 1999; "Condo Growth Irks Residents," *New Orleans City Business* (June 12, 2000); "Quarter Condos Spur Sales, Conflict," *Times-Picayune* (April 12, 2003).

7. Greater New Orleans Community Data Center (compilers), "U.S. Census Bureau, Census 2000 Full-Count Characteristics (SF1)," at www.gnocdc.org (accessed June 1, 2005).

8. See my article, Kevin Fox Gotham, "Tourism Gentrification: The Case of New Orleans's Vieux Carre (French Quarter)," *Urban Studies* 42 (2005): 1099–1121. According to the U.S. Census Bureau, the Vieux Carre consists of census tracts 38, 42, and 47. In census tract 38, median housing value in constant 2000 dollars increased more than seven times, from $64,474 in 1950 to $460,000 in 2000. The cost of rent also increased dramatically after 1950, from $193.82 per month in census tract 38 to $549 per month in 2000. Census tracts 42 and 47 show similar trends.

9. Chris Rose, "Larry Flynt: The 60-Second Interview," *Times-Picayune* (May 27, 2004), E1, E7.

10. Figures on the growth of hotel rooms in the French Quarter from 1960 to 1982 are reported in Rick Raber, "Laws Can't Stop Hotel Expansion in the French Quarter," *Times-Picayune* (July 31, 1983).

11. "French Quarter Groups Sue To Stop Marriott," Associated Press News Release (August 29, 2000); "Resident, Developers Trade Barbs over Hotel," *New Orleans City Business* (October 23, 2000); "Quarter Residents to Fight Hotel," *New Orleans City Business* (December 11, 2000).

12. Bruce Eggler, "Quarter Hotel Conversion Gets Panel OK; Plan Needs Waiver of 35-Year Ban," *Times-Picayune* (August 11, 2004).

13. Mark Gottdiener, *Theming of America: Dreams, Visions, and Commercial Spaces,* second edition (New York: Westview, 2001); Paul Chatterton and Robert Hollands, *Urban Nightscapes: Youth Cultures, Pleasure Spaces, and Corporate Power* (London: Routledge, 2003).

14. Iris Kelso, "A Clear Choice," *Times-Picayune* (May 18, 1986).

15. VCPORA advertisement opposing the Aquarium of the Americas, *Times-Picayune* (November 3, 1986), A7.

16. "Orleans Zoo Chief Loves Challenges," *Times-Picayune* (November 16, 1986).

17. Marks Lewis Torre and Associates, *Report on the Existing Conditions on Bourbon Street* (New Orleans: Marks Lewis Torre and Associates, 1977).

18. Vesey, "Tourism Impacts in the Vieux Carre."

19. Quoted in Michael J. Smith, "Quarter's Keepers," *Times-Picayune* (June 21, 1998), B1.

20. One major symposium titled "Selling the City . . . Without Selling Out," March 24–26, 1988, brought together local, national, and international groups to "explore the issues and opportunities surrounding economic development through the planned management of tourism around heritage and cultural sites." Sponsored by the National Trust for Historic Preservation, the symposium examined "the consequences of increased tourism on the Vieux Carre" and noted the need to "seek community strategies to expand tourism while protecting valuable cultural resources" (Letter from Ann Masson, Symposium Coordinator, to Mrs. Mary Morrison, February 18, 1988, in Williams Research Center, Historic New Orleans Collection, Mary Meeks Morrison and Jacob Morrison Papers, Box 39, MS 553).

21. Speech by Mary Morrison to the New Orleans Association of University Women, Tulane University, May 27, 1972, in Williams Research Center, Historic New Orleans Collection, Mary Meeks Morrison and Jacob Morrison Papers, Folder: "Then and Now Speech," MS 553.

22. Interview with J. F. B., New Orleans, June 12, 2003.

23. Interview with B. E. D., New Orleans, July 13, 2003.

24. Interview with M. M. M., New Orleans, July 24, 2003.

25. Interview with J. F. B., New Orleans, May 14, 2005.

26. Interview with H. S. S., New Orleans, May 14, 2003.

27. Interview with B. E. D., New Orleans, April 16, 2005.

28. Cosimo Matassa, interview with Michael Hurtt, *OffBeat Magazine* (June 2004), 64.

29. Maria Kefalas, *Working Class Heroes: Protecting, Home, Community, and Nation in a Chicago Neighborhood* (Berkeley: University of California Press, 2003).

30. Elijah Anderson, *Streetwise: Race, Class, and Change in an Urban Community* (Chicago: University of Chicago Press, 1990); Mitchell Duneier, *Slim's Table* (Chicago: University of Chicago Press, 1992); Philip Kasinitz, "The Gentrification of 'Boerum Hill': Neighborhood Change and Conflicts over Definitions," *Qualitative Sociology* 11 (1988): 163–82; Bryan S. Turner, "A Note on Nostalgia," *Theory, Culture, and Society* 4 (1987): 147–56.

31. Quoted in David Frisby, *Cityscapes of Modernity* (New York: Polity, 2001), 114.

32. Robert A. Beauregard, *Voices of Decline: The Postwar Fate of U.S. Cities* (New York: Routledge, 1993), 37.

33. Erving Goffman, *Frame Analysis: An Essay on the Organization of Experience* (New York: Harper, 1974), 21.

34. Philip Kasinitz and David Hillyard, "The Old-Timer's Tale: The Politics of Nostalgia on the Waterfront," *Journal of Contemporary Ethnography* 24 (1995): 156.

35. Interview with M. C. V., New Orleans, June 6, 2004.

36. Interview with H. S. L., New Orleans, June 13, 2004.

37. Anthropologist Victor Turner introduced the idea of liminal space as an "in-between" space, a space of transformation between phases of estrangement/separation and integration/belonging (Victor Turner, *Dramas, Fields, and Metaphors: Symbolic Action in Human Society* [Ithaca, N.Y.: Cornell University Press, 1975]). Geographer Rob Shields and sociologist Sharon Zukin have used the concept liminal space to refer to practices, cultures, and identities that are positioned between the global and local, the sacred and profane, and the public and private spaces (Rob Shields, *Places on the Margin* [London: Routledge, Chapman Hall, 1991]; Sharon Zukin, *Landscapes of Power* [Berkeley: University of California Press, 1991]; Sharon Zukin, "Postmodern Urban Landscapes: Mapping Culture and Power," in *Modernity and Identity*, edited by Scott Lash and John Friedman [New York: Blackwell, 1992], 221–47).

38. Interview with R. L. L., New Orleans, August 12, 2004.

39. Interview with L. F. S., New Orleans, April 29, 2004.

40. Interview with P. G. G., New Orleans, March 29, 2005.

41. Interview with N. C. C., New Orleans, June 19, 2005.

42. Interview with G. N. C., New Orleans, June 10, 2005.

43. New Orleans Spring Fiesta Association, at http://www.springfiesta.com/ (accessed September 12, 2006).

44. Interview with D. S. S., New Orleans, June 2, 2005.

45. Quoted in New Orleans International Music Colloquium (NOIMC), at http://www.noimc.org/ (accessed September 12, 2006).

46. Interview with S. S. L., New Orleans, December 2, 2003.

47. Interview with with J. L. C., New Orleans, May 4, 2005.

48. Pierre Bourdieu, *In Other Words: Essays Toward a Reflexive Sociology,* translated by Matthew Adamson (Stanford, Calif.: Stanford University Press, 1990), 130.

49. Daniel J. Boorstin, *The Image: A Guide to Pseudo-Events in America* (New York: Harper and Row, 1964); Dean MacCannell, *Empty Meeting Grounds: The Tourist Papers* (New York: Routledge, 1992); Dean MacCannell. *The Tourist: A New Theory of the Leisure Class* (New York: Schocken, 1976).

50. Susan Fainstein, Lily M. Hoffman, and Dennis R. Judd, "Making Theoretical Sense of Tourism," in *Cities and Visitors: Regulating People, Markets, and City Space,* edited by Lily M. Hoffman, Susan S. Fainstein, and Dennis R. Judd (New York: Blackwell, 2003), 240–53.

51. Pierre Bourdieu, "Social Space and Symbolic Power," *Sociological Theory* 7 (1989): 14–25.

52. For example, Michael Sorkin (editor), *Variations on a Theme Park: The New American City and the End of Public Space* (New York: Hill and Wang, 1992); Alan Bryman, "Disneyization of Society," *Sociological Review* 47 (1999): 25–47. For an overview of the Disneyfication thesis, see Bart Eeckhout, "The 'Disneyification' of Times Square: Back to the Future?" in *Critical Perspectives on Urban Redevelopment,* edited by Kevin Fox Gotham (New York: Elsevier, 2001), 379–428.

53. In 1968, *Harper's Magazine* columnist Walker Percy warned of the French Quarter turning into "Disneyland Francaise of high rise slave quarters full of Yankee tourists looking out at other Yankee tourists" (Walker Percy, "New Orleans Mon Armour," *Harper's Magazine* [September 1968], 86). For more recent ruminations about the so-called Disneyization of the French Quarter, see "French Quarter: Perils of Prosperity," *Times-Picayune* (May 15, 1994); "Protection: Tensions Mount between Agency, Critics," *Times-Picayune* (May 18, 1994).

54. The concept of "tourist bubble" comes from the work of political scientist, Dennis Judd: "The tourist bubble is like a theme park, in that it provides entertainment and excitement, with reassuringly clean and attractive surroundings" (Dennis Judd, "Constructing the Tourist Bubble," in *The Tourist City,* edited by Dennis R. Judd and Susan S. Fainstein [New Haven, Conn.: Yale University Press, 1999], 39).

NOTES TO CHAPTER 8

1. Interview with E. J. S., New Orleans, May 14, 2003.

2. Interview with Y. S. W., New Orleans, June 7, 2003.

3. *Mardi Gras New Orleans,* at http://www.experienceneworleans.com/mardi gras/quartermardi.html (accessed May 12, 2006).

4. Jeff Duncan, "The Good Times Roll Again in New Orleans, as Carnival Is Deemed a Critical Success," *Times-Picayune* (March 2, 2006).

5. Trymaine Lee, "Indian Tradition Marches on in Devastated Neighborhoods: Spiritual Songs Embody Resilience of City's Tribes," *Times-Picayune* (March 1, 2006).

6. Duncan, "Good Times Roll Again."

7. James J. McLain, "Mardi Gras 2000: Its Economic Impact," *Louisiana Business Survey* 31 (2000): 2–4, 8. McLain also reported that Mardi Gras 2003 generated $20.5 million in direct tax revenues for the city of New Orleans while costing $4.6 million for city services such as police overtime and trash collection (Bob Dart, "Party Pays, Dispels Qualms about Storm," *Atlanta Journal-Constitution* [February 26, 2006], 15A).

8. "For New Orleans, Mardi Gras Is Becoming an All-Year Cash Cow," *New York Times* (February 7, 1999), 6.

9. Alfred Charles, "Revelers Made 1994 a Carnival to Bank On," *Times-Picayune* (January 28, 1995).

10. Krewe of Endymion, *Endymion Krewe History,* at http://www.endymion .org/history.php (accessed September 21, 2006).

11. Vincent Randazzo, " 'King' Danny Kaye to Upset Tradition at the Mardi Gras," *New York Times* (February 9, 1969), 25.

12. Interview with E. L. K., New Orleans, July 7, 2003.

13. Interview with J. B. K., New Orleans, August 16, 2003.

14. Audrey Warren and Geoffrey A. Fowler, "Mardi Gras Bead Mania Bewilders Chinese," *Wall Street Journal* (February 24 200); Siona LaFrance, "The Chinese Connection," *New Orleans Times-Picayune* (February 21, 2001). For an insightful analysis of the global production of Mardi Gras beads, see David Redmon's film, *Mardi Gras: Made in China,* at http://www.mardigrasmadein china.com/ (accessed June 15, 2006).

15. "Going for the Purple, Green, and Gold," *Times-Picayune* (September 7, 2003).

16. Kern Studios, at http://www.kernstudios.com/news/html (accessed May 5, 2004).

17. Arjun Appadurai, *Modernity at Large: Dimensions of Globalization* (Minneapolis: University of Minnesota Press, 1996); Ulf Hannerz, *Cultural Complexity* (New York: Columbia University Press, 1992).

18. Caroline Senter, "Carnival of Errors, *Nation* (April 13, 1992), 496.

19. Larry Rohter, "Bias Law Casts Pall over New Orleans Mardi Gras," *New York Times* (February 2, 1992).

20. Frances Frank Marcus, "New Orleans Outlaws Bias by Mardi Gras Parade Clubs," *New York Times* (December 21, 1991), 7.

21. Quoted in Senter, "Carnival of Errors," 496.

22. Quoted in Marcus, "New Orleans Outlaws Bias," 7

23. Ibid.

24. Rohter, "Bias Law Casts Pall."

25. "The Grinch That Stole Mardi Gras," *Time Magazine* (February 17, 1992), 34.

26. The Krewe of Proteus returned to the streets for Mardi Gras 2000, and local rumor has it that some members of the Krewe of Momus formed the Krewe of Chaos, which started rolling in 2002.

27. Senter, "Carnival of Errors," 496.

28. Rohter, "Bias Law Casts Pall."

29. Quoted in Reid Mitchell, *All on a Mardi Gras Day: Episodes in the History of New Orleans Mardi Gras* (Cambridge: Harvard University Press, 1995), 193.

30. Frances Frank Marcus, "A Sulky Undercurrent at Mardi Gras," *New York Times* (February 14, 1993), 1.

31. Quoted in Alan Sayre, "Krewe Joins Parade of Dropouts: Mardi Gras Club Says 'Fun Is Gone,' " *Houston Chronicle* (August 19, 1992).

32. Senter, "Carnival of Errors," 496.

33. Ibid.

34. Quoted in "Grinch That Stole Mardi Gras," 34.

35. Quoted in Rohter, "Bias Law Casts Pall."

36. Quoted in Marcus, "New Orleans Outlaws Bias," 7.

37. Quoted in Senter, "Carnival of Errors."

38. "New Orleans Weakens Mardi Gras Bias Law," *New York Times* (February 7, 1992), A17.

39. U.S. District Court for the Eastern District of Louisiana, 1994 U.S. District Court, March 10, 1994, *Louisiana Debating and Literary Association, et al., v. City of New Orleans, et al.*, Civil Action No. 93-658 and Consolidated Cases 93-660, 93-661, and 93-685 Section "AD"(4); U.S. District Court of Appeals for the Fifth Circuit, January 26, 1995, *Louisiana Debating and Literary Association, et al., v. City of New Orleans, et al.* 42 F.3d 1483; U.S. District Court for the Eastern District of Louisiana, 1995 U.S. District Court, August 23, 1995, *Louisiana Debating and Literary Association, et al., v. City of New Orleans, et al.*, Civil Action No. 93-0658 and Consolidated Cases Section "D."

40. Michael Omi and Howard Winant, *Racial Formation in the United States: From the 1960s to the 1980s*, second edition (New York: Routledge, 1994), 98.

41. The cost of riding on a float varies enormously by parade. For some smaller krewes, riders might spend $300 on annual dues and $200 to $500 on throws. In the largest parades, riders might spend $700 to $850 in dues, plus a large one-time initiation fee, and anywhere from $200 to $2,500 on throws. In all the krewes, people typically spend additional money on balls, formal attire for parties, cabs, hotel rooms for parade or ball night, costumes, food, and alcohol.

42. Interview with R. L. I., New Orleans, April 19, 2003.

43. Article III, Sec. 34-7, M.C.S., Ord. 19, 314, 1, July 15, 1999.

44. "Talk of the South: Did New Orleans Sell Soul by Marketing Mardi Gras? 'Official' Trademark Seen as Slap at Tradition," *Atlanta Journal and Constitution* (February 2, 1994); "Idea for Mardi Gras Sponsorship on Hold," *Times-Picayune* (February 14, 1994); "Mardi Gras Inc: New Orleanians Outraged over Deal for 'Official' Sponsors," *San Francisco Chronicle* (February 13, 1994); "Mardi Gras Licensing Attacked: Mayor Peppered with Questions," *Times-Picayune* (December 17, 1993).

45. Rebecca Mowbray, "Glad Products to Back, and Bag, Carnival in N.O.; But with Time Winding Down, There's No 'Presenting Sponsor,'" *Times-Picayune* (February 7, 2006), 1; Gordon Russell, "Orleans Seeks Backers to Defray Carnival," *Times-Picayune* (September 6, 2006).

46. Zulu Lundi Gras Festival, at http://www.lundigrasfestival.com/ (accessed 23 April 2006).

47. Websites accessed April 23, 2006; see also Rebecca Mowbray, "Corporate Perks on Parade," *Times-Picayune* (March 2, 2003).

48. Interview with S. L. M., New Orleans, November 6, 2003.

49. Lynne Jensen and Susan Finch, "Want to Ride? It's Membership Decimated by the Hurricane, Zulu Seeks Paraders," *Times-Picayune* (January 11, 2006), 1.

50. Interview with A. H. T., New Orleans, July 16, 2003.

51. Interview with T. S. E., New Orleans, August 12, 2003.

52. Interview with E. L. I., New Orleans, June 24, 2003.

53. Interview with H. S. L., New Orleans, July 19, 2003.

54. "Krewe Controversy: Changing Times," *Times-Picayune* (August 17, 1997), B1; "Beware Creeping Commercialism," *Times-Picayune* (August 20, 1997), B7; "Mardi Gras for Sale," *Times-Picayune* (August 22, 1997), B6; "New Money on Parade," *Economist* (February 21, 1998).

55. The phrase "web of group affiliations" comes from the work of Georg Simmel. Among other works, see his "Metropolis and Mental Life," in *Georg Simmel: On Individuality and Social Forms*, edited by Donald N. Levine (Chicago: Chicago University Press, [1903] 1971), 324–39.

56. Ann Swidler, *Talk of Love: How Culture Matters* (Chicago: University of Chicago Press, 2001).

57. Interview with E. L. I., New Orleans, June 24, 2003.

58. Pierre Bourdieu, *Outline of a Theory of Practice* (London: Cambridge University Press, 1977), 78–87.

59. Eric Hobsbawm and Terence Ranger (editors), *The Invention of Tradition* (Cambridge: Cambridge University Press, 1983).

NOTES TO CHAPTER 9

1. Bruce Eggler, "Different Paths All Leading to New Orleans's Recovery," *Times-Picayune* (November 30, 2005), 1.

2. For an overview of the Urban Land Institute's 's report and the Bring New Orleans Back Commission recommendations, see Molly Reid, "Together at Last? A Recap of the City's Rebuilding Plans," *Times-Picayune* (October 7, 2006), 1.

3. Coleman Warner, "Panel Queried on the Future of N.O.; 'Shrunken Footprint' Worries Residents," *Times-Picayune* (October 13, 2006), 1.

4. Coleman Warner, "Neighbors Protest Housing for Former Addicts," *Times-Picayune* (September 11, 2006), 1.

5. Paul Rioux, "St. Bernard Sued over Rent Limit; Group Says New Law Upholds Segregation," *Times-Picayune* (October 4, 2006), 1.

6. Meghan Gordon, "More Housing for Poor Opposed; Roberts Says That Those from City Are Unwelcome," *Times-Picayune* (October 19, 2006).

7. Laura Maggi and Gwen Filosa, "A Grand Scheme for Reinventing Public Housing Is in the Works, but Displaced Residents Want Action Now," *Times-Picayune* (October 18, 2006).

8. John Pope, "Evoking King, Nagin Calls N.O. 'Chocolate City': Speech Addresses Fear of Losing Black Culture," *Times-Picayune* (January 17, 2006).

9. Adrianna G. Garcia, "Hispanic Laborers Pave Way for City's Return," *Times-Picayune* (October 19, 2005); James Varney, "Nuevo Orleans? An influx of Hispanic Workers in the Wake of Hurricane Katrina Has Some Officials Wondering Why Locals Aren't on the Front Lines of Recovery," *Times-Picayune* (October 18, 2005).

10. Robert Travis Scott, "LA Gets $28.5 Million for Tourism; Area Agencies Get Lion's Share of Aid," *Times-Picayune* (September 20, 2006).

11. Mary Foster, "Shootings Tarnish New Orleans Image," Associated Press Report (July 30, 2006).

12. John Urry, *Consuming Places* (London: Routledge, 1995).

13. Chris Rojek and John Urry (editors), *Touring Cultures: Transformations of Travel and Theory* (London: Routledge, 1997); Mark Gottdiener, "The Consumption of Space and the Spaces of Consumption," in *New Forms of Consumption: Consumers, Culture, and Commodification,* edited by Mark Gottdiener (Lanham, Md.: Rowman and Littlefield, 2000), 265–84; Sharon Zukin,

The Culture of Cities (London: Blackwell, 1995); Richard Lloyd and Terry Nichols Clark, "The City as an Entertainment Machine," in *Critical Perspectives on Urban Redevelopment,* edited by Kevin Fox Gotham (New York: Elsevier, 2001), 357–78.

14. Richard Lloyd argues that city dwellers "do not leave entertainment only to visitors but use their city 'as if tourists,' aggressively pursuing urban consumption opportunities" (Richard Lloyd, *Neo-Bohemia: Art and Commerce in the Postindustrial City* [New York: Routledge, 2006], 126).

15. For example, Michel Picard and Robert E. Wood (editors), *Tourism, Ethnicity, and the State in Asian and Pacific Society* (Honolulu: University of Hawaii Press, 1997); Michel Picard, *Bali: Cultural Tourism and Touristic Culture* (Singapore: Archipelago Press, 1996).

16. Richard Peterson, *Creating Country Music, Fabricating Authenticity* (Chicago: University of Chicago Press, 1997).

17. David Grazian, *Blue Chicago: The Search for Authenticity in Urban Blues Clubs* (Chicago: University of Chicago Press, 2003).

18. Joseph Schumpeter, *Capitalism, Socialism and Democracy* (New York: Harper, [1945] 1975), 82–85.

19. The example of the super krewes is illustrative of Cohen's notion of "emergent authenticity," whereby a "a cultural product or trait thereof, which is at one point generally recognized as inauthentic may, in the course of time, become gradually recognized as authentic, even by experts" (Erik Cohen, "Authenticity and Commodification in Tourism," *Annals of Tourism Research* 15 [1988]: 379).

20. Karl Marx, "The Eighteenth Brumaire of Louis Bonaparte," in *Marx-Engels Reader,* edited by Robert C. Tucker, second edition (New York: Norton, [1952] 1978), 595.

21. Sharon Zukin, "Cultural Strategies of Economic Development and the Hegemony of Vision," in *Urbanization of Injustice,* edited by Andy Merrifield and Erik Swyngedouw (New York: New York University Press, 1997), 241.

22. I thank sociologist Peter Kivisto for suggesting these points to me.

23. New Orleans Jazz and Heritage Foundation, at www.jazznet.org and www.nojazzfest.com (accessed January 3, 2007).

24. Urban Conservancy, at http://urbanconservancy.info/ (accessed December 21, 2006).

25. Interview with C. R. C., New Orleans, November 5, 2005.

26. For an insightful analysis of racial heritage tourism, see Michelle Boyd, "Reconstructing Bronzeville: Racial Nostalgia and Neighborhood Redevelopment," *Journal of Urban Affairs* 22 (2000): 107–22.

27. Gerald D. Suttles, "The Cumulative Texture of Local Urban Culture," *American Journal of Sociology* 90 (1984): 283–304.

28. Ann Swidler, "Culture in Action: Symbols and Strategies," *American Sociological Review* 51 (1986): 273–86.

29. Joane Nagel, "Constructing Ethnicity: Creating and Recreating Ethnic Identity and Culture," *Social Problems* 41 (February 1994): 162.

30. "Explosion of authenticities" is a paraphrase of Henri Lefebvre's "explosion of spaces" terminology (Henri Lefebvre, *The Production of Space* [New York: Blackwell, 1991]).

31. The term "connective tissues" comes from the work of Harvey Molotch and colleagues, who suggest that scholars focus on the networked connections linking civic organizations, neighborhood coalitions, and other local groups to understand the production of place character (Harvey Molotch, William Freudenberg, and Krista E. Paulsen, "History Repeats Itself, but How? City Character, Urban Tradition, and the Accomplishment of Place," *American Sociological Review* 65 [2000]: 791–823).

32. Barbara Eckstein argues that the widely read literature about New Orleans has over the decades shaped public memory and intervened in the framing of the city's problems, the proposed solutions to these problems, and the perceived effectiveness of those solutions (Barbara Eckstein, *Sustaining New Orleans: Literature, Local Memory, and the Fate of a City* [New York: Routledge, 2005]).

Selected Bibliography

ARCHIVAL SOURCES

Loyola University Archives, Lafcadio Hearn Collection: Mayor Moon Landrieu's papers and other manuscripts pertaining to the postwar era
New Orleans Public Library, City Archives: 1984 Louisiana Exposition Collection
Ohio Historical Center Archives Library, Newspaper Roll no. 4427
Tulane University, Howard-Tilton Memorial Library: *Times-Picayune* Index
Tulane University, Howard-Tilton Memorial Library, Special Collections, Blanche F. Mysing Papers
Tulane University, Howard-Tilton Memorial Library, Special Collections: Vertical Files on New Orleans history, culture, and tourism
University of New Orleans, Earl K. Long Library, Louisiana Collection: Vieux Carre Property Owners, Residents, and Associates
University of New Orleans, Louisiana and Special Collections: New Orleans Chamber of Commerce Collection (cited as MSS 66, NOCC, UNO)
Williams Research Center, Historic New Orleans Collection: Federal Writers Project of the Works Progress Administration (WPA); Mary Meeks Morrison and Jacob Morrison Papers; William Russell Jazz Collection; World's Industrial and Cotton Centennial Exposition, 1883–1885

REFERENCES

Allen, Theodore Allen. *The Invention of the White Race*. New York: Verso, 1994.
Almaguer, Tomas. *Racial Fault Lines: The Historical Origins of White Supremacy in California*. Berkeley: University of California Press, 1994.
Alsayyad, Nezar (editor). *Consuming Tradition, Manufacturing Heritage: Global Norms and Urban Forms in the Age of Tourism*. London: Routledge, 2001.
Anderson, Elijah. *Streetwise: Race, Class, and Change in an Urban Community*. Chicago: University of Chicago Press, 1990
Appadurai, Arjun. *Modernity at Large: Cultural Dimensions of Globalization*. Minneapolis: University of Minnesota Press, 1996.

Augustin Advertising and Information Bureau. *Mardi Gras in New Orleans 1798–1908*. New Orleans: Augustin Advertising Bureau, 1908.

Bakhtin, Mikhail. *Rabelais and His World*. Translated by Helene Iswolsky. Bloomington: Indiana University Press, 1984.

Barthel, Diane. *Historic Preservation: Collective Memory and Historical Identity*. New Brunswick, N.J.: Rutgers University Press, 1996.

Baumbach, Richard O., and William Borah. *The Second Battle of New Orleans: A History of the Vieux Carre Riverfront Expressway Controversy*. Birmingham: University of Alabama Press, 1981.

Beauregard, Robert A. *Voices of Decline: The Postwar Fate of U.S. Cities*. New York: Routledge, 1993.

Beck, Ulrich. *What Is Globalization?* Cambridge, Mass.: Polity, 1999.

Benjamin, Walter. *Reflections, Essays, Aphorisms, Autobiographical Writing*. New York: Harcourt Brace, 1978.

Bennett, James B. *Religion and the Rise of Jim Crow in New Orleans*. Princeton, N.J.: Princeton University Press, 2005.

Bernard, Karl. *Travels through North America during the Years 1825 and 1826*. Philadelphia: Carey, Lea and Carey, 1828.

Bernardi, Daniel (editor). *The Birth of Whiteness: Race and the Emergence of U.S. Cinema*. New Brunswick, N.J.: Rutgers University Press, 1996.

Biles, Roger. "The Urban South in the Great Depression." *Journal of Southern History* 56 (1990): 71–100.

Blassingame, John W. *Black New Orleans, 1860–1880*. Chicago: University of Chicago Press, 1976.

Bolding, Gary. "Change, Continuity, and Commercial Identity of a Southern City: New Orleans, 1850–1950." *Louisiana Studies* 14 (1975): 161–78.

Bolding, Gary A. "New Orleans Commerce: The Establishment of the Permanent World Trade Mart." *Louisiana History* 8 (1967): 351–61.

Bonilla-Silva, Eduardo. *White Supremacy and Racism in the Post–Civil Rights Era*. Boulder, Colo.: L. Rienner, 2001.

Boorstin, Daniel. *The Image: A Guide to Pseudo-Events in America*. New York: Harper and Row, 1964.

Bourdieu, Pierre. *In Other Words: Essays Toward a Reflexive Sociology*. Translated by Matthew Adamson. Stanford, Calif.: Stanford University Press, 1990.

Bourdieu, Pierre. *Outline of a Theory of Practice*. London: Cambridge University Press, 1977.

Bourdieu, Pierre. "Social Space and Symbolic Power." *Sociological Theory* 7 (1989): 14–25.

Boyd, Michelle, "Reconstructing Bronzeville: Racial Nostalgia and Neighborhood Redevelopment." *Journal of Urban Affairs* 22 (2000): 107–22.

Boyer, Christine M. *The City of Collective Memory: Its Historical Imagery and Architectural Entertainments*. Cambridge, Mass.: MIT Press, 1994.

Brodkin, Karen. *How Jews Became White Folks: And What That Says about Race in America.* New Brunswick, N.J.: Rutgers University Press, 1998.

Brookings Institution. *New Orleans after the Storm: Lessons from the Past, a Plan for the Future.* Washington, D.C.: Brookings Institution, 2005.

Brown, Laura Clark. "New Orleans Modernism: The Arts and Crafts Club in the Vieux Carre, 1919–1939." *Louisiana History* 41 (2000): 317–43.

Bryman, Alan. "Disneyization of Society." *Sociological Review* 47 (1999): 25–47.

Bryman, Alan. *The Disneyization of Society.* Thousand Oaks, Calif.: Sage, 2004.

Canclini, N. G. *Hybrid Cultures: Strategies of Entering and Leaving Modernity.* Minneapolis: University of Minneapolis Press, 1995.

Carter, Dan T. *When the War Was Over: The Failure of Self-Reconstruction in the South, 1865–1867.* Baton Rouge: Louisiana State University Press, 1985

Castells, Manuel. "Materials for an Exploratory Theory of the Network Society." *British Journal of Sociology* 51(January/March 2001): 5–24.

Castells, Manuel. *The Rise of the Network Society.* Cambridge, Mass.: Blackwell, 1996.

Chang, T. C. "Renaissance Revisited: Singapore as a 'Global City for the Arts.'" *International Journal of Urban and Regional Research* 24 (December 2000): 818–31.

Chatterton, Paul, and Robert Hollands. *Urban Nightscapes: Youth Cultures, Pleasure Spaces, and Corporate Power.* London: Routledge, 2003.

Clark, Terry Nichols, Richard Lloyd, Kenneth K. Wong, and Pushpam Jain, "Amenities Drive Urban Growth." *Journal of Urban Affairs* 24 (2002): 493–515.

Cocks, Catherine. *Doing the Town: The Rise of Urban Tourism in the United States, 1850–1915.* Berkeley: University of California Press, 2001.

Cohen, Erik. "Authenticity and Commodification in Tourism." *Annals of Tourism Research* 15 (1988): 371–86.

Coleman, William H. *Historical Sketch Book and Guide to New Orleans and Environs.* New York: N.p., N.d.

Couch, Randal R. "The Public Masked Balls of Antebellum New Orleans: A Custom of Masque outside the Mardi Gras Tradition." *Louisiana History* 34 (1994): 403–31.

Davis, Fred. *Yearning for Yesterday: A Sociology of Nostalgia.* New York: Free Press, 1979.

Debord, Guy. *The Society of the Spectacle.* Translated by Donald Nicholson-Smith. New York: Zone Books, 1994.

Desmond, Jane C. *Staging Tourism: Bodies on Display from Waikiki to Sea World.* Chicago: University of Chicago Press, 1999.

Domínguez, Virginia R. *White by Definition: Social Classification in Creole Louisiana.* New Brunswick, N.J.: Rutgers University Press, 1986.

Donaldson, Gary A. "A Window on Slave Culture: Dances at Congo Square in New Orleans, 1800–1962." *Journal of Negro History* 69 (1984): 63–72.

Douglas, George A. *All Aboard! The Railroad in American Life.* New York: Paragon House, 1992.

Dubois, W. E. B. *Black Reconstruction in America, 1860–1880.* New York: Free Press, 1935.

Duneier, Mitchell. *Slim's Table.* Chicago: University of Chicago Press, 1992.

Durkheim, Emile. *Elementary Forms of Religious Life.* Translated by Karen E. Fields. New York: Free Press, [1912] 1995.

Eade, J. (editor). *Living the Global City: Globalization as Local Process.* London: Routledge, 1997.

Eckstein, Barbara. *Sustaining New Orleans: Literature, Local Memory, and the Fate of a City.* New York: Routledge, 2005.

Edmonson, Munro. "Carnival in New Orleans." *Caribbean Quarterly* 4 (1956): 233–45.

Eeckhout, Bart. "The 'Disneyification' of Times Square: Back to the Future?," pp. 379–428 in *Critical Perspectives on Urban Redevelopment,* edited by Kevin Fox Gotham. New York: Elsevier, 2001.

Eriksen, Thomas Hylland. "Creolization and Creativity." *Global Networks* 3 (2003): 223–37.

Evans, Nicholas M. *Writing Jazz: Race, Nationalism, and Modern Culture in the 1920s.* New York: Garland, 2000.

Fainstein, Susan S., and David Gladstone. "Evaluating Urban Tourism," pp. 21–34 in the *Tourist City,* edited by Dennis R. Judd and Susan S. Fainstein. New Haven, Conn.: Yale University Press, 1999.

Fainstein, Susan S., and Dennis R. Judd. "Global Forces, Local Strategies, and Urban Tourism," pp. 1–20 in *Tourist City,* edited by Dennis R. Judd and Susan S. Fainstein. New Haven, Conn.: Yale University Press, 1999, 1–20.

Fainstein, Susan, Lily M. Hoffman, and Dennis R. Judd. "Making Theoretical Sense of Tourism," pp. 240–53 in *Cities and Visitors: Regulating People, Markets, and City Space,* edited by Lily M. Hoffman, Susan S. Fainstein, and Dennis R. Judd. New York: Blackwell, 2003.

Fairall, Herbert. *World's Industrial and Cotton Centennial Exposition, New Orleans, 1884–1885.* Iowa City: Republican Publishing, 1885.

Faircloth, Adam. *Race and Democracy: The Civil Rights Struggle in Louisiana, 1915–1972.* Athens: University of Georgia Press, 1995.

Farrow, Lee A. "Grand Duke Alexei and the Origins of Rex, 1872: Myth, Public Memory, and the Distortion of History." *Gulf South Historical Review* 18 (2002): 6–30.

Featherstone, Mike, Scott Lash, and Roland Robertson (editors). *Global Modernities.* Thousand Oaks, Calif.: Sage, 1995.

Fine, Gary Allen. *Difficult Reputations: Collective Memories of the Evil, Inept, and Controversial.* Chicago: University of Chicago Press, 2001.

Fischer, Roger A. "A Pioneer Protest: The New Orleans Streetcar Controversy of 1867." *Journal of Negro History* 53 (1968): 219–33.

Fischer, Roger A. "Racial Segregation in Ante Bellum New Orleans." *American Historical Review* 74 (1969): 926–57.

Foley, John. "Neighborhood Movements, Identity, and Change in New Orleans's French Quarter." Ph.D. Dissertation, University of New Orleans, 1999.

Foley, John, and Mickey Lauria. "Historic Preservation in New Orleans French Quarter: Unresolved Racial Tensions," pp. 67–90 in *Knights and Castles: Minorities and Urban Regeneration,* edited by Huw Thomas and Francesco L. Piccolo. Burlington, Conn.: Ashgate, 2003.

Foley, John, and Mickey Lauria. "Plans, Planning, and Tragic Choices." *Planning Theory and Practice* 1 (2000): 219–33.

Foner, Eric. *Reconstruction: America's Unfinished Revolution, 1863–1877.* New York: Harper and Row, 1988.

Fortier, Alcee. "The French Language in Louisiana and the Negro-French Dialect." *Transactions* 1 (1884–1885): 98

Franklin, Adrian, and Mike Crang. "The Trouble with Tourism and Travel Theory." *Tourist Studies* 1 (2001): 5–22.

Frisby, David. *Cityscapes of Modernity.* New York: Polity, 2001.

Gallas, Walter. "Neighborhood Preservation and Politics in New Orleans: Vieux Carré Property Owners, Residents and Associates, Inc. and City Government, 1938–1983." M.A. Thesis, University of New Orleans, 1996.

Gans, Herbert. *The Urban Villagers: Group and Class in the Life of Italian-Americans.* New York: Free Press, 1962.

Gay, Patricia. "The 1984 World's Fair, the Warehouse District, and the Preservation Industry." *Preservation in Print* (June/July 2004): 6.

Geertz, Clifford. *The Interpretation of Cultures.* New York: Basic Books, 1973.

Gill, James. *Lords of Misrule: Mardi Gras and the Politics of Race in New Orleans.* Jackson: University Press of Mississippi, 1997.

Gillette, William. *Retreat from Reconstruction, 1869–1879.* Baton Rouge: Louisiana State University Press, 1979.

Goffman, Erving. *Frame Analysis: An Essay on the Organization of Experience.* New York: Harper, 1974.

Gotham, Kevin Fox. *Race, Real Estate, and Uneven Development: The Kansas City Experience, 1900–2000.* Albany: State University of New York Press, 2002.

Gotham, Kevin Fox. "Tourism Gentrification: The Case of New Orleans's Vieux Carre (French Quarter)." *Urban Studies* 42 (2005): 1099–1121.

Gottdiener, Mark, "The Consumption of Space and the Spaces of Consumption," pp. 265–84 in *New Forms of Consumption: Consumers, Culture, and*

Commodification, edited by Mark Gottdiener. Lanham, Md.: Rowman and Littlefield, 2000.

Gottdiener, Mark. *Theming of America: Dreams, Visions, and Commercial Spaces.* Second Edition. New York: Westview, 2001.

Gottdiener, Mark, Claudia C. Collins, and David R. Dickens. *Las Vegas: The Social Production of an All-American City.* Malden, Mass.: Blackwell, 1999.

Grazian, David. *Blue Chicago: The Search for Authenticity in Urban Blues Clubs.* Chicago: University of Chicago Press, 2003.

Greenberg, Miriam. "Branding Cities: A Social History of the Urban Lifestyle Magazine." *Urban Affairs Review* 36(2) (November 2000): 228–62.

Greenberg, Miriam. *Branding New York.* New York: Routledge, 2008.

Greenberg, Miriam. "The Limits of Branding: The World Trade Center, Fiscal Crisis, and the Marketing of Recovery." *International Journal of Urban and Regional Research* 27(2) (June 2003): 386–416.

Greenwood, D. "Culture by the Pound: An Anthropological Perspective on Tourism as Cultural Commoditization," pp. 129–39 in *Hosts and Guests: The Anthropology of Tourism,* edited by V. Smith. Philadelphia: University of Pennsylvania, 1997.

Griswold, Wendy, and Nathan Wright. "Cowbirds, Locals, and the Endurance of Regionalism." *American Journal of Sociology* 109 (2004): 1411–51.

Hale, Grace Elizabeth. *Making Whiteness: The Culture of Segregation in the South, 1890–1940.* New York: Pantheon, 1998.

Hall, C. Michael, Allan M. Williams, and Alan A. Lew (editors). *A Companion to Tourism.* New York: Blackwell, 2004.

Hall, Gwendolyn Midlo. *Africans in Colonial Louisiana: The Development of Afro-Creole Culture in the Eighteenth Century.* Baton Rouge: Louisiana State University Press, 1992.

Haney-Lopez, Ian. *White by Law: The Legal Construction of Race.* New York: New York University Press, 1996.

Hanger, Kimberly S. *Bounded Lives, Bounded Places: Free Black Society in Colonial New Orleans, 1769–1803.* Durham, N.C.: Duke University Press, 1997.

Hannerz, Ulf. *Cultural Complexity.* New York: Columbia University Press, 1992.

Hannerz, Ulf. *Transnational Connections.* London: Routledge, 1996.

Hannigan, John. *Fantasy City: Pleasure and Profit in the Postmodern Metropolis.* New York: Routledge, 1998.

Harlan, Louis R. "Desegregation in New Orleans Public Schools during Reconstruction." *American Historical Review* 68 (April 1962): 663–75.

Harris, Kerr, Forster and Company. *Trends in the Hotel-Motel Business: Twenty-Eighth Annual Review.* Atlanta: Harris, Kerr, Forster, 1964.

Harvey, David. *The Condition of Postmodernity: An Enquiry into the Origins of Cultural Change.* New York: Blackwell, 1987.

Harvey, David. "From Space to Place and Back Again: Reflections on the Condition of Postmodernity," pp. 3–29 in *Mapping the Future: Local Cultures, Global Change*, edited by J. Bird, B. Curtis, T. Putnam, G. Robertson, and L. Tucker. London: Routledge, 1993.

Harvey, David. "Voodoo Cities." *New Statesman and Society* 1 (September 30, 1988): 33–35.

Hennick, Louis C. *The Streetcars of New Orleans*. Gretna, La.: Pelican, 1965.

Hirsch, Arnold R. "New Orleans: Sunbelt in the Swamp," pp. 100–37 in *Sunbelt Cities: Politics and Growth since World War II*, edited by Richard M. Bernard and Bradley R. Rice. Austin: University of Texas Press, 1983.

Hirsch, Arnold R. "Simply a Matter of Black and White: The Transformation of Race and Politics in Twentieth Century New Orleans," pp. 262–319 in *Creole New Orleans: Race and Americanization*, edited by Arnold R. Hirsch and Joseph Logsdon. Baton Rouge: Louisiana State University Press, 1992.

Hirsch, Arnold R., and Joseph Logsdon (editors). *Creole New Orleans: Race and Americanization*. Baton Rouge: Louisiana State University Press, 1992.

Hobsbawn, Eric. *Industry and Empire: An Economic History of Britain since 1750*. London: Weidenfeld and Nicolson, 1968.

Hobsbawm, Eric. "Introduction: Inventing Traditions," pp. 1–14 in *The Invention of Tradition*, edited by Eric Hobsbawm and Terence Ranger. Cambridge: Cambridge University Press, 1992.

Hobsbawm, Eric, and Terence Ranger (editors). *The Invention of Tradition*. Cambridge: Cambridge University Press, 1983.

Hummon, David. *Commonplaces: Community, Ideology, and Identity in American Culture*. Albany: State University of New York Press, 1990.

Ignatiev, Noel. *How the Irish Became White*. New York: Routledge, 1995.

Inger, Morton. *Politics and Reality in an American City: The New Orleans School Crisis of 1960*. New York: Center for Urban Education, 1969.

Jackson, Joy. *New Orleans in the Gilded Age: Politics and Urban Progress, 1880–1896*. Baton Rouge: Louisiana State University Press, 1969.

Jacobson, Matthew Frye. *Whiteness of a Different Color: European Immigrants and the Alchemy of Race*. Cambridge: Harvard University Press, 1998.

Jewell, Edwin L. *Jewell's Crescent City Illustrated: The Commercial, Social, Political and General History of New Orleans—Including Biographical Sketches of Its Distinguished Citizens, Together with a Map and a General Strangers' Guide*. New Orleans: Edwin L. Jewell, 1873.

Johnson, Jerah. "Jim Crow Laws of the 1890s and the Origins of New Orleans Jazz: Correction of an Error." *Popular Music* 19 (2000): 243–51.

Judd, Dennis. "Constructing the Tourist Bubble," pp. 35–53 in *The Tourist City*, edited by Dennis R. Judd and Susan S. Fainstein. New Haven, Conn.: Yale University Press, 1999.

Kasinitz, Philip. "The Gentrification of 'Boerum Hill': Neighborhood Change and Conflicts over Definitions." *Qualitative Sociology* 11 (1988): 163–82.

Kasinitz, Philip, and David Hillyard. "The Old-Timer's Tale: The Politics of Nostalgia on the Waterfront." *Journal of Contemporary Ethnography* 24 (1995): 139–64.

Kaufman, Randi. "The Social Impacts of Condominium Conversion in the Vieux Carre Neighborhood." Master's Thesis, University of New Orleans, 1999.

Kearns, Gerry, and Chris Philo (editors). *Selling Places: The City as Cultural Capital, Past and Present.* Oxford: Pergamon, 1993.

Kefalas, Maria. *Working Class Heroes: Protecting, Home, Community, and Nation in a Chicago Neighborhood.* Berkeley: University of California Press, 2003.

Kein, Sybil (editor). *Creole: The History and Legacy of Louisiana's Free People of Color.* Baton Rouge: Louisiana State University Press, 2000.

Kendall, John Smith. *History of New Orleans.* Chicago: Lewis, 1922.

Kern, Stephen. *The Culture of Time and Space, 1880–1918.* Cambridge: Harvard University Press, 1983.

King, Grace Elizabeth. *Memories of a Southern Woman of Letters.* New York: Macmillan, 1932.

King, Grace Elizabeth. *New Orleans: The Place and the People.* New York: Macmillan, 1895.

Kinser, Samuel. *Carnival, American Style: Mardi Gras at New Orleans and Mobile.* Chicago: University of Chicago Press, 1990.

Knopp, Lawrence. "Exploiting the Rent Gap: The Theoretical Significance of Using Illegal Appraisal Schemes to Encourage Gentrification in New Orleans." *Urban Geography* 11 (1990): 48–64.

Knopp, Lawrence. "Some Theoretical Implications of Gay Involvement in an Urban Land Market." *Political Geography Quarterly* 9 (1990): 337–52.

Kraidy, Marwan M. *Hybridity, or the Cultural Logic of Globalization.* Philadelphia: Temple University Press, 2005.

Laborde, Errol. *Marched the Day God: A History of the Rex Organization.* New Orleans: School of Design, 1999.

Laborde, Errol. "The Men Who Made Mardi Gras." *New Orleans City Business* 36 (February 2002): 45–50.

Lachance, Paul. "The Formation of a Three-Caste Society: Evidence from Wills in Antebellum New Orleans." *Social Science History* 18 (1994): 211–42.

La Cour, Arthur Burton, and Stuart Omer Landry. *New Orleans Masquerade: Chronicles of Carnival.* New Orleans: Pelican, 1957.

Lamont, Michele (editor). *The Cultural Territories of Race: Black and White Boundaries.* Chicago: University of Chicago Press, 1998.

Larsen, Lawrence H. *The Rise of the Urban South.* Lexington: University of Kentucky Press, 1985.

Lash, Scott, and John Urry. *Economies of Signs and Space.* London: Sage, 1994.

Latrobe, Benjamin Henry. *Impressions Regarding New Orleans: Diaries and Sketches, 1818–1820.* New York: Columbia University Press, 1951.

Lauria, Mickey. "The Implications of Marxian Rent Theory for Community-Controlled Redevelopment Strategies." *Journal of Planning Education and Research* 4 (1984): 16–24.

Lauria, Mickey, Robert K. Whelan, and Alma H. Young. "Revitalization of New Orleans," pp. 102–27 in *Urban Revitalization: Policies and Programs,* edited by Fritz W. Wagner, Timothy E. Joder, and Anthony J. Mumphrey Jr. Thousand Oaks, Calif.: Sage, 1995.

Leach, William. *Land of Desire: Merchants, Power, and the Rise of a New American Culture.* New York: Pantheon, 1993.

Leathem, Karen Trahan. "'A Carnival according to Their Own Desires': Gender and Mardi Gras in New Orleans, 1870–1941." Ph.D. Dissertation, University of North Carolina at Chapel Hill, 1994.

Lefebvre, Henri. *The Production of Space.* New York: Blackwell, 1991.

Lewis, Pierce F. *New Orleans: The Making of an Urban Landscape.* Second Edition. Charlottesville: University of Virginia Press, 2005.

Lloyd, Richard. *Neo-Bohemia: Art and Commerce in the Postindustrial City.* New York: Routledge, 2006.

Lloyd, Richard, and Terry Nichols Clark, "The City as an Entertainment Machine," pp. 357–78 in *Critical Perspectives on Urban Redevelopment,* edited by Kevin Fox Gotham. New York: Elsevier, 2001.

Logsdon, Joseph, and Caryn Cosse Belle. "The Americanization of Black New Orleans, 1850–1900," pp. 201–61 in *Creole New Orleans: Race and Americanization,* edited by Arnold Hirsch and Joseph Logsdon. Baton Rouge: Louisiana State University Press, 1992.

Long, Alecia P. *The Great Southern Babylon: Sex, Race, and Respectability in New Orleans, 1865–1920.* Baton Rouge: Louisiana State University Press, 2004.

Luders, Joseph. "The Economics of Movement Success: Business Responses to Civil Rights Mobilization." *American Journal of Sociology* 111 (January 2006): 963–92.

Lyell, Sir Charles. *A Second Visit to the United States of North America.* Volume 2. London: John Murray, 1849.

MacCannell, Dean. *Empty Meeting Grounds: The Tourist Papers.* New York: Routledge, 1992.

MacCannell, Dean. "Staged Authenticity: Arrangements of Social Space in Tourist Settings." *American Journal of Sociology* 79 (1973): 589–603.

MacCannell, Dean. *The Tourist: A New Theory of the Leisure Class.* New York: Schocken, 1976.

Marks Lewis Torre and Associates. *Report on the Existing Conditions on Bourbon Street.* New Orleans: Marks Lewis Torre and Associates, 1977.

Martinot, Steve. *The Rule of Racialization: Class, Identity, Governance.* Philadelphia: Temple University Press, 2002.

Marx, Karl. *Capital.* Volume 1. Translated by Ben Fowlkes. New York: Vintage, [1867] 1978.

Marx, Karl. "The Eighteenth Brumaire of Louis Bonaparte," pp. 594–617 in *Marx-Engels Reader,* edited by Robert C. Tucker. Second Edition. New York: Norton, [1952] 1978).

McLain, James J. "Mardi Gras 2000: Its Economic Impact." *Louisiana Business Survey* 31 (2000): 2–4, 8.

Meethan, Kevin. *Tourism in Global Society: Place, Culture, and Consumption.* New York: Palgrave, 2001.

Mele, Christopher. *Selling the Lower East Side: Culture, Real Estate, and Resistance in New York City.* Minneapolis: University of Minnesota Press, 2002.

Milligan, Melinda. "Displacement and Identity Discontinuity: The Role of Nostalgia in Establishing New Identity Categories." *Symbolic Interactionism* 26 (2003): 381–403.

Mitchell, Reid. *All on a Mardi Gras Day: Episodes in the History of New Orleans Mardi Gras.* Cambridge: Harvard University Press, 1995.

Molotch, Harvey, William Freudenberg, and Krista E. Paulsen. "History Repeats Itself, but How? City Character, Urban Tradition, and the Accomplishment of Place." *American Sociological Review* 65 (2000): 791–823.

Murji, Karim, and John Solomos (editors). *Racialization: Studies in Theory and Practice.* Oxford: Oxford University Press, 2005.

Mystick Krewe of Comus. *One Hundred Years of Comus.* New Orleans: Mystick Krewe of Comus, 1956.

Nagel, Joane. "Constructing Ethnicity: Creating and Recreating Ethnic Identity and Culture." *Social Problems* 41 (February 1994): 152–76.

Nagel, Joane. *Race, Ethnicity, and Sexuality: Intimate Intersections, Forbidden Frontiers.* New York: Oxford University Press, 2003.

Newman, Harvey. *Southern Hospitality: Tourism and the Growth of Atlanta.* Tuscaloosa: University of Alabama Press, 1999.

Norman, Benjamin Moore. *Norman's New Orleans and Environs.* New Orleans: B. M. Norman, 1845.

Olick, Jeffrey K. (editor). *States of Memory: Continuities, Conflicts, and Transformations in National Retrospection.* Durham, N.C.: Duke University Press, 2003.

Omi, Michael, and Howard Winant. *Racial Formation in the United States: From the 1960s to the 1980s.* Second Edition. New York: Routledge, 1994.

Osborne, Mitchell. *1984 World's Fair, New Orleans: The Official Guidebook.* Edited by Linda C. Delery. New Orleans: Picayune, 1984.

Peterson, Richard. *Creating Country Music, Fabricating Authenticity.* Chicago: University of Chicago Press, 1997.

Picard, Michel. *Bali: Cultural Tourism and Touristic Culture.* Singapore: Archipelago Press, 1996.

Picard, Michel, and Robert E. Wood (editors). *Tourism, Ethnicity, and the State in Asian and Pacific Society.* Honolulu: University of Hawaii Press, 1997.

Raeburn, Bruce. "Early New Orleans Jazz in Theaters." *Louisiana History* 43 (2002): 41–52.

Ralph, Julian. "New Orleans, Our Southern Capital." *Harper's New Monthly Magazine* 86 (February 1893): 365–66.

Rambuss, Richard. "Spenser and Milton at Mardi Gras: English Literature, American Cultural Capital, and the Reformation of New Orleans Mardi Gras." *Boundary* 27 (Summer 2000): 61–62.

Rand, McNally and Company. *The World's Industrial and Cotton Centennial Exposition at New Orleans.* Chicago: Rand, McNally, 1885.

Reeves, Sally K. "Making Groceries: Public Markets and Corner Stores in Old New Orleans." *Gulf South Historical Review* 16 (2000): 20–47.

Reichl, Alexander J. *Reconstructing Times Square: Politics and Culture in Urban Development.* Lawrence: University Press of Kansas, 1999.

Reinders, Robert C. *End of an Era: New Orleans, 1850–1860.* New Orleans: Pelican, 1964.

Richmond and Danville Railroad, Piedmont Airline, and Atlantic Coast Line. *Our Great All Around Tour for the Winter of '84–'85.* New York: Leve and Alden Printing, 1884–1885.

Ritzer, George. *Enchanting a Disenchanted World: Revolutionizing the Means of Consumption.* Second Edition. Thousand Oaks, Calif.: Pine Forge, 2005

Ritzer, George. *The Globalization of Nothing.* Thousand Oaks, Calif.: Pine Forge, 2004.

Roach, Joseph. *Cities of the Dead: Circum-Atlantic Performance.* New York: Columbia University Press, 1996.

Robertson, Roland. *Globalization: Social Theory and Global Culture.* Thousand Oaks, Calif.: Sage, 1996.

Rojek, Chris, and John Urry (editors). *Touring Cultures: Transformations of Travel and Theory.* London: Routledge, 1997.

Rosenberg, Daniel. *New Orleans Dockworkers: Race, Labor, and Unionism, 1892–1923.* Albany: State University of New York Press, 1988.

Rosendahl, Patricia. "New Orleans' Own Silent Films." *Southern Quarterly* 23 (1984): 40–46.

Rothman, Hal. *Devil's Bargains: Tourism in the Twentieth Century American West.* Lawrence: University Press of Kansas, 1998.

Rydell, Robert W. *All the World's a Fair: Visions of Empire at American International Expositions, 1876–1916.* Chicago: University of Chicago Press, 1984.

Rydell, Robert W. "The Culture of Imperial Abundance: World's Fairs in the Making of American Culture," pp. 191–216 in *Consuming Visions: Accu-*

mulation and Display of Goods in America, 1880–1920, edited by Simon J. Bronner. New York: Norton, 1989.

Schindler, Henri. *Mardi Gras, New Orleans.* Paris: Flammarion, 1997.

Schudson, Michael. *Watergate in American Memory.* New York: Basic Books, 1992.

Schumpeter, Joseph A. *Capitalism, Socialism, and Democracy.* New York: Harper [1942] 1975.

Schuth, Wayne H. "The Image of New Orleans on Film." *Southern Quarterly* 19 (1981): 240–45.

Schuth, Wayne H. "The Images of Louisiana in Film and Television." *Southern Quarterly* 23 (1984): 5–17.

Schwartz, Barry. *Abraham Lincoln and the Forge of National Memory.* Chicago: University of Chicago Press, 2000.

Scott, Allen J. *The Cultural Economy of Cities: Essays on the Geography of Image-Producing Industries.* London: Sage, 2000.

Sears, John. *Sacred Places: American Tourist Attractions in the Nineteenth Century.* Oxford: Oxford University Press, 1989.

Shaffer, Marguerite. *See America First: Tourism and National Identity, 1905–1930.* Washington, D.C.: Smithsonian Institution, 2001.

Sheller, Mimi, and John Urry (editors). *Tourism Mobilities: Places to Play, Places in Play.* New York: Routledge, 2004.

Shepherd, Robert. "Commodification, Culture, and Tourism." *Tourist Studies* 2 (2002): 183–201.

Shepherd, Samuel C. "A Glimmer of Hope: The World's Industrial and Cotton Centennial Exposition, New Orleans, 1884–1885." *Louisiana History* 26 (1985): 271–90.

Shields, Rob. *Places on the Margin.* London: Routledge, Chapman Hall, 1991.

Simmel, Georg. "The Berlin Trade Exhibition," pp. 255–58 in *Simmel on Culture: Selected Writings,* edited by David Frisby and Mike Featherstone. London: Sage, [1896] 2000.

Simmel, Georg. "Metropolis and Mental Life," pp. 324–39 in *Georg Simmel: On Individuality and Social Forms,* edited by Donald N. Levine. Chicago: Chicago University Press, [1903] 1971.

Smalley, Eugene. "In and Out of the New Orleans Exposition." *Century Magazine: A Popular Monthly* 30 (June 1885): 194. Available at http://cdl.library.cornell.edu (accessed May 1, 2005).

Smart, Tristine Lee. "Prestige Symbol Manipulation: Controlling Form and Meaning—Prestige Symbols, Carnival, Louisiana, Earthwork Complexes, Ohio." Ph.D. Dissertation, University of Michigan, Ann Arbor, 1999.

Smith, Michael Peter, and Marlene Keller. " 'Managed Growth' and the Politics of Uneven Development in New Orleans," pp. 126–66 in *Restructuring the City: The Political Economy of Urban Redevelopment,* edited by Susan Fainstein, Norman I. Fainstein, Richard Child Hill, Dennis Judd, and Michael Peter Smith. New York: Longman, 1986.

Snewmaker, Kenneth E., and Andrew K. Prinz (editors). "A Yankee in Louisiana: Selections from the Diary and Correspondence of Henry R. Gardiner, 1862–1866." *Louisiana History* 5 (1964): 271–95.

Somers, Dale A. "Black and White in New Orleans: A Study in Urban Race Relations, 1865–1900." *Journal of Southern History* 40 (1974): 19–42.

Sorkin, Michael (editor). *Variations on a Theme Park: The New American City and the End of Public Space.* New York: Hill and Wang, 1992.

Spain, Daphne. "Race Relations and Residential Segregation in New Orleans: Two Centuries of Paradox." *Annals of the American Academy of Political and Social Science* 441 (1979): 82–96.

Stanonis, Anthony J. *Creating the Big Easy: New Orleans and the Emergence of Modern Tourism, 1918–1945.* Atlanta: University of Georgia Press, 2006.

Starr, S. Frederick (editor). *Inventing New Orleans: The Writings of Lafcadio Hearn.* Jackson: University Press of Mississippi, 2001.

Strawn, Lydia (compiler). *World's Industrial and Cotton Centennial Exposition.* Chicago: General Passenger Department, Illinois Central Railroad, n.d.

Suttles, Gerald D. "The Cumulative Texture of Local Urban Culture." *American Journal of Sociology* 90 (1984): 283–304.

Swidler, Ann. "Culture in Action: Symbols and Strategies." *American Sociological Review* 51 (1986): 273–86.

Swidler, Ann. *Talk of Love: How Culture Matters.* Chicago: University of Chicago Press, 2001.

Swidler, Ann. "What Anchors Cultural Practices," pp. 74–92 in *The Practical Turn in Contemporary Theory,* edited by Theodore R. Schatzki, Karin Knorr-Cetina, and Eike von Savigny. London: Routledge and Kegan Paul, 2001.

Tasistro, Louis Fitzgerald. *Random Shots and Southern Breezes Containing Critical Remarks on the Southern States and Southern Institutions with Semi-Serious Observations on Men and Manners.* New York: Harper Brothers, 1842.

Taylor, Joe Gray. *Louisiana Reconstructed, 1863–1877.* Baton Rouge: Louisiana State University Press, 1974.

Tomlinson, John. *Globalization and Culture.* Chicago: University of Chicago Press, 1996.

Tregle, Joseph. "Creoles and Americans," pp. 131–88 in *Creole New Orleans: Race and Americanization,* edited by Arnold Hirsch and Joseph Logsdon. Baton Rouge: Louisiana State University Press, 1992.

Tregle, Joseph. "Early New Orleans Society: A Reappraisal." *Journal of Southern History* 18 (1952): 20–36.

Tuffly, Ellis L. "The New Orleans Cotton Exchange, the Formative Years, 1870–1880." *Journal of Southern History* 39 (1973): 545–64.

Tunnel, Ted. *Crucible of Reconstruction: War, Radicalism, and Race in Louisiana, 1862–1877.* Baton Rouge: Louisiana State University Press, 1984.

Turner, Bryan S. "A Note on Nostalgia." *Theory, Culture, and Society* 4 (1987): 147–56.

Turner, Victor. *Dramas, Fields, and Metaphors: Symbolic Action in Human Society.* Ithaca, N.Y.: Cornell University Press, 1975.

University of New Orleans, College of Urban and Public Affairs. *Changing Land Use in the Vieux Carre: Managing Growth to Preserve a National Landmark District.* New Orleans: University of New Orleans, 1992.

Urry, John. *Consuming Places.* London: Routledge, 1995.

Urry, John. *The Tourist Gaze.* Second Edition. Thousand Oaks, Calif.: Sage, 2002.

Vandal, Giles. "Nineteenth-Century Municipal Responses to the Problem of Poverty: New Orleans' Free Lodgers, 1850–1880, as a Case Study." *Journal of Urban History* 19 (1992): 30–59.

Vandal, Giles. "The Origins of the New Orleans Riot of 1866, Revisited." *Louisiana History* 22 (Spring 1981): 135–65.

Vandercock and Company. *Illustrated Guide to the Winter Resorts for Health and Pleasure in the Southern States and Florida: The World Exposition at New Orleans, La.* Chicago: Vandercock, 1884.

Vesey, Catherine. "Tourism Impacts in the Vieux Carre: An Analysis of Cultural Issues, Residential Perspectives, and Sustainable Tourism Planning." Ph.D. Dissertation, University of New Orleans, 1999.

Wagner, Jacob A. "The Myth of Liberty Place: Race and Public Memory in New Orleans, 1874–1993." Ph.D. Dissertation, University of New Orleans, 2004.

Wagner-Pacifici, Robin, and Barry Schwartz. "The Vietnam Veterans Memorial: Commemorating a Difficult Past." *American Journal of Sociology* 97 (September 1991): 376–420.

Waldo, J. Curtis. *The History of the Carnival in New Orleans from 1857–1882.* New Orleans: Chicago, St. Louis, and New Orleans Railroad, 1882.

Walton, John. *Storied Land: Community and Memory in Monterey.* Berkeley: University of California Press, 2001.

Warner, Charles Dudley. "Impressions of the South." *Harper's New Monthly Magazine* 71 (September 1885): 550. Available at Cornell University, "Making of America," http://cdl.library.cornell.edu/ (accessed May 1, 2005).

Watson, G. Llewellyn, and Joseph P. Kopachevsky. "Interpretations of Tourism as Commodity." *Annals of Tourism Research* 21 (1994): 643–60.

Watson, Thomas D. "Staging the 'Crowning Achievement of the Age': Major Edward A. Burke, New Orleans, and the Cotton Centennial Exposition." *Louisiana History* 25 (1984): 341–66.

Weber, Max. *The Protestant Ethic and the Spirit of Capitalism.* New York: Scribner's, [1902] 1958.

Wellman, Barry. "The Community Question: The Intimate Networks of East Yonkers." *American Journal of Sociology* 84 (March 1979): 1201–31.

Wellman, Barry. "Network Analysis: Some Basic Principles." *Sociological Theory* 1 (1983): 155–200.

Wells, Steve, and Jim Stodder. "A Short History of New Orleans Dockworkers." *Radical America* 10 (1976): 43–69.

Whelan, Robert K., and Alma Young. "New Orleans: The Ambivalent City," pp. 132–48 in *Big City Politics in Transition*, edited by H. V. Savitch and John Clayton Thomas. Newbury Park, Calif.: Sage, 1991.

Wright, Beverly. "Black New Orleans: The City That Care Forgot," pp. 45–74 in *In Search of the New South: The Black Urban Experience in the 1970s and 1980s*, edited by Robert Bullard. Tuscaloosa: University of Alabama Press, 1989.

Young, Perry. *Carnival and Mardi Gras in New Orleans*. New Orleans: Harmanson's, 1939.

Zerubavel, Eviatar. "The Standardization of Time: A Sociohistorical Perspective." *American Journal of Sociology* 88 (1982): 1–23.

Zerubavel, Eviatar. *Time Maps: Collective Memory and the Social Shape of the Past*. Chicago: University of Chicago Press, 2003.

Zukin, Sharon. "Cultural Strategies of Economic Development and the Hegemony of Vision," pp. 223–43 in *Urbanization of Injustice*, edited by Andy Merrifield and Erik Swyngedouw. New York: New York University Press, 1997.

Zukin, Sharon. *The Culture of Cities*. London: Blackwell, 1995.

Zukin, Sharon. *Landscapes of Power*. Berkeley: University of California Press, 1991.

Zukin, Sharon. "Postmodern Urban Landscapes: Mapping Culture and Power," pp. 221–47 in *Modernity and Identity*, edited by Scott Lash and John Friedman. New York: Blackwell, 1992.

Zukin, Sharon. "Urban Lifestyles: Diversity and Standardization in Spaces of Consumption." *Urban Studies* 35 (1998): 825–39.

Index

About the Author

Kevin Fox Gotham is Associate Professor of Sociology at Tulane University in New Orleans. He is the author of *Race, Real Estate, and Uneven Development: The Kansas City Experience, 1900–2000* and the editor of *Critical Perspectives on Urban Redevelopment*.